Isaac Bashevis Singer: Conversations

Literary Conversations Series

Peggy Whitman Prenshaw
General Editor

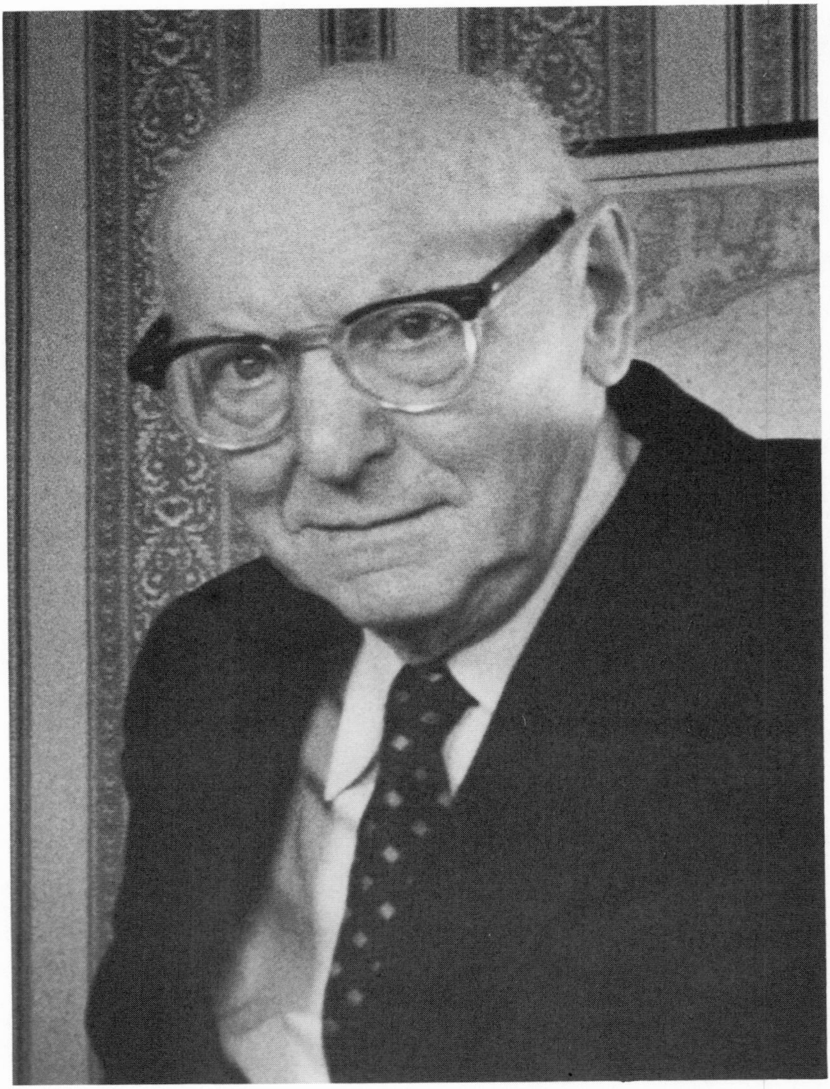

Grace Farrell

Isaac Bashevis Singer: Conversations

Edited by
Grace Farrell

University Press of Mississippi
Jackson and London

Copyright © 1992 by the University Press of Mississippi
All rights reserved
Manufactured in the United States of America

95 94 93 92   4 3 2 1

The paper in this book meets the guidelines for permanence and durability
of the Committee on Production Guidelines for Book Longevity of the Council
on Library Resources.

Library of Congress Cataloging-in-Publication Data

Singer, Isaac Bashevis, 1904–1991
    Isaac Bashevis Singer : conversations / edited by Grace Farrell.
        p.   cm. — (Literary conversations series)
    Includes index.
    ISBN 0-87805-589-4 (cloth). — ISBN 0-87805-590-8 (paper)
    1. Singer, Isaac Bashevis, 1904–1991—Interviews.   2. Authors,
Yiddish—United States—Interviews.   I. Farrell, Grace.   II. Title.
III. Series.
PJ5129.S49Z463   1992
839′.0933—dc20   92-19281
                                                     CIP

British Library Cataloging-in-Publication data available

Books in English by Isaac Bashevis Singer

The Family Moskat. New York: Alfred A. Knopf, 1950.
Satan in Goray. New York: Noonday Press, 1955.
Gimpel the Fool and Other Stories. New York: Noonday Press, 1957.
The Magician of Lublin. New York: Noonday Press, 1960.
The Spinoza of Market Street and Other Stories. New York: Farrar, Straus and Cudahy, 1961.
The Slave. New York: Farrar, Straus and Cudahy, 1962.
Short Friday and Other Stories. New York: Farrar, Straus and Giroux, 1964.
The Family Moskat. New York: Farrar, Straus and Giroux, 1965.
In My Father's Court. New York: Farrar, Straus and Giroux, 1966.
Zlateh the Goat and Other Stories. New York: Harper and Row, 1966.
Selected Short Stories of Isaac Bashevis Singer. Ed. Irving Howe. New York: Modern Library, 1966.
The Fearsome Inn. New York: Scribner, 1967.
The Manor. New York: Farrar, Straus and Giroux, 1967.
Mazel and Shlimazel, or The Milk of a Lioness. New York: Farrar, Straus and Giroux, 1967.
When Shlemiel Went to Warsaw and Other Stories. New York: Farrar, Straus and Giroux, 1968.
The Seance and Other Stories. New York: Farrar, Straus and Giroux, 1968.
A Day of Pleasure: Stories of a Boy Growing Up in Warsaw. New York: Farrar, Straus and Giroux, 1969.
The Estate. New York: Farrar, Straus and Giroux, 1969.
Elijah the Slave. New York: Farrar, Straus and Giroux, 1970.
A Friend of Kafka and Other Stories. New York: Farrar, Straus and Giroux, 1970.
Joseph and Koza or The Sacrifice to the Vistula. New York: Farrar, Straus and Giroux, 1970.
Topsy-Turvy Emperor of China. New York: Harper and Row, 1971.
Drawings of Tully Filmus (with George A. Perret). Philadelphia: Jewish Publication Society, 1971.
Alone in the Wild Forest. New York: Farrar, Straus and Giroux, 1971.
An Isaac Bashevis Singer Reader. New York: Farrar, Straus and Giroux, 1971.
Enemies, A Love Story. New York: Farrar, Straus and Giroux, 1972.
The Hasidim. New York: Crown Publishers, 1972.
The Wicked City. New York: Farrar, Straus and Giroux, 1972.

A Crown of Feathers. New York: Farrar, Straus and Giroux, 1973.
The Fools of Chelm and Their History. New York: Farrar, Straus and Giroux, 1973.
Why Noah Chose the Dove. New York: Farrar, Straus and Giroux, 1974.
Passions and Other Stories. New York: Farrar, Straus and Giroux, 1975.
A Tale of Three Wishes. New York: Farrar, Straus and Giroux, 1976.
Naftali the Storyteller and His Horse, Sus. New York: Farrar, Straus and Giroux, 1976.
A Little Boy in Search of God (with Ira Moskowitz). New York: Doubleday, 1976.
Yentl: A Play (stage adaptation with Leah Napolin). New York: Samuel French, Inc. 1977.
Shosha. New York: Farrar, Straus and Giroux, 1978.
A Young Man in Search of Love. New York: Doubleday, 1978.
Old Love. New York: Farrar, Straus and Giroux, 1979.
Nobel Lecture. New York: Farrar, Straus and Giroux, 1979.
The Power of Light. New York: Farrar, Straus and Giroux, 1980.
Reaches of Heaven: A Story of the Baal Shem Tov. New York: Farrar, Straus and Giroux, 1980.
Lost in America. New York: Doubleday, 1981.
The Collected Stories. New York: Farrar, Straus and Giroux, 1982.
Three Complete Novels. New York: Avenel Books, 1982.
The Golem. New York: Farrar, Straus and Giroux, 1982.
The Penitent. New York: Farrar, Straus and Giroux, 1983.
Yentl the Yeshiva Boy. New York: Farrar, Straus and Giroux, 1984.
Love and Exile. New York: Doubleday, 1984.
Stories for Children. New York: Farrar, Straus and Giroux, 1984.
Teibele and Her Demon (stage adaptation with Eve Friedman). New York: Samuel French, Inc., 1984.
The Image and Other Stories. New York: Farrar, Straus and Giroux, 1985.
The Death of Methuselah and Other Stories. New York: Farrar, Straus and Giroux, 1988.
The King of the Fields. New York: Farrar, Straus and Giroux, 1988.
Scum. New York: Farrar, Straus and Giroux, 1991.

For Alma Singer

Contents

Introduction

Once when I apologized to Isaac Bashevis Singer for asking questions which must have been asked before, he replied, "I will try to give you different answers or I will give you the same answers but to different questions!" Several times, while reading scores of interviews in preparation for this collection, I came across similar responses to similar apologies. The interviews collected here are representative of the many he gave over a twenty-five year period. In them Singer displays a remarkable consistency in giving answers to questions concerning the nature of his writing, its ethnic roots, his demonology, the importance of free will, and the place of storytelling in human life.

It becomes clear from this collection that Singer loved to give interviews. They were a social counterpoint to the solitary work of writing. In 1964 he told Reena Sara Ribalow about the loneliness of his work: "Nobody asks the eternal questions more than an artist— why are we here, why do we suffer, why is there death? We all ask these same questions but the real artist can never forget them. This is why he is lonely, because a man who can never forget these questions, who is always asking, does not really belong. . . . [this makes him] completely lonely and not a part of society." Singer was famous, however, for encouraging interruptions of his lonely task. He routinely worked from 9 to 12 in the morning, the same hours which were "the best time to call." As he said to Kenneth Turan, "I write between one phone call and another. This is not a joke" (1976). He kept his number listed in the New York directory until shortly after winning the Nobel Prize, when, with great reluctance, he had it unlisted. He told Harold Flender in 1968, "I am interviewed, and otherwise interrupted. But somehow I manage to keep on writing. . . . I think that being disturbed is part of life, and sometimes it's useful to be disturbed because while you are busy with something else, your perspective changes or the horizon widens. All I can say about myself is that I have never written in peace . . ."

These twenty-four welcomed disturbances to his writing are representative of the many he allowed from fellow writers, well-known critics, young people just beginning their careers, and stringers from local newspapers. As with other books in the Literary Conversations series, the interviews are reprinted uncut and are arranged chronologically. For the glimpse it provides of both Singer's erudition and his humor, the selection seeks to achieve a balance between scholarly interview and portraiture. We learn of his wide-ranging self-education in classical and modern literature and philosophy as well as his free-flying pet parakeets and his Yiddish typewriter. For its usefulness to scholarship, the selection is comprehensive in its chronological range and provides both important academic discussions and newspaper interviews.

The chronological arrangement of the pieces often reveals a progressive refinement of Singer's thought, for, as the same questions are asked, he develops his answers along a uniform line until he reaches a version which seems final to him; then he repeats it in subsequent interviews with little revision. It would seem that for the author this is one of the primary values of the interview; the questions posed enable him to reveal to himself his own thought and in collaboration with a series of interviewers, to shape, articulate, modify, and arrive at a more satisfactory version of these thoughts. For instance, Singer insists to Melvin Maddocks in 1967, that literature is entertainment rather than an intellectual force for social change: "My old-fashioned aim is to entertain. I avoid gimmicks. I try to avoid page after page of repeating, of blowing up the smallest detail. That awful 'modern' garrulousness—it's a result of the writer's futile desire to teach, to explain, to change society. Actually, the force of the novelist and poet is a force without direction. It stirs the soul, but it doesn't lead to action." To Cyrena Pondrom, whose comprehensive interview was originally published in two issues of *Contemporary Literature* (1969) and is here reprinted for the first time in its entirety, Singer says, "Literature is a force, it's a vector which goes not straight but around and around—like the waves of the oceans, they keep on going, but they go nowhere. Literature stirs the mind; it makes you think about a million things, but it does not lead you." By 1972 Singer gives a more concise and more eloquent statement to Herbert

Lottman, "Art is a force, but without a vector. Like the waves of the sea it flows forward and backward, but the net result is static."

While the chronological sequencing of the interviews reveals Singer refining his thought, the collection itself, bringing together an array of interviews previously dispersed, sets up an interactive dialogism whereby the threads of new meaning are woven in the spaces between the interviews. For the scholar, this is one of the primary values of a collection of interviews, because when read together they build a new context which may lead to new perspectives. For example, through this collection, Singer's insistence upon the entertainment function of storytelling becomes reciprocally linked with his resistance to political activism. He discusses each in terms of power. To Cryena Pondrom, Singer says that, "a sociological function, a function to build a better society and so on. I don't believe that literature has this power." During his 1973 dialogue with Irving Howe on Yiddish and Jewish literary traditions, Singer explains that he is a stranger in the midst of Yiddishists because Yiddishism is strongly influenced by socialism and Marxism. When Howe comments that although Singer writes in Yiddish and Howe in English, paradoxically Howe is closer to the Yiddishist tradition than is Singer, Singer agrees: "I think so because you write your articles in *Dissent*; you still have hope that by your dissent and by the dissent of some other people like you, you can change things. I have lost this illusion." In Singer's 1963 interview with Joel Blocker and Richard Elman, he connects his resistance to any form of political activism with his unwillingness to appropriate to himself any form of power over others. He insists that his skepticism embraces both religious and political dogma, because he is opposed to systems which exert power over individuals; even the power of reviewing books is one which he seeks to avoid. He explains to Harold Flender that "power is a great temptation, and those who have power will sooner or later stumble into injustice" (1968).

This unwillingness to appropriate power to himself or to his storytelling is rhetorically connected to his cosmology; again and again he discusses the supernatural in terms of "powers" over which the human has no control: "There are powers which control us, powers which we do not know or recognize" (Ribalow 1964). What has been called his "quietism" is connected with his conviction that we not only do not know enough about the possible effects of our actions in the world to be confident about taking action, but that in trying to do good we may open ourselves up to evil: "In a way, I'm not far from the Buddhist and the Indian way of thinking that the best thing you can do is run away from evil, not fight it, because the moment you begin to fight evil, you become a part of evil yourself" (Howe 1973). Even his vegetarianism, seen in this dialogic context formed from the interviews, can be viewed, like his storytelling, as yet another way in which Singer refuses to assert power over other living beings. His philosophical perspective on life, his critical perspective on literature, and his mode of living emerge as parts of a consistent whole.

The question of Singer's belief in and use of the demonic repeatedly arises. To Blocker and Elman (1963) he asserts, "I truly believe that there are forces and spirits in this world, about which we know very little, which influence our lives. . . . I find it very easy to believe in reincarnation, possession by devils, and other such things." He goes on to make a distinction between his belief and his literary use of the supernatural. His use of the demonic is "a kind of spiritual stenography," a way of characterizing human behavior. Pondrom's interview enlarges the discussion by foregrounding the psychological nature of the demonic. And while Singer acquiesces that his demons can be approached from a variety of perspectives, he continually maintains a belief in their substantive reality. Most frequently he connects his use of the demonic with free will: "The material world is a combination of seeing and blindness. This blindness we call Satan. If we would become all seeing, we would not have free choice anymore. Because if we would see God, if we would see His greatness, there would be no temptation or sin. And since God wanted us to have free will this means that Satan, in other words, the principle of evil, must exist. Because what does free choice mean? It means freedom to choose between good and evil. If there is no evil there is no freedom" (Farrell 1976). In *Conversations with Isaac Bashevis Singer,* Richard Burgin talks at length with Singer about the supernatural and its relationship to free will, human passions, and the thought of Schopenhauer, Spinoza and the Kabbalah. A chapter from his book is reprinted here.

The collection should provide a corrective to the view that Singer was a naive storyteller, unsophisticated because he embraced folklore and because he avoided both political issues and technical innovation. These interviews reveal him as easily conversant over a wide range of world literature and as keenly aware of the socio-political forces at play in the Warsaw literary community of his young adulthood. His was a conscious choice to keep his fiction out of any political realm and to focus on traditional elements of storytelling. When Laurie Colwin, a fiction writer and a translator with Singer of his fiction, asks if he is preserving a vanished culture, Singer responds: "People tell me this, and while they tell me this I have a moment of feeling, yes, it is so. But I never sit down to write with this idea. I wouldn't be a writer if I would sit down to preserve the Yiddish language, or life in Poland, or make a better world or bring peace. I don't have all these illusions. I know that my story will not do anything else but entertain a reader for half an hour. And this is enough for me." And as he resists political significance, so he resists self-conscious technical innovations in fiction: "I'm against [literary criticism] when the writer himself is his own critic, while he writes. . . . I don't believe the writer should interpret, just as I feel it would be a very bad thing if a rose would explain exactly what colors it used and how it is to become a rose. The beauty of the rose is its silence, its *being* a rose. And I think this is really what Gertrude Stein meant when she said, 'A rose is a rose is a rose.' It meant that you cannot say more" (Pondrom 1969).

On the often asked questions regarding translation, Singer gives Blocker and Elman an often repeated answer: "be prepared to lose at least 40 per cent in translation, and to make sure that the other 60 per cent has some worth. Or better still, write something 140 per cent [good]. . . . To me the translation becomes as dear as the original." Facetiously, Singer explains his loyalty to the Yiddish language: "I like to write ghost stories and nothing fits a ghost better than a dying language. The deader the language the more alive the ghosts. Ghosts love Yiddish, and as far as I know, they all speak it. . . . I am sure that millions of Yiddish-speaking ghosts will rise from their graves one day and their first question will be, 'Is there any new book in Yiddish to read?' " (Noble 1978).

Singer's impish sense of humor is present throughout the collection. In fact, the sequence of interviews reveals that it becomes more pronounced as time goes on and he becomes more assured of his popularity, increasing in a pronounced way after he wins the Nobel Prize. In 1984 the imp becomes a bit of a devil in Singer's own interview with himself about Barbra Streisand's musical version of "Yentl the Yeshiva Boy," a production of which he was not fond. The collection reveals that there is a fierce side to Singer which stands in contrast to the frail appearance of this gentle lover of uncaged parakeets. "Modern literature gives off the smell of confession. The novel has become a couch," he complained to Melvin Maddocks in 1967. "Never before in the history of literature have the readers been so fooled, so hypnotized against their will, to call mediocrity greatness. The net result is that we have many so-called celebrities, but there is nothing to celebrate" (Turan 1976). "If I weren't a writer, I'd do some work that is not ambiguous, that is of some use to someone. . . . [There is] so much real garbage lying around which is not collected."[1]

It is that fierceness which must have sustained Singer through many years of work during which he had limited recognition and perhaps even less acceptance: Yiddishists often faulted him for refusing to use his talent as a force for change in the world, Jewish readers often deplored his use of pre-Enlightenment folk material, academics could not take too seriously a writer who insisted on telling stories which emphasize plot and character. "I would have done the same thing if I had not gotten any recognition," Singer tells Tom Teicholz (1983). "I would still do my work." Not too many years before his death, he acknowledged to Linda Matchan (1985) that it might be a struggle to write, "But I like to struggle. You can only be victorious if you fight, so if I struggle and I think that I have managed to do what I wanted, to me this is a little victory."

Like a thread present in the background texture of the conversations, is the figure of Alma Singer. Isaac's wife for over 51 years, she appears first in parentheses in Herbert Lottman's 1972 interview, glossing Singer's response to Paris: "The people here would never have done anything for you. America gave you everything." At other moments she appears briefly—breaking the news of the Nobel Prize

---

[1]Israel Shenker. "Isaac Bashevis Singer Scoffs." *Atlantic Monthly* (July 1970), 99.

(Noble 1978), bearing freshly squeezed orange juice (Berkley 1983), or packing "Duelly's" lunch to take to his class at the University of Miami (Matchan, 1985). In 1982 *People* magazine reported that Alma "manages everything from finances to a glass of tea. And, says Isaac, 'she is a very good editor.' " Singer goes on to say, " 'My wife is a saint. For the 42 years of our marriage she had to put up with a lot of nonsense, including supporting my writing as a buyer for department stores in the days when one article for the *Jewish Daily Forward* earned $25. Alma is like my Rock of Ages.' " Or, he adds facetiously, " 'the Rockette of Ages.' "[2] In my 1981 conversation with the Singers, Alma reveals her own powers of storytelling and presents herself as skeptic in contrast to her believing husband, who talks of the telepathic *esprit* which he believes flows between them. Because of her dedication to him, this collection is dedicated to Alma Singer.

The last interview in the collection was published shortly after Singer's death. He had spoken with Valerie Wells about the inde-structibility of the human spirit and about how he would like to be remembered: as a good writer, as a good man. "But whether this will come out," he quipped, "is a big question." I would like to think that this collection helps to answer that big question on both counts.

I wish to thank a variety of individuals at Butler University for support in preparing this collection. My student Jean Ulhir gave me hours of help—in locating and photocopying interviews, in typing, in cutting and pasting, in verifying details, and in providing enthusiasm down to the wire. Bill Walsh, Dean of the College of Arts and Sciences, generously offered to finance the student help I needed. Sharon Lewis, research librarian, helped to locate many of the interviews; Renee Reed, reference librarian, helped to locate authors and publishers; in the English Department, Eileen Cornelius, secretary, helped with typing, xeroxing and mailing; Shirley Daniell, projects director, offered aid in a variety of ways from retyping interviews to performing the miracles of both faxing and calming frayed nerves. Bob Stalcup helped with last minute photography. In compiling the chronology I have relied on, in addition to my own conversations over a fifteen-year span with Alma and Isaac Singer, a wide variety of

2*People* (17 May 1982), 99.

sources including newspaper and journal accounts, biographies and
autobiographies. For dating some of Singer's earliest work, I found
David Neal Miller's *Bibliography,* published by Peter Lang, very
useful. I offer thanks to Seetha A-Srinivasan, my editor at the University Press of Mississippi, and to the community of editors, publishers,
writers, agents, and friends of I. B. Singer who gave me permission
to reprint, help in locating one another, and encouragement for this
project. My thanks to Giancarlo Maiorino and my gratitude always to
my children, Matthew and Elizabeth.

Chronology

1904   Isaac Bashevis Singer is born in Leoncin in the province of Warsaw, Poland on 21 November (his passport, used for entry into the United States, would mistakenly list 14 July, 1904 as his date of birth, a mistake which Singer never thought important enough to correct); the third surviving child of Bathsheba Zylberman, daughter of the rabbi of Bilgoray in the province of Lublin, and Pinchas Mendel Singer, Hasidic rabbi from Tomaszow. His sister Hinde Esther had been born in 1891, his brother Israel Joshua in 1893, and his brother Moishe would be born in 1906.

1907–14   The family moves to Radzymin in 1907 and then, in 1908, to Warsaw, where his father is the rabbi of Krochmalna Street, which Singer chronicles in his memoir *In My Father's Court*. Singer attends local *cheders*, religious primary schools.

1914–17   Singer's education continues in the study house under his father's tutelage. Hinde Esther marries Abraham Kreitman and moves to Antwerp. When war breaks out, Israel Joshua goes into hiding to escape conscription; Isaac visits him in an artist's studio and has his first, vivid, experiences of a secular world. In 1915 the Germans occupy Warsaw and the Singers suffer extreme poverty and hunger.

1917–23   To escape the hardships of an occupied city, Singer, with his mother and younger brother Moishe, leave Warsaw to return to his mother's family in Bilgoray. Singer studies the Talmud and learns modern Hebrew, which he then teaches in private homes. During this period, he is immersed in the rural Hasidic folk culture which will permeate his work. Although it was forbidden, he studies the Kabbalah. At the same time he pursues secular studies including German and Polish and reads Spinoza. He begins to write secular literature which he publishes in a Hebrew newspaper. In 1921 Singer enrolls in Warsaw's Tachkemoni Rabbinical Seminary, but returns to Bilgoray the following year, where he again teaches Hebrew, before joining his parents and younger brother in nearby Dzikow.

1923   Singer returns to Warsaw when offered a job as proof-reader for *Literarishe bleter,* a journal which his brother, Israel Joshua coedits. He writes reviews and begins a series of translations into Yiddish, which, by 1935, include Knut Hamsun's *Pan* and *Victoria,* Remarque's *All Quiet on the Western Front,* Mann's *The Magic Mountain.* He also translates novels for a variety of Warsaw newspapers. It is during this period that he frequents the Warsaw Writers Club and he loses his faith in religious dogma. His belief in a God who is completely unknown and forever silent leads him from agnosticism to a personal mysticism which becomes central to his fiction.

1924–25   Singer meets Runia or Rachel, the mother of his only child, Israel. They separate in 1935, when he emigrates to the United States and she to Russia, divergent paths which reflect their serious political differences.

1925–28   In 1925 Singer makes his fiction debut in Yiddish with a short story, "Oyf der elter" (In Old Age) which wins a prize in *Literarishe bleter's* literary contest. It is published under the pseudonym "Tse" and, in 1935, is reprinted in *The Jewish Daily Forward.* His second published story, "Nerot" (Candles) appears in 1925 in *Ha-yom* and is signed Isaac Bashevis, a variant of his mother's name; its use is both a tribute to her and an attempt to distinguish himself from his brother, who by now is well-known as a writer. Other early works include "Vayber" (Women) published that same year in *Literarishe bleter;* "Eyniklekh" (Grandchildren) published in *Varshever shriftn,* 1926–7; "Verter oder bilder" (Words or Pictures) published in *Literarishe bleter* 1927; and "Oyfn oylem-hatoye" (In the World of Chaos) in *Di yidishe velt,* 1928. "Two Corpses Go Dancing," published in Yiddish in 1943 and in English in 1968 in the collection *The Seance,* is one of a number of variations which Singer wrote on "In the World of Chaos."

1929   Singer's father dies in Dzikow; his son Israel is born.

1932   Singer edits, with Aaron Zeitlin, a magazine called *Globus,* which prints several of Singer's short stories, including "A Zokn" (The Old Man), later translated and included in *Gimpel the Fool and Other Stories* (1959).

1933   *Globus* serializes Singer's first novel, *Satan in Goray.* Israel Joshua, his wife and son Joseph emigrate to New York where he works for the *Jewish Daily Forward.* Before leaving Warsaw his older son dies of pneumonia.

1934   Singer also writes for a Yiddish newspaper in Paris, the *Parizer haynt,* and, through his brother, begins to sell stories to the *Jewish Daily Forward.*

1935   The Warsaw P. E. N. Club publishes *Satan in Goray* in book form. Assisted by his brother, Singer emigrates to New York, arriving 1 May, to work as an unsalaried free-lance journalist for Abraham Cahan at the *Forward.* He assumes the pen names I Warshawsky (1939 ff) and D. Segal (1943 ff), and has a regular column called, "It's Worthwhile Knowing." In the early 1940s he joins the staff as a salaried writer.

1935–36   *Der zindiker meshiekh (Messiah the Sinner)* is serialized in the *Forward,* but is not considered a success.

1937   Singer meets Alma Haimann Wasserman at a summer
           resort in the Catskills. She had emigrated from Germany
           the previous year. They marry on 14 February 1940. A
           well-educated woman, Alma helps to support Singer's
           writing by working for many years in sales positions in
           New York department stores. She also serves as one of
           his translators.

1939   Singer's mother and younger brother Moishe are de-
           ported from Dzikow in a cattle car; reportedly they freeze
           or starve to death that winter.

1939–43   In the Forward, Singer writes essays about grass widows,
           dybbuks, and split personality—topics which reappear in
           his fiction. His titles range from "Love, the Eternal
           Riddle—The Whims of its Victims" to "People Who Like
           to Torture and People Who Like to Suffer" and "We Also
           Dream While Awake—How." He writes war-related
           essays, such as "The War is Really a Moral Issue" and
           "Algeria, Tunisia, Morocco—What about these Countries
           our Army is Liberating from the Nazis?"

1943   Singer becomes a United States citizen; Farlag Matones
           (New York) publishes Satan in Goray and Other Tales in
           Yiddish. He begins writing short stories again, publishing
           "Zaydlus der ershter" in the Forward, which is later
           translated as "Zeidlus the Pope" and collected in Short
           Friday (1964) and "Der roye veeyne-nire," translated as
           "The Unseen," and collected in Gimpel the Fool (1957).

1944   On February 10, having dined with Isaac and Alma at
           their apartment the night before, Singer's beloved older
           brother and mentor, Israel Joshua, dies of a heart attack
           at age 51. His son, Joseph Singer, later became a fre-
           quent translator of his uncle's work. "The Spinoza of
           Market Street" is published in Yiddish; it later appears
           in Esquire (1961) and as the title story of a collection
           (1961).

1945   "Der kurtser fraytik" (Short Friday) appears in Yiddish,
            later to be the title story in a 1964 collection. "Gimpl
            tam" (Gimpel the Fool), perhaps Singer's most famous
            story, is published in *Yidisher kemfer.* Other stories
            published this year in Yiddish and later collected in
            English translations include "The Little Shoemakers"
            and "The Wife-Killer."

1946–52   In 1946, *The Family Moskat* begins a three-year serializa-
            tion in the *Forward*. It is also serialized over New York
            radio's WEVD's "Forward Hour." Before the book is
            completed, Alfred A. Knopf buys translation rights for
            The Family Moskat. In 1950, the novel, dedicated to
            Israel Joshua Singer, is published by Knopf in English
            (translated by Abraham Gross, Nancy Gross, and Singer)
            and by Morris S. Sklarsky in Yiddish. In 1949, "A Tale of
            Two Liars," which, in 1961, appears in *The Spinoza of
            Market Street,* is published in the *Forward*. In 1952, *The
            Manor* begins serialization in the *Forward*. In preparation
            for an anthology of Yiddish literature, Eliezer Greenberg
            reads "Gimpl tam" to Irving Howe. Saul Bellow translates
            the story and Howe sends it to *Partisan Review.*

1953   The appearance of "Gimpel the Fool" in the May issue of
            Partisan Review is a critical breakthrough for Singer.
            During the fifties and thereafter, his work appears widely
            in English, in such magazines as *Partisan Review, Com-
            mentary, The New Yorker, Harper's,* and *Esquire.* In
            an interview in 1967, Singer says: "I considered myself
            unknown to American readers. Then in 1953, *Partisan
            Review* published 'Gimpel the Fool,' in a translation by
            Saul Bellow. This story brought me so much popularity—
            somehow I have the strange feeling that all the literary
            people in America read that one issue of *Partisan Review.*
            From this point, writers and editors began to call me and
            be interested in me" (from Dick Adler. "The Magician of
            86th Street." *Book World* [29 October 1967], 8).

1954   "Gimpel the Fool" is reprinted in *A Treasury of Yiddish
            Literature,* edited by Irving Howe and Eliezer Greenberg
            (Viking Press). Singer's sister Hinde Esther Kreitman, who
            also became a writer, dies.

1955   Noonday Press publishes *Satan in Goray,* translated by
            Joseph Sloan in collaboration with Singer, Cecil Hemley
            and Elaine Gottlieb Hemley.

1956   *Mayn tatn's bes-din shtub* (the Yiddish original of *In My
            Father's Court*) is published by Kval Publishers.

1957   *Shadows by the Hudson* is serialized in the *Forward.
            Gimpel the Fool and Other Stories,* Singer's first collec-
            tion of stories in English, is published by Noonday. Except
            for "The Old Man," which was published in *Globus* in
            1932, the stories were written in New York between
            1942–57. Portions of *Mayn tatn's bes-din shtub* is
            dramatized at the Folksbeine Theatre in Manhattan.

1958   *A Ship to America* is serialized in the *Forward.*

1959   *The Magician of Lublin* is serialized in the *Forward.*

1960   Noonday publishes the English version of *The Magician
            of Lublin,* translated by Elaine Gottlieb and Joseph Singer
            in collaboration with Singer. This same year Noonday
            Press is bought up by Farrar, Straus, and Cudahy, and
            Farrar Straus begins its long affiliation with Singer. He
            reads at Brandeis University and attracts the attention
            of critic and man of letters, Edmund Wilson.

1961   *The Slave* is serialized in the *Forward* and *The Spinoza of
            Market Street,* Singer's second collection of short stories
            in English, is published by FS&C.

1962   *The Slave,* translated by Singer and Cecil Hemley is
            published by FS&C. For the first time Singer is listed in

the Modern Language Association Bibliography of scholarly publications. J. A. Eisenberg's essay, "Isaac Bashevis
Singer—Passionate Primitive or Pious Puritan" (*Judaism*), is listed under the heading "Yiddish." This is also
the year that Singer, who has avoided animal food for
years, becomes a vegetarian.

1963   Richard Hall adapts "Gimpel the Fool" as a one-act play
        which is produced at the Mermaid Theater in New York
        City. The Central Yiddish Culture Organization publishes
        Gimpel Tam un Anderer Dertailunger.

1964   *Short Friday and Other Stories* is published by Farrar,
        Straus and Giroux. Singer is elected to the National
        Institute of Arts and Letters and is nominated for the
        Nobel Prize by Edmund Wilson.

1965   FS&G reissues *The Family Moskat.*

1966   *Sonim, di geshichte fun a liebe,* later translated as
        Enemies, a Love Story (1972), is serialized in the
        Forward. FS&G brings out Singer's first collection of
        memoirs, *In My Father's Court,* based on his childhood
        years and previously published in Yiddish in 1956 as
        Mayn tatn's bes-din shtub. His first in a long series of
        illustrated tales for children is published by Harper and
        Row; *Zlateh the Goat and Other Stories* is translated by
        Singer and Elizabeth Shub and is illustrated by Maurice
        Sendak. It wins Singer's first Newbery Award. Irving
        Howe edits and introduces *Selected Short Stories of Isaac
        Bashevis Singer* for Modern Library.

1967   *The Manor,* translated in collaboration with Joseph
        Singer and Elaine Gottlieb, is published by FS&G and
        receives a nomination for the National Book Award.
        Singer is awarded a National Arts Council grant. With the
        publication on 25 November of "The Slaughterer," Singer
        begins his long relationship with *The New Yorker* and his

collaboration there with Rachel MacKenzie who becomes his editor. Two more volumes for children appear: *The Fearsome Inn,* illustrated by Nonny Hogrogian, which wins the Newbery Award, and *Mazel and Shlimazel; or, The Milk of a Lioness,* illustrated by Margot Zemach, which is named an American Library Association Notable. The difficulty in categorizing Singer, an American citizen from Poland who writes in Yiddish, is reflected in this year's annual Modern Language Association Bibliography of scholarly publications: Irving H. Buchen's "Isaac Bashevis Singer and the Revival of Satan" (*Texas Studies in Language and Literature*) is listed under "Yiddish," while Richard A. Newman's "Isaac Bashevis Singer" (*Hibbert Journal*) is found under the heading "American."

1968   *The Seance and Other Stories,* dedicated to the memory of Singer's sister Hinde Esther, is published by FS&G along with the children's collection *When Shlemiel Went to Warsaw and Other Stories,* illustrated by Margot Zemach.

1969   *Shlemiel* wins the Newbery Award and is named an American Library Association Notable. FS&G publishes *The Estate* (sequel to *The Manor*), translated in collaboration with Joseph Singer, Elaine Gottlieb, and Elizabeth Shub, as well as a children's version of his memoirs, *A Day of Pleasure: Stories of a Boy Growing Up in Warsaw* with photographs by Roman Vishniac.

1970   Singer wins his first National Book Award for *A Day of Pleasure.* FS&G publishes *A Friend of Kafka and Other Stories* and, for children, *Elijah the Slave,* illustrated by Antonio Frasconi, and *Joseph and Koza; or, The Sacrifice to the Vistula,* illustrated by Symeon Shimin. *The Manor* and *The Estate* are purchased by the Book-of-the-Month Club. In May at the Whitney Museum, Singer is presented with Brandeis University's Creative Arts Award Medal for 1970.

1971   *An Isaac Bashevis Singer Reader* is published by FS&G. *Alone in the Wild Forest,* illustrated by Margot Zemach, and *The Topsy-Turvy Emperor of China* are published for children. The Jewish Publication Society publishes George A. Perret's and Singer's *Drawings of Tully Filmus.*

1972   *Enemies, A Love Story* is published by FS&G and *The Hasidim* by Crown. With a grant from the American Film Institute, Bruce Davidson produces *Isaac Singer's Nightmare and Mrs. Pupko's Beard,* which appears on Public Television and wins first prize in its class at the 1972 American Film Festival. *The Wicked City,* illustrated by Leonard Everett Fisher, is published for children and named an American Library Association Notable.

1973   *A Crown of Feathers and Other Stories* appears. Yale Repertory Theater produces *The Mirror* adapted from the story of the same name which was first published in *New World Writing* (1955) and included in *Gimpel the Fool.* Another book for children appears: *The Fools of Chelm and Their History,* illustrated by Uri Shulevitz.

1974   Singer wins his second National Book Award for *A Crown of Feathers. Baal Tshuve (The Penitent)* is serialized in the *Forward.* In April, Yale Repertory produces *Shlemiel the First,* based on portions of *The Fools of Chelm.* The Chelsea Theater produces *Yentl* at the Brooklyn Academy of Music. Leah Napolin collaborates with Singer on the script. *Why Noah Chose the Dove* appears for children.

1975   *Passions and Other Stories* is published. In July Singer receives an honorary degree from the Hebrew University in Jerusalem during the celebrations of the university's Golden Jubilee. In September, the S. Y. Agnon Gold

Medal is bestowed upon him by the American Friends of the Hebrew University. And in October *Yentl* opens on Broadway at the Eugene O'Neill Theater, starring Tovah Feldshuh as Yentl and John Shea as Avigdor. Later that year, Singer receives the Maggid Award from the American Jewish Public Relations Society.

1976   *Naftali the Storyteller and His Horse, Sus,* published by FS&G and illustrated by Margot Zemach, is named an American Library Association Notable. Doubleday publishes *A Little Boy in Search of God: Mysticism in a Personal Light* with illustrations by Ira Moskowitz.

1978   In the Spring *Teibele and Her Demon,* staged in collaboration with Eve Friedman, opens in Minneapolis at the Guthrie Theater. FS&G publishes *Shosha.* A film version of *The Magician of Lublin* is produced by Menahem Golan and Yoram Globus, starring Alan Arkin, Louise Fletcher, Valerie Perrine and Shelley Winters. Singer's second volume of memoirs, *A Young Man in Search of Love,* illustrated by Raphael Soyer is published by Doubleday. And in the fall, Singer wins the Nobel Prize for Literature.

1979   FS&G publishes Singer's *Nobel Lecture* in a bilingual edition, as well as a collection of stories, *Old Love* which takes its title from a story in *Passions.*

1980   FS&G publishes *The Power of Light: Eight Stories for Hanukkah,* illustrated by Irene Lieblich and *The Reaches of Heaven,* a study of the Baal Shem Tov, illustrated with twenty-four original etchings by Ira Moskowitz.

1981   *Lost in America,* Singer's third volume of memoirs, is illustrated with paintings and drawings by Raphael Soyer for Doubleday.

1982   *The Collected Stories* is published by FS&G and is sold
           as the Main Selection of the Book-of-the-Month Club.
           Three Complete Novels, an unabridged collection of *The
           Slave, Enemies, A Love Story,* and *Shosha* is published
           by Avenel Books. FS&G brings out *The Golem,* illus-
           trated by Uri Shulevitz, for children.

1983   Barbra Streisand produces, directs and stars in the film
           version of *Yentl,* based on "Yentl the Yeshiva Boy," from
           the collection *Short Friday.* The story had previously
           been adapted for the stage by Singer in collaboration
           with Leah Napolin, and had a Broadway run in 1975.
           The Penitent, a translation of *Baal Tshuve,* is published
           by FS&G.

1984   *A Play for the Devil* performs off Broadway. *Love and
           Exile,* Singer's collection of memoirs, including *A Little
           Boy in Search of God, A Young Man in Search of Love,*
           and *Lost in America,* is published by Doubleday with a
           new introduction, "The Beginning." Previously published
           children's stories are collected and published by FS&G as
           Stories for Children. The stage adaptation of "Teibele and
           Her Demon" is published with Eve Friedman by Samuel
           French, Inc. An edition of "Yentl the Yeshiva Boy" with
           woodcuts by Antonio Frasconi is published by FS&G.

1985   *The Image and Other Stories,* translated with Lester
           Goran, is published by FS&G. *Der ver aheim (The Way
           Home)* is serialized in the *Forward.*

1988   Singer's last collection of short stories, *The Death of
           Methuselah and Other Stories,* and a novel, *The King of
           the Fields* (a translation of *Der Kenig vun di felder*) are
           published by FS&G.

1989   The American Academy and Institute of Arts and Letters
           bestows its highest award, the Gold Medal, on Singer. A
           film version of *Enemies, A Love Story* is produced and

directed by Paul Mazursky, and stars Ron Silver, Angelica
Houston, and Lena Olin. Because Singer's health is
failing, Alma Singer attends the New York opening alone.
The Singers now spend most of the year in their ocean-
side condominium in Florida.

1991   Singer's last novel, *Scum,* a translation by Rosaline
         Dukalsky of *Shoym,* is published by FS&G. On 24 July
         Isaac Bashevis Singer dies in Surfside, Florida.

Isaac Bashevis Singer: Conversations

An Interview with Isaac Bashevis Singer

Joel Blocker and Richard Elman/1963

From *Commentary*, 36 (November 1963), 364–72. Reprinted from *Commentary*, November 1963, by permission; all rights reserved. (Richard Elman's latest work is the novel *Tar Beach*.)

Interviewers: Perhaps we could begin by asking you some questions about what has happened to Yiddish literature. Yiddish literature was, in its prime, a body of work which was very close to the masses by whom it was read—in language, in point of view, and in drawing from a common basis of experience. The annihilation of six million Jews during World War II changed all that drastically. The Yiddish-reading audience was decimated and continues now to dwindle from attrition. How, then, do you feel about writing in Yiddish today?

Singer: You don't feel very happy about writing in a language when you know it dies from day to day. Although I don't feel that Yiddish will die completely, it's a fact that the number of readers is becoming smaller and smaller, and we—I mean Yiddish writers—are all conscious of it. The only thing is, I don't have this feeling while I write; I don't choose to remember it. I think that's a lucky thing because if I did remember while I was writing that some of my readers were dying and others were not being born to replace them, it might have some influence on me. Writers, as a rule, don't think about their readers while they write. As a matter of fact, thinking about the reader is a terrible pitfall for a writer. A writer should not think about who is going to read him because the moment he thinks about this, some other power interferes. In my case, writing Yiddish and thinking about the readers would really destroy the writer completely. But happily I never think about such things. When I sit down to write I have a feeling that I'm talking maybe to millions or maybe to nobody.

Interviewers: Nevertheless, are you and other Yiddish writers disturbed by this tragedy—not at the moment of writing, but in general?

Singer: We are all conscious of it when we are not writing. There is a lot of discussion about it in the Yiddish papers and in meetings of the PEN Club. We all feel the same thing and we express it in Yiddish by saying: "We talk to the wall." We sometimes have the feeling that we are talking to nobody. On the other hand, I can tell you that those people who still read Yiddish are a peculiarly sensitive group. No writer gets the response a Yiddish writer does, if the readers really like him. The Yiddish reader, as a rule, is either very bad or very good. There is no such thing as a neutral reader. Either he loves the writer or he hates him. I have had good luck writing in the Yiddish paper, the *Jewish Daily Forward.* This paper still has eighty or ninety thousand readers and many of them—as a matter of fact, most of them—are readers of fiction. I still have a lot of readers and have the feeling sometimes that I am talking to thousands of people. I know, for example, that my novel, *The Slave,* which the *Forward* ran in its week-end literary supplement, had an audience of twenty thousand readers. Not many writers have such an immediate audience.

Interviewers: Then writing in Yiddish today has its advantages as well? You're not completely "talking to the wall"? In fact, you're probably better off than most serious American writers today who have no immediate mass audience of that size. If a writer in this country does enjoy such readership, it is not of the same kind as your Yiddish-reading audience.

Singer: I must say that the *Jewish Daily Forward* has a tradition of publishing good fiction. Its editors have always considered it a very important part of the newspaper. Our readers ask for fiction. It isn't like American newspapers. The New York *Daily News,* for example, also publishes fiction, but I don't think the *News* would lose many readers if it stopped publishing stories. The Yiddish reader is accustomed to reading novels and stories in the newspapers. For him, it's a must. In this respect, we are lucky.

Interviewers: Do you see any future for Yiddish literature?

Singer: The future looks very black. They say that if a Yiddish reader dies, there is no one to replace him. This is true. How it happens that the *Forward* still has eighty to a hundred thousand readers today, and the *Jewish Day Journal,* another Yiddish newspaper, has close to fifty thousand is a riddle to me because twenty-five or even thirty-five years ago they said the Yiddish press

would only last another five years. One of the greatest pessimists then
was Abraham Cahan who helped build the *Forward*. He said that the
first generation of Jews in this country would speak Yiddish, but the
second generation would not. It was so, but somehow the Yiddish
press goes on living. It's like the Jews generally. They die all the time
and they keep on living all the time.

Interviewers: If that's the case, who then are you writing for—
this still considerable Yiddish audience, a different audience in
English and other languages, or both?

Singer: As I said before, I'm not very conscious of the audience.
The only audience I'm conscious of—you may laugh at me—is
myself. I have to please myself. After I have written something I am
the first reader. I'm most interested in pleasing myself. It's not modest
to say so, but I think this is so with every writer. In my case this is
especially important because Yiddish readers are not a homogeneous
audience. They are of different kinds, some very educated, some not
educated at all. For example, we have readers who will read good
fiction, but their intelligence is so small and their taste so dubious that
you just don't know how they will judge and what they will accept.
We get letters at the *Forward* from readers who say, "I read the
wonderful novel of Sholem Asch. I also read the wonderful novel
of—," referring to some mediocre detective story we might publish
at the same time. To him they are both alike. Yet we also have very
many perceptive readers who know world literature and are very
sensitive to literary values. That's why when a Yiddish writer worries
about his audience he gets all mixed up.

Interviewers: You don't at all—somewhere in the back of your
mind—have an image of someone reading you in a foreign language—English, for example?

Singer: That's a very important question. They accused Sholem
Asch of writing for the translator. I don't say the accusation was true,
but there were those who pointed to specific passages in Asch's work
and said: "You see these lines. They were written for the English, not
for the Yiddish reader." I take great care not to think about the reader
in English or French or any other language. Nothing can spoil a writer
more than writing for the translator. He must feel that he writes for
people who know everything he knows—not for the stranger. It's
only when you write for your own people and when you don't think

about anybody else that the other people reading in a foreign language will appreciate your work and like it. Can you imagine Gogol writing for the French or the American reader? He was a Russian and wrote like a Russian and assumed that the reader knew everything he knew. You know, many of my Yiddish readers complain that I am too Jewish. They say: "We have already forgotten about all these things." "You remind us of things we would like to forget." But this doesn't bother me. I assume that the reader knows as much about Jewishness and Jewish life as I do.

Interviewers: Would it be fair to say that you are actually writing in a somewhat artificial or illusionary context, as if none of the terrible things that happened to the Jewish people during the last two decades really did occur?

Singer: Yes, very fair. There was a famous philosopher, Vaihinger, who wrote a book called *The Philosophy of "As If,"* in which he showed that we all behave "as if." The "as if" is so much a part of our life that it really isn't artificial. After all, what could be more artificial than marriage? When a man marries a woman he assumes that she's going to be devoted to him and he acts as if his wife will treat him in this fashion. And so on and so on . . . Every man assumes he will go on living. He behaves *as if* he will never die. So I wouldn't call my attitude artificial. It's very natural and healthy. We have to go on living and writing.

Interviewers: But you do agree that at the heart of your attitude there is an illusion which is consciously sustained?

Singer: Yes. But take the case of a mathematician who writes a book and knows that there are only ten or twenty other mathematicians who will understand him. Still he doesn't write for twenty people. He knows there will be mathematicians in later generations. Every man who creates something does not and should not worry about being understood. I would say I write for the best possible reader no matter how many readers there really are.

Interviewers: Then you're not really a popular writer in Yiddish, just as in English those critics who originally acclaimed your work were part of an avant-garde rather than a mass audience?

Singer: No. I'm not a popular writer among Yiddish readers. As a matter of fact I had many quarrels with Abe Cahan who told me: "You write well, but it's not for our readers." Even my present editor at the *Forward* sometimes complains that my language is too difficult, my subjects too obscure. And when I write about devils and ghosts, for instance, he asks: "Who among our readers remembers such things?" No, I'm not a popular writer. But the truth is, in spite of this, I have become, to a degree, "popular." Still, my work is only published in the week-end supplements which are devoted to literary works, rather than the regular week-day pages in which appears conventionally popular fiction.

Occasionally, however, I write more popular work under a different name—under the name of Warshofsky. Generally I sign my name in the *Forward* Isaac Bashevis, but once in a while I publish under the name of Isaac Warshofsky. When I write under the name of Warshofsky I take less care, but I never publish such things in book form. I use a different name to distinguish between two different kinds of writing. Since I must write a great deal and I cannot work on every piece of writing the way I work on the stories which I take very seriously, I publish some pieces which I consider belle-lettristic journalism. It sometimes happens that some of them come out well. In fact, one of my books, *Mein Taten's Bes-din Shtub* ("My Father's Courtroom") is a compilation of this kind of work, published under the name of Warshofsky. Only later I adopted it, as it were, and signed the name Bashevis . . . after I cleaned it up and worked on it.

Interviewers: Is it a common practice among Yiddish writers to use pseudonyms?

Singer: It's not uncommon. I. L. Peretz wrote under many different names. Some say as many as fifty pseudonyms.

Interviewers: And you make a definite distinction between your literary and your journalistic work?

Singer: Yes I do. I must say I don't work very hard on my journalism. I just write it and let it go. I write memoirs of my boyhood, reviews, *feuilletons,* and all kinds of things. As a matter of fact many of my readers like my journalism better than my stories, and some of my best stories were never published in the *Forward.* For example, "Gimpel the Fool" was first published in a Yiddish literary magazine.

Interviewers: About this business of names again. What is your real name?

Singer: My real name is Isaac Singer. My brother's name was Israel Joshua Singer. In Yiddish I sign my fiction Isaac Bashevis. For some reason this name is sacred to me, and I won't sign my journalism with it. Perhaps it's because Bashevis is derived from my mother's name. Her name was Bathsheba.

Interviewers: To come back to Yiddish literature for a few moments. Do you regard yourself as writing within that specific tradition, or do you feel that you have been more influenced by non-Jewish European authors?

Singer: I'll tell you, I feel myself naturally a part of the Jewish tradition. Very strongly so! But I wouldn't say I feel myself a part of the Yiddish tradition. Somehow I always wanted to write in my own way, and I never felt that I was somebody's disciple. For instance, Sholem Aleichem, who was a great writer, always used to say that he was a disciple of Mendele Mocher Seforim. That was very modest. But I don't have these feelings. The only person I have a lot to thank for—from whom I learned a great deal—was my brother, I. J. Singer, who was ten years older than I. But even here I wouldn't say I was my brother's disciple. I would almost say that I tried to create my own tradition, if one can use such words.

Interviewers: Then what do you think you *did* learn from your brother?

Singer: My brother wrote a number of novels—*The Brothers Ashkenazi,* which was translated into English; also *Yoshe Kalb,* which was translated under the name of *The Sinner,* and many others. I learned a lot from my brother, particularly in regard to construction. I consider him a great master of construction, and his writing was always quite close to me. Much more so than Sholem Asch's, for example. So whatever there was to learn from my brother I learned, and I think it was a lot. My brother always used to say to me that a writer should not mix the essay with fiction. Many writers are half essayists and half fiction writers. Thomas Mann, for example. He writes a story, and in the middle of the story he inserts an essay or an article. He is himself both the writer and the critic. Even a writer like Dostoevski used to do this. In *The Brothers Karamazov,* while he is describing Father Zosima, he suddenly inserts a whole essay on what a saint is and what a saint should be. It is the old-fashioned way of writing. My brother always used to call this a literary mannerism. It's true that the great novelists used this in a successful way. But for a young writer, a modern writer, it's not the best model. I avoid these things. When I tell a story, I tell a story. I don't try to discuss, criticize, or analyze my characters.

Interviewers: Apparently, your brother was very much aware of Flaubert's dicta on the purity of the novel?

Singer: Yes, you're right. I think in this case I also agree one hundred per cent with Flaubert—when you tell a story, tell a story. Use the words that give information about your characters, but don't talk about them. When I write about a character I will say that he looked so and so and behaved so and so, but I won't say he was a good man. Sometimes I read writers who say their characters are "noble" men. To me this is ridiculous. If the man was truly noble this should come across from what you tell about him. It's up to the reader to judge.

Interviewers: Along these lines, then, do you consider yourself to be a "modern" or a "modernistic" writer? The American critic, Irving Howe, has tried to define this modernistic element in your work. Do you feel this was just?

Singer: When I read Mr. Howe's piece I was greatly surprised to find myself described as modernistic. First of all, it never occurred to me that I was a "modernist." Secondly, I don't know what a modernist is. This word . . . you cannot define it. What is modern today will be traditional twenty years from now. When Mr. Howe called me modernistic, I assume he meant that I write in a way similar to other contemporary writers. Maybe you could tell me. What does it mean to be a "modernist"?

Interviewers: Well, perhaps it means your work is different from traditional Yiddish writing. For instance, there are certain conventions that Sholem Aleichem uses that don't appear in your writing. One example would be the "dear reader" device, the writer addressing the reader directly.

Singer: Yes. I try not to use the "dear reader." It's curious, however, when I write under the name of Warshofsky in an article or memoir, then it pops up when I need to make a connection of some sort. But in real fiction the "dear reader" device is always a trick, a substitute for telling the story. It's only when the writer can't think of anything else or has some spiritual interruption that he resorts to "dear reader"—as if to say, "Dear reader, forgive me for not telling the story the right way."

Interviewers: Do you mind if we ask a few biographical questions at this point? You were born in 1904 in Poland and grew up in Warsaw. Warsaw at that time, during the first two decades of the century, was a center of Yiddish writing. Did you go to the University in Warsaw?

Singer: No. But I studied in a rabbinical seminary which was a kind of college.

Interviewers: How old were you?

Singer: I must have been about eighteen.

Interviewers: What did the studies encompass?

Singer: We studied secular as well as religious subjects and the Hebrew language. I never finished the seminary because a lot of the things they taught there I knew already. My knowledge of secular subjects was backward, but in religious matters I knew a great deal. My family was very religious. My father was a rabbi. So were both of my grandfathers.

Interviewers: Were they Hasidic rabbis?

Singer: My father was and his father as well. But my maternal grandfather was an anti-Hasid, a *misnaged.* There was always a conflict between my father and my mother about Hasidism because my mother was a little bit of a skeptic where that was concerned— especially about the *zaddikim,* "the wonder-rabbis." My father always used to say that if you don't believe in the *zaddikim* today, tomorrow you won't believe in God. My mother would say, it's one thing to believe in God and another to believe in a man. My mother's point of view is also my point of view.

Interviewers: But did your family want you to be a rabbi?

Singer: Very much so. But I made up my mind very early not to be one because I began to doubt, not the power of God, but all the traditions and dogmas. I saw how one sentence in the Bible was made into volumes and volumes in the Talmud and later books. From my earliest childhood I had a feeling that one thing was God and the Higher Powers, which are above us and with us, and another thing is what human beings make of the divine. I think that many of the misunderstandings of religion stem from this . . . the failure to distinguish between God and man.

Interviewers: What kind of boyhood did you have? Many of your books portray urban lower-class Jewry in Poland. Were you, a rabbi's son, exposed to this as a boy?

Singer: Yes. We lived on a very poor street in Warsaw, Kroch-malna Street. Naturally I was in contact with poor people. Many of them used to come to my father for advice. Many of their questions were religious and moral, but they had a direct bearing on everyday life. Many of the women used to come and tell stories of woe to my mother. I always listened, and I had plenty of chances to listen, to poor people and rich people. My father was a *dayan*, a kind of a judge. So people used to come with all kinds of business problems and conflicts, and I remember trying to decide for myself which of them was honest and which of them was dishonest.

Interviewers: Well, is the clan you describe in *The Family Moskat* a family you knew in the Warsaw of that day, or is it purely invention?

Singer: No. It was invented. It is true that there was such a rich family in Warsaw in those days, and many people have thought that I was describing this family, but it isn't so. *The Family Moskat* is a composite of many families I knew.

Interviewers: What do you think first impelled you to write?

Singer: There was one important circumstance: My brother was a writer. My father was also a writer. He published religious books. So writing and publishing were always familiar. However, the real reason for wanting to write was that I very often met situations which baffled me, and from the moment I knew that there was such a thing as literature, I thought how wonderful it would be to be able to describe such things. Incidentally, some of these situations now seem not as unusual as they seemed at the time. When I was about twelve years old I began to read worldly books. Before that I had read only Hebrew books. Well, the first worldly book that I read was a Sherlock Holmes collection by Conan Doyle in a Yiddish translation, and I cannot tell you how delighted I was with this book. I'm afraid even today to try and read it again because I know I would be disap-pointed. Every story of Sherlock Holmes sounded to me then like heavenly music. Something only an angel could write. As a matter of fact, I tried to imitate Sherlock Holmes. I considered myself a detective. I remember once walking in Warsaw and seeing a man who I immediately thought was suspicious. I said to myself, this man is suspicious. There was no reason whatsoever for me to believe this, but I followed him over half of Warsaw. After a while the man began to look back. At that moment I was Sherlock Holmes and I hoped that he would commit a murder and that I would catch him, and so on and so on.

Interviewers: This familiarity with criminals and their behavior comes across very strongly in *The Magician of Lublin*. . . .

Singer: Now that you say so, I think you are right, but it would never have occurred to me. This is the reason that critics sometimes know more than writers.

Interviewers: When did you begin to write seriously?

Singer: Let me continue with what I was saying before. One day my brother brought home a copy of Dostoevski's *Crime and Punishment* in Yiddish . . .

Interviewers: Also a detective story. . . .

Singer: Yes. But I understood very little of it. I was just too young. I knew that the hero had committed a murder, but that's all. There is one moment in the book where the District Attorney speaks to Raskolnikov and Raskolnikov suddenly gets up and is ready to leave and then he sits down again. When I read these few lines I thought how wonderful this was. I don't know why this made such an impression on me. . . . Now you ask, when did I begin to write: When I was about sixteen I began to write in Hebrew, not in Yiddish. I wrote terrible poems, although they were admired because the Hebrew was good. Then, after a while, I began to write stories, again in Hebrew. I even published a few in a Hebrew newspaper. But later I saw that writing Hebrew was an artificial thing because there was a lot of dialogue in my writing, and as my characters spoke Yiddish, I had to translate what they said into Hebrew—which was not a living language at that time. So, after a while, I said to myself: What am I, a writer or a translator? And I came to the conclusion that I must write in Yiddish because it was my mother language and the language of the people I wanted to write about. Since then I have written mostly in Yiddish. Wait—here's something more I remember, a very interesting thing. Even before I learned to read and write, as a child, I liked to imitate my father and my brother. I used to take a pen and scribble on paper. All week long I would scribble and when Saturday came I had to stop. This for me was an ordeal—to have to wait until the

Sabbath ended so that I could continue my smearing. Why? I don't know even today.

Interviewers: You once told us that during your adolescence you spent three or four years in your grandfather's village, and that this was a strong influence in determining your future as a writer.

Singer: Yes. Because this town was very old-fashioned. Not much had changed there in many generations. In this town the traditions of hundreds of years ago still lived. There was no railroad nearby. It was stuck in the forest and it was pretty much the same as it must have been during the time of Chmielnicki. I learned a lot about Jewishness in this town. The town was called Bilgoray. I could have written *The Family Moskat* (which takes place in Warsaw) without having lived in Bilgoray, but I could never have written *Satan in Goray* or some of my other stories without having been there.

Interviewers: Why? What did you do there?

Singer: I studied the Talmud. I studied the Bible. I studied Cabbala, although it was forbidden. According to the Law, a man should not study Cabbala before he is thirty, but I used to remove the books from the study house. In fact, I almost stole them. I took them to my house and read them often. I was fascinated by the Cabbala.

Interviewers: Considering all this, how did your parents react to your wanting to be a writer?

Singer: It was a great shock to them. They considered all the secular writers to be heretics, all unbelievers—they really were too, most of them. To become a *literat* was to them almost as bad as becoming a *meshumed,* one who forsakes the faith. My father used to say that secular writers like Peretz were leading the Jews to heresy. He said everything they wrote was against God. Even though Peretz wrote in a religious vein, my father called his writing "sweetened poison," but poison nevertheless. And from his point of view, he was right. Everybody who read such books sooner or later became a worldly man and forsook the traditions. In my family, of course, my brother had gone first, and I went after him. For my parents, this was a tragedy.

Interviewers: You and your brother left Poland about 1935, your brother first. Why did you leave, and were you able to pick up right away and continue writing?

Singer: Yes. We were both pessimists. We both believed that it was inevitable after Hitler came to power that the Germans would invade Poland.

When I came to this country I lived through a terrible disappointment. I felt then—more than I believe now—that Yiddish had no future in this country. In Poland, Yiddish was still very much alive when I left. When I came here it seemed to me that Yiddish was finished: it was very depressing. The result was that for five or six or maybe seven years I couldn't write a word. Not only didn't I publish anything in those years, but writing became so difficult a chore that my grammar was affected. I couldn't write a single worthwhile sentence. I became like a man who was a great lover and is suddenly impotent, knowing at the same time that ultimately he will regain his power. I shouldn't have even tried to write anything, but I did try, again and again, without success. The novel I tried to write then I eventually threw away. In later years when I looked at it I was startled to find that it was the work of an illiterate man—and this was after I had written *Satan in Goray* and knew Yiddish fairly well. It was a real case of amnesia. One has to get a very great blow to act in such a way. But after a while I got over it, just like that lover whom I spoke of. I've seen this phenomenon at work in other writers. For example, those Yiddish writers who went to Russia, hoping that Communism would help them in some way, became so disappointed that some of them could not even write a single worthwhile sentence. Bergelson, who was a good writer, published a book in Russia called *Birobijan*. When I read this book I had the same feeling that I had in reading the stuff I wrote upon first coming to America. The man couldn't write a word. It wasn't merely a question of style.

Interviewers: At that time, did it ever occur to you to write in English?

Singer: I used to play with the idea, but never seriously. Never. I always knew that a writer has to write in his own language or not at all.

Interviewers: Did you ever think of going to Palestine in 1935?

Singer: Yes. I did think about it. But since I wanted to write in Yiddish and I knew that in Palestine Hebrew was the spoken and written language of the Jews, I decided not to. I could never really think seriously about going to Palestine even though I knew that Yiddish had no real future here. Perhaps I was selfish. I chose Yiddish not because I was a *Yiddishist,* but because I felt that this was the best way for me to express myself.

Interviewers: About the time that you were growing up in Warsaw, Jewish radical movements of one sort or another had a very strong influence. Jewish socialism in the form of Bundism was a powerful movement, and of course the Zionist movement was burgeoning. Did you ever feel yourself attracted to any of these groups?

Singer: For some strange reason, just as I was skeptical about religious dogma, so was I skeptical about political dogmas. Certainly I was very close to these people, and maybe that was the trouble: you know, sometimes when you see the cook, the food doesn't seem very appetizing. While the ideologies sounded very attractive, I was close enough to see who was preaching them and how these people fought for power among themselves. The truth is, if you ask me, that the aches and troubles of this world cannot be cured by any system. Nevertheless, there are better and worse systems. Democracy seems to me to be one of the better systems, and there is no system which gives more power to the devil than Communism.

As for Zionism, I always believed in it. I think that Israel is a great hope for the Jewish people. But it is true that just as I knew the socialist cooks, I knew some of the Zionist cooks in Poland. . . . Yet, in the case of Zionism, I felt that whoever the cook was, the food was wholesome. It is true that when I was in Israel five years ago, I found there things which I didn't like. But you find these things in your own home or in your own heart. Am I so delighted with myself and with my writing?

I always felt about the Soviet Union that it would never come to any good. From its very beginning it was a butcher shop, and it has remained so even today . . . even if there has been some "improvement." When people have extreme power over other people, it's a terrible thing. I always pray to God (and I do pray because I am in my way a religious man), don't give me any power over any other human beings. I have always avoided this kind of power like the plague. As a book reviewer, I sometimes have some power and it is my hope that someday I will be able to stop reviewing books, because even this little bit of power I inevitably abuse. You know, I review the easier books first or I leave the more difficult ones for last. I do what is easier for me, and in this way I abuse my power.

Interviewers: Can we talk a little about translations now, the translations of your books? Do you feel that much of what you have written comes across in English translation?

Singer: I am very happy about my books being translated into English. In English my audience is a very real one. I don't have to assume or imagine it. It's not *as if.* And of course many of my English readers are intelligent Jews who know no other language, and I am very happy to reach them. I always take this business of being translated seriously. I am very scrupulous about English translations. Even though my knowledge of English is small, I always felt from the moment I found an American publisher that I wanted to work hard on the translations, because when I read some of the Yiddish writers in English, particularly some of Sholem Aleichem, I knew how bad translation could be. It was so bad you couldn't read it. So I made up my mind that I would contribute as much as I could to the effort. For years I worked together with the translators on *The Family Moskat.* Incidentally, by working on that translation, I learned the little English I know. Since that time I have taken part in the translation of every one of my books. I think only in this way can a translation come out bearable. I say "bearable," because you know just as much as I do that writers inevitably lose a great deal in translation. A friend of mine, also a Yiddish writer, once came to me for some advice. He thought that because I had been translated into English I could advise him on a translation of his own book. I told him that he must be prepared to lose at least 40 per cent in translation, and to make sure that the other 60 per cent had some worth. Or better still, to write something 140 per cent. . . .

Translation is an endless process, really. Every translation, like every book, is a problem in itself. The same translator can do a good job on one book and a bad job on another. Nevertheless, good translation is possible, but it involves hard work for the writer, the translator, and the editor. I don't think that a translation is ever really finished. To me the translation becomes as dear as the original.

Interviewers: Well, you've been a translator yourself, haven't you? Did you take as much care with other men's work?

Singer: I must confess, no. I did most of my translations as a young man, and frankly I don't think they are very good. I translated *The Magic Mountain,* Stefan Zweig, Remarque, all these from the

German. I also translated from Polish and Hebrew. Although my translations were generally praised, I really didn't work as hard on them as I should have. I think *now* I would do a much better job because I have learned what it can mean.

Interviewers: What did you do with that chapter in French in *The Magic Mountain?* Did you leave it in French, as was done in the English translation?

Singer: No. I didn't because French can't be transliterated easily into Yiddish, which uses Hebrew characters. But since it was bad French I had to translate it into bad Yiddish. You don't have to make a great effort to write bad Yiddish.

Interviewers: While we're on the subject of translations, it seems that the six books of yours which have been translated into English fall into two categories. One of these is the kind of writing best exemplified by *The Family Moskat,* that is, rather straightforward, realistic narrative; in this case, a family chronicle. *The Magician of Lublin* is also somewhat like this. But *Satan in Goray* and most of your stories seem to have a different quality altogether. They are much more stylized; they emphasize folk elements, particularly the demonic and the supernatural. Now our question is this: is this division of your translated work, as we've outlined it, representative of your total output?

Singer: In asking the question that way, you also answer it. . . . It is true that my work does fall into two such categories. The reason is simple: sometimes I feel like writing about the supernatural, in a symbolic way, and I also feel that there is a place for the realistic method. These two categories are not mutually exclusive; they are only two sides of the same coin. The world can be looked at one way or another, and the theme of a story determines its style. What I have had translated thus far is a good part of my work, but there are still many things which have not been translated and published. For instance, I have written a novel called *Der Hoyf* in Yiddish. In English I originally wanted to call it *The Beginning,* because it deals with what we spoke about earlier: the beginning of socialism and Zionism in Poland. But it will probably be called *The Manor.* The translation is now being completed. It is a large book written more or less in the style of *The Family Moskat.* There is another book which I have written about Jewish life in America. It's called *Shadows by the*

Hudson and it's again written in a different style, a kind of combination of the two styles.

Interviewers: Why don't you tell us something about *Shadows by the Hudson.* Isn't this one of the very few things you've written about America?

Singer: Yes. *Shadows by the Hudson* is a story of a group of people who came to this country at the end of the Second World War or immediately thereafter and settled on the Upper West Side of New York—on Riverside Drive, West End Avenue, Broadway and so forth. While they live here, their minds and spirits are still in the old country, although, at the same time, they take roots here in New York. The times are mixed up and they are mixed up, and their story is full of confusion, unusual love stories. In fact, I think it's an unusual kind of novel.

Interviewers: What are you working on now?

Singer: A book called *A Ship to America.* This is the first time I've ever written a novel in the first person. It has autobiographical elements, but it isn't autobiography. It begins in Poland in 1935, but most of the book takes place in New York. It's the story of a writer who comes to this country, loses his passport, and becomes, against his own will and intentions, an illegal visitor. In 1939, he gets his first papers and a permit to go abroad. On the eve of the Second World War, he goes back to Poland to marry his lover and bring her, and his son by another woman, back to America. I won't tell you the end, because the book is now being serialized in the *Forward* on Fridays and Saturdays.

As for the style, I would say it's different from anything I've done before. Writing in the first person is a new experience for me, and creates new problems in description and construction. The idea that writing in the first person is easier than in the third person is far from true. It is a style with many possible pitfalls and demands more caution from a writer. One of the chief dangers of such a novel is that it always threatens to become a mere memoir.

Interviewers: Now what about this folk element in your work? What use do you feel you are making of it, and how do you regard the so-called demonic trait?

Singer: There are two reasons for this: one is literary and the other is more than literary. The more than literary reason is that I really believe there are spirits in this world, and that man has a soul, and that the soul is not the only spiritual entity in this world. I really believe that. Of course, many people, Jews and Christians alike, have believed in demons and spirits. But that's not why I believe in them. I truly believe that there are forces and spirits in this world, about which we know very little, which influence our lives. A hundred years from now, when people know more about other things, they will also know more about these spiritual powers. I believe that psychical research is a science of the future, not the past. I find it very easy to believe in reincarnation, possession by devils, and other such things. We have many proofs that these things exist.

Interviewers: Then why is it that you are so cynical about Hertz Yanovar and his group of spiritists in *The Family Moskat?*

Singer: *I* am not. It is my characters who are skeptical about this group. All the skepticism belongs to Asa Heshel and his wife. Still, I myself am a little skeptical about spiritism. Why? Because this is already a planned business. You sit down at a table and call forth a spirit. I don't believe that a spirit can just be called forth to order. In the same way, I don't believe that a man can just sit down and write a great poem. It won't work; it's not so easy. Spiritism has become a money-making thing, a kind of church, a dogma. So I don't believe in it; but I do believe that it is possible for a human being to *see* a spirit in a spontaneous way. This perhaps explains why I write critically about spiritism in *The Family Moskat.*

Interviewers: Just for the record, have you yourself ever had what you would call a spiritual or supernatural experience?

Singer: Never, really. But other people, whom I trust, have. And I have read a lot about such things. If there is any field of knowledge in which I am some kind of scholar, it is psychic research. I have read a great deal on this subject, in English and other languages.

Interviewers: Are you familiar with Yeats's mysticism, with theosophy and Rosicrucianism?

Singer: No, I don't know Yeats. But I've read Madame Blavatsky. But let me come back to the literary reason for my use of the demonic and supernatural. First, it helps me to express myself. For example, by using Satan or a demon as a symbol, one can compress a great many things. It's a kind of spiritual stenography. It gives me more freedom. For another thing, the demons and Satan represent to me, in a sense, the ways of the world. Instead of saying this is the way things happen, I will say, this is the way demons behave. Demons symbolize the world for me, and by that I mean human beings and human behavior; and since I really believe in their existence—that is, not only symbolically but substantively—it is easy to see how this kind of literary style was born. I really love this style and I am always finding new symbols and new stories. In *The Slave,* for example, I was unable to write about Jewish demons because this was primarily a story about Polish gentiles. Consequently, I found out all about Polish demonology. It fascinated me. Writers, as a matter of fact, fall in love with things like that, just as men fall in love with women. And certain things repeat themselves in every serious writer. I would say that every serious writer is possessed by certain ideas or symbols, and I am possessed by my demons and they add a lot to my vision and my expression.

Interviewers: You say that these demons and Satan symbolize the world for you. Now in many of your stories—like *Satan in Goray,* "The Mirror," and "The Diary of One Not Yet Born"—these imps, demons, devils, and what have you triumph either partially or completely. This would seem to make you a kind of "devil's advocate." Perhaps you mean to imply that evil is triumphing over good in man.

Singer: In many cases, it does; and in many cases, it doesn't. From experience we know that it happens often in this world—I'm not speaking now of the next world—that evil is victorious. Wouldn't you say that Hitler's success was the triumph of evil? Certainly, he almost reached his goal. And those Germans who went along with him, in his evil ways, have not been punished. On the other hand, the good sometimes prevails. In my story, "Gimpel the Fool," Satan tells Gimpel to do a nasty thing. Gimpel does so, and then reneges on the devil. So you see, I make no rules; evil doesn't always triumph and it isn't always defeated. Once you establish a rule, it's against literature and against life.

Interviewers: What you're saying is that you are writing morality stories, more realistic examples, perhaps, than some of the old-fashioned morality tales, but in essence, stories of good and evil.

Singer: I would not characterize my stories as morality tales, but rather as being constructed around a moral point of view. Perhaps only *The Magician of Lublin* could be called a true morality tale. In

this book, I had more of an "axe to grind." It's true that when I write
I don't look at the world as if it is beyond judgment. I do judge, not
always explicitly, but more often implicitly. I even would go so far as
to say that any writer who does not think in terms of good and evil
cannot go very far in his writing. This is a tragedy in much of modern
writing; authors have ceased to look upon life from the eternal point
of view of good and evil. They look upon life in a purely scientific
way; they say that such circumstances create such people and such
people behave so. The moment a writer begins to regard life from a
behavioristic point of view, the writing falls flat and the writer
descends to the level of his own characters. As the Talmud expresses
it: *les din, les dayan,* there is no judgment and no judge. My judgment is that good does not always triumph, that this is very far from
being the best of all possible worlds. That's why all my Jews are not
good Jews. Why should they be any different than anybody else?
The Cabbalists say this world is the worst of all possible worlds. They
believe there are millions of worlds, but the worst is this one. Here is
the very darkness itself. How can you expect that in the blackest
darkness, in the deepest abyss of all, everything should turn out nice
and proper? From a Cabbalistic point of view, I'm a very realistic
writer. . . .

Interviewers: This is the second time you've mentioned the
Cabbala. Have you read other mystical or occult works?

Singer: Well, I've read all the classic works of spiritism and
occultism—not only the old ones, but the modern scientific books.
The Phantasms of the Living by Gurney and Myers, which is a
classic; there's another one, too, about life after death. These were
both written in the 1880's in England, when the Society for Psychical
Research was created. These were people of great integrity, and they
did a great deal of research. You would be surprised at some of the
things they discovered. Nowadays psychic research is undergoing a
kind of crisis; but at the end of the last century it flourished. Yet even
today there are many serious people engaged in it. You know that
William James believed in occultism. Once you begin to study these
things you are faced with the fact that here is an uncharted ocean of
knowledge.

Interviewers: Do you know personally many of the people
engaged in psychic research?

Singer: No, I do not. And I will tell you why: there is no field in which so many liars and charlatans abound as in this one. Let's not fool ourselves: there are so many that it is incredible. But they have somehow managed not to utterly destroy legitimate psychic research, just as literature has not been destroyed by its numerous bad practitioners, by, say, the two hundred or so bad writers scribbling away in Brooklyn or the Bronx, in Paris and San Francisco. Both of these fields are good ones for liars and charlatans; they can really go to town. In the case of psychic research people, there is much obvious nonsense. They publish magazines about people who visit other planets and come down to tell whom they met there. I am not so foolish as to believe all these fakers. Still, I do read their magazines. I find their lies interesting. If nothing else, they are revealing fantasies. I do believe, however, in phenomena like clairvoyant dreams, extrasensory perception, and the like. And I think these things are all reflections of Higher Powers, whether divine or otherwise, of powers which surround us and are at work all the time.

Interviewers: Of course, then, you believe in God.

Singer: Yes, I do. I'm not, however, an observant Jew. I believe in God but not in man insofar as he claims God has revealed himself to him. If a man came to me and tells me he has been to the planet Mars, I would call him a liar, but I would not stop believing in the existence of the planet. I believe that the Higher Powers do not reveal themselves so easily; you have to search for them. Consequently, I have no faith in dogmas of any kind; they are only the work of men. Man is born to free choice, to believe, to doubt, or to deny. I choose to believe. I also believe in the power of personal prayer. While I shun organized prayer and religion, I would call myself a religious man. The Higher Powers, I am convinced, are always with us, at every moment, everywhere, except, perhaps, at the meetings of Marxists and other left-wingers. There is no God there; they have passed a motion to that effect.

A Visit to Isaac Bashevis Singer

Reena Sara Ribalow/1964

From *The Reconstructionist*, 30 (29 May 1964), 19–26. Reprinted by permission.

It was a cold, brittle day and the wind bit through me and made me catch my breath. I ran, shivering, into the elaborate corridor of the marble-faced apartment building, empty save for two listless rubber plants and a stuffed gold sofa with spindly legs. Standing in front of a list of tenants I ran my finger down each line of small, black cards until I found the one I wanted. It was a black card, exactly like the rest, except that it was a little crooked. 14C, it read, I. B. Singer.

The hall of the fourteenth floor was surprisingly dim and dingy. I peered through the dimness at another little black card attached to the door. As I rang the doorbell I noticed that this card was also crooked. There was a shuffle of feet behind the locked door. Someone fumbled with the latch and mumbled something. When the door opened I couldn't really see anyone, but a quiet, almost rustling voice said, "Come in, come in. I am very pleased to have you in my house." I had come to the home of Isaac Bashevis Singer, one of the world's great novelists, who produces remarkable works of fiction in the Yiddish language.

As the door closed behind me, something whizzed over my head and I looked up, startled. But Mr. Singer first shook my hand, then walked ahead of me, leading me into his study. He seemed to notice nothing extraordinary. Just before I entered his study, something again flapped over my head and I turned quickly.

"Those are just my birds," Mr. Singer explained. His gentle voice suited his meek, frail appearance. "They are never kept in a cage. I keep their food in the cage but they are free. They might get into accidents this way; they would be safer in a cage but in a cage their life is miserable." He shrugged. "So there is the choice. It is better they should be free." One of the parakeets warbled and Mr. Singer smiled a faint smile. "Their names are Shnooky and Vacky. That's Vacky singing—the boy. We had another boy—Motsy. He left us. Flew in one day through the window and then a year later he flew out. He sang all day. Wonderful bird. He could say anything. Since he left Shnooky stopped singing. She lets this one peck at her but she never sings." There was a dampness around his eyes. "Ach, the sweetest creatures in the world, these birds. So sweet." Mr. Singer sighed, then entered the study and invited me in.

"Sit down, sit down." Mr. Singer's voice had a lilt, a Yiddish inflection. He stood in front of a huge bookcase, stuffed with papers, magazines and books. On his right was a large desk, piled high with papers and galleys. Before him was a table strewn with magazines, newspapers and more papers. Scattered around the room on top of the bookcases were sketches of him and propped up against the wall was one oil painting. I glanced at it briefly and thought it was a good likeness. At least, the painting was a pale, quiet man, a few wisps of white all but invisible hair on his narrow, delicately-shaped head and pale-rimmed glasses veiling his faded blue eyes.

When Mr. Singer saw me looking at the bookcase, he eagerly drew out several books. I recognized the American edition of his latest work, *The Slave*. There was a paperback edition of the same book. "It isn't out yet, " he added, "In a few weeks it will be available." I was glad to see that Mr. Singer's books were in paperback editions. But what surprised and impressed me most was the pile of books Mr. Singer then pulled out. "See, this is a French translation of *The Slave. L'Esclave*. I don't read French too well, but even I found mistakes in it. It got good reviews in France, though. It's nice to see." Stamped across the pink cover were the words, "*Roman Yiddishe par* Isaac Bashevis Singer."

Mr. Singer, knowing of my interest in his work, pointed to a paperback with an imaginative Botticelli-like cover. "This is *Satan in Goray* in Italian, and here is a copy of *Gimpel the Fool* in Swedish. Imagine! Swedish! And this is *Satan in Goray* in French. All my books are out in English editions—I mean, from England."

In addition to the many translations of his work, Mr. Singer has been included in several short story collections and textbooks. There was one collection of many volumes put out by the *Encyclopedia*

Britannica called *World's Greatest Short Stories.* Mr. Singer delight-
edly told me that he was the only living writer in the collection.
"They put me between Pushkin and Chekhov," he said, with unmistakable pride. "That's not bad, is it?"

A copy of the Sunday *Herald Tribune* Paperback Book Section
was on the table. Mr. Singer leafed through it and indicated an article
where several prominent literary figures had been asked which ten
paperback titles they would recommend. "See, Karl Shapiro. You
know of him? He mentioned me. I never thought . . . See, he lists
Gimpel the Fool." "Gimpel the Fool" is the title story of a collection
of Mr. Singer's short stories. "That's very nice of him, isn't it? And he
says he doesn't see what it could have lost in the translation." He
paused for a moment. "But I tell you, you always lose a great deal in
translation. Always. I try to write so I shouldn't lose too much. I write
in Yiddish but I go over the translations and sometimes, like with *The
Slave,* I help to translate."

I mentioned that he had had tremendous success with his translations.

"Yes, that is true, I have been lucky. The critics are nice to me, but
I still earn most of my living by writing for the Yiddish paper, *The
Forward.* But I am lucky with my English translations."

He showed me a copy of *Partisan Review* which had first published
Saul Bellow's translation of "Gimpel the Fool." It was this story which
brought Mr. Singer to the attention of noted American literary critics.
Slowly, a cult of admirers developed and today Isaac Bashevis Singer
is internationally known.

Mr. Singer, like many writers, takes pride in the magazines in which
his work appears. Because he writes in Yiddish, he seems to marvel
that English-language editors are interested in his stories and in his
novels, and that American critics devote long essays to his world and
his talent.

He called my attention to his stories in *Mademoiselle, Esquire,
Harper's, Gentleman's Quarterly, Partisan Review* and other quality
magazines. His finger rested on a copy of *The Saturday Evening
Post.* "Four stories of mine they printed in one issue. So much
money they sent me!" I asked how much and reluctantly he admitted
"They sent me $3,500! So much! Then someone told me, 'They
cheated you!' I said, 'What? This you call cheating?'" He twisted his

pale lips in a grimace. "One shouldn't pay writers so much. I don't believe in it. Then they get conceited and they think every word is holy."

He reflected for a moment. I had the impression that he was talking more to himself than to me. He was thinking through his experiences as a writer who, creating in the Yiddish language, yet managed to make contact with the wider American audience.

"Someone told me," he said, "that Henry Miller wrote an introduction to a book called *The Best of H. E. Bates,* in which he said the only two short story writers he can read are H. E. Bates and Isaac Bashevis Singer." He looked pleased. "I want to buy that book. I never read Bates. You know, it would be interesting."

I sensed his need for approval, for recognition. There was no conceit or superiority in it; it was a simple and almost childlike delight at seeing his work in print and, above all, seeing the influence it had on others. The amazing circulation and acceptance of his books seem to bear out the claim, made by many critics and literary experts, that Mr. Singer's is a world talent and that he may be nominated for the Nobel Prize in literature one of these days.

I had heard that Mr. Singer was writing a new book, and asked him about it. He was pleased to discuss it. "Well, it was called *The Court* in Yiddish, but in English it will be called *The Manor.* It is a realistic book, a chronicle." Mr. Singer differentiates between his symbolic works and his realistic ones. Most of them, however, are symbolic. "It begins in 1863, the year of the Polish uprising and continues to the end of the century. It is like my book *The Family Moskat*—it ends where *The Family Moskat* begins. I suppose you would call it a story of Zionism and Socialism—ideas which were prevalent at that time. But of course it's also a story of people—of life and of love, as all stories are. Otherwise they would mean nothing. I hope it will be out this November."

I wondered if he had written anything about America, if he planned to deal only with the past, and to draw from his past.

"Oh, yes, I've written some stories about America and a novel also, but they've never been translated into English. One was about some old men in Miami, called "Alone." That was translated and printed in *Mademoiselle.* The novel, about immigrants, was printed serially in *The Forward.* It is called *Shadows by the Hudson.*

Somehow I don't write much about America. I do draw from the past—from my past life—my life in Poland. You know, in parts of Poland life is like it was 200 years ago. The people are very primitive. My own house was medieval and my father, my mother—they lived in the past, too. I take stories from my immediate experience."

I asked about *The Slave,* which is set in 13th century Poland. "I got the idea for *The Slave* when I visited a town in Poland named Zavoya, and on a mountain I found a barn exactly like the barn I used in *The Slave.* Exactly as it was in the 13th century. In the barn there was a girl living and sleeping with the cows and with the sheep. Even then, I thought, what a good book this will make. Those mountains in Poland are especially primitive. Of course, I had to do some research but even something like *The Slave* was taken from my own experience. It is for the same reason that I write about Jews. It is not that I think they are special but that I know them best; but it is not that they are better. For the same reason I write sometimes about Poles. I know them well."

I asked if he wrote for his own personal satisfaction or to communicate something to his readers. Mr. Singer smiled and shrugged, a gesture he used often and which seemed natural to his narrow, stooped shoulders. "Many writers say they write only for themselves. They are hypocrites. If men would stay on an island, all alone, and they knew that nobody would ever publish anything they wrote, they would write nothing. When you write, the reader is always there. Of course, I actually come first because I have to like it. But I know that if I like it there will always be one reader—someone else who will like it. We write and always we know that others will read us and judge us. The reader is always there."

He chewed on his glasses as he spoke, his eyes a darker blue, his look faraway and intent. I wondered how I ever could have thought him meek. His words and his voice were confident. "Whatever you write, even if you want to say something, it will very often come out very differently. Your writing sometimes means or says things to readers that you never meant to say. I believe that the hero and the situation rule themselves and rule you. You do not really control what you write. It shapes itself."

He rubbed his forehead and his hands were blunt but almost transparently white, and delicately veined with blue. The only color in his face was the burning, darkened color of his eyes. "Things do not always go according to reason. There are powers which control us, powers which we do not know or recognize. We call them anything— God, demons, angels, divine powers. But they have a power beyond us. I believe that even as Jacob struggled with the angel, we are always struggling against these powers."

"Certainly," he said, in answer to a further question, "I use ghosts and demons and spirits in my stories as symbols. But I also believe in them. Even though we give them these names—demons, angels, ghosts—we do not know what these powers are. But I believe that humans are not the highest form of life, that millions of other beings exist, both above and below the human. Some are evil and some are divine. Men deny them but I am sure of their existence. As a matter of fact," his smile was humorless and there was no laughter in his eyes, "when it is dark I am always afraid of them."

His voice was gentle, serious. "They are a part of God, perhaps you can call them God. But I have known atheists—if you would put them in a room with a corpse or leave them to sleep in a cemetery they would tremble like a leaf." He arched one eyebrow and chewed on his glasses and for a minute he looked almost unearthly.

I thought of one of his stories . . . "Shiddah and her child Kuzibah were sitting nine yards under the earth . . . Shiddah's body was made of cobwebs; her hair reached down to her anklebones; her feet were like those of a chicken; and she had the wings of a bat. Kuzibah, who looked like his mother, had, in addition, donkey ears and wax horns . . . Every half hour his mother gave him medicine made of devil's dung mixed with copper juice, the darkness of a ditch, and the droppings of a red cow . . ."

I looked at Mr. Singer watching me quietly and asked him whether he preferred to write short stories or novels. "I'll tell you the truth, short stories are what I like best of all because a novel must always have flaws. It must, because of their size and scope. In a short story, I can satisfy my desire for perfection. A short story can be perfect and I can make it exactly what I want it to be and keep it from having flaws. Short stories, I believe, are my real strength. When I write realistic novels," he added, "like *The Family Moskat,* I write almost like my brother, I. J. Singer." Mr. Singer's brother was a famous Yiddish writer. "I always say that my brother was my teacher and master. But he never wrote symbolically. Yiddish writers are very

shocked by my writing, actually. They say my treatment of the
relationship between men and women is too open and too radical.
Maybe," he said, his eyes suddenly glinting behind his glasses,
"That's why Henry Miller likes me." He sighed. "Still, I'm a Yiddish
writer. That's one reason I couldn't live in Israel. They have a wonderful thing—a miracle and I think it's wonderful that we have
our own country again. But I couldn't live there because it's too small
and because they're against Yiddish. Not so much now as they were.
But I write in Yiddish, even if I do shock Yiddish readers and
writers."

By now I could believe that this was the man who had written the
violent and weird stories I had admired. Then I remembered the
anecdote I had read in Leonard Lyons' column. Norman Mailer was
supposed to appear on a David Susskind discussion show, with
Bernard Malamud. Malamud couldn't make it and Mr. Singer was
asked to take his place. When told he would receive no fee, Mr.
Singer said, "For nothing I don't talk to Mailer."

"I called up Leonard Lyons about that," Mr. Singer commented.
He looked worried. "I didn't mean to insult anyone. I was just
making a joke. Listen, why should I hurt people? So Mr. Lyons told
me that Mailer said nice things to him about me. He wasn't hurt." Mr.
Singer looked glad. "I don't like to hurt anyone," he said and that
partly answered something I had been curious about. I had been told
that he was a vegetarian. Why? I asked.

"That," he said, nodding with approval, "is a serious question."
He was excited and rubbed a worn patch on his shabby suit. "I even
wrote an article about it. People are vegetarians because they say
they don't like meat or because they say it is unhealthy. I always liked
meat and I think it is perfectly healthy. But I feel animals are not
made to be killed. I have my two birds, they are such lovely creatures—the thought of someone eating them makes me sick. I realize
that in this world things are made so animals and people have to kill
each other. It can't be helped. But it is not my duty to help in this
destruction." His voice was still soft but it was urgent and he talked
quickly. "No human being has what animals have. They should be
our teachers and masters, not our food. They are humble, they have
humility, they are sincere. They are not something to eat, they are
God's beautiful creation."

Mr. Singer is a Jewish writer, but is not a particularly observant

Jew. What he feels constitutes a Jew is someone "whose Jewishness
is his life. This is a maximum Jew. To me there are maximum and
minimum Jews. My father was a maximum Jew. He would never say
'I have to eat.' He would say 'A Jew has to eat.' His Judaism was his
way of life, his belief. Just as there are writers who can barely squeeze
out a sentence and then there are masters, it's the same with Jews.
There are minimum Jews who were just born Jews—but they are all
Jews. I myself am somewhere in between. I do think that as a philosophy, Judaism has unrevealed treasures which no other religion has.
And it has never before happened in history that a nation has been
exiled for 2,000 years and then come back and formed a country.
And this with the return of Hebrew, the rebirth of the language,
proves that the Almighty has a purpose for the Jewish people."

Somehow, in the course of our conversation we got around to
psychiatrists. Some girl hadn't wanted to go to a certain college, and
had been disturbed. Her parents had called a psychiatrist. Mr. Singer
grimaced again and shrugged. "Listen," he said, "if I went to a
psychiatrist every time I was disturbed, I would do nothing else." His
humor was a light, gentle, elusive thing, sometimes seeming to dart
out from behind the glint of his glasses, and revealing the life in his
eyes. But it was sometimes sharp and bitter and this hadn't been
entirely a joke.

"Do you think," I asked, watching him carefully, "that writers are
set apart from other people?" He made a deprecating gesture. "No,
we're all made of the same stuff," he said. "There is no difference."

I looked at the frail man, perched at the edge of his seat, his hand
clutching one of his books. He looked small in this big room
surrounded by the papers and words that were his whole life. He
seemed utterly lonely. I repeated, "Don't you think that writers, of
necessity, have to be lonely and different from others?" For a
moment he didn't answer. Then in his gentle voice he said, "Well,
now that you phrase it that way . . . I . . . well, yes, I suppose that is
true. All artists are basically rebels, not against society but against
God. They have a quarrel with the Almighty. This is because a real
artist is a builder. Destruction, death, is something he cannot
understand and accept. Nobody asks the eternal questions more
than an artist—why are we here, why do we suffer, why is there
death? We all ask these same questions but the real artist can never

forget them. This is why he is lonely, because a man who can never forget these questions, who is always asking, does not really belong. When he is always asking and is never answered, this alone makes him alone, completely lonely and not a part of a society."

He was quiet for a long time, staring out the window, his hands absently stroking his glasses. I looked at the painting. It had the paleness of the exterior man but it had not caught the passion, the liveliness, the humor, the suffering. It had tried to capture the loneliness but made it look like a meekness, which isn't there. Mildness was there, perhaps, but coupled with the mildness was also a violence and wildness of imagination and emotion. And above all an utter loneliness. The painting was not Isaac Bashevis Singer because it was the shell of an aging, delicate man—not the fiery, lonely and great artist within. And Isaac Bashevis Singer is, above all, an artist.

Mr. Singer walked through the crowded living room, past the two parakeets perched on a picture frame and into the hall.

"It was my pleasure," he said with a courtly semi-bow. He smiled warmly and said "Goodbye to you." He stood in the door, a slender figure outlined against a bookcase which was standing in the hall.

Then I was down in the corridor with the spindly gold couch. I noticed for the first time that there was a faded mural on the wall. I looked again at the row of little black cards, seeing only one. I. B. Singer, it read. And it was just like the rest, except that it was a little crooked.

He Builds Bridges to the Past

Melvin Maddocks/1967

From *The Christian Science Monitor* (28 October 1967), 9.

The contemporary novelist holds his talent together rather like a political coalition. He is, so to speak, the final compromise among a number of conflicting half-likes, or perhaps half-dislikes.

Part of him is drawn to some tradition; part of him is inspired to kick viciously or antically against it. He feels the beat of modernity— and yet in his heart often despises it. Frequently he cannot stand his own country. But in the end, he can't stand anyone else's either.

This state of intellectual and moral suspension has been fashionably called "alienation" and thought of as a negative or even self-indulgent state. Very occasionally a writer comes along who turns the same conditions into a strength—who converts the quicksand, as it were, into his own kind of cement. Isaac Bashevis Singer is such a writer.

The stresses Singer has had to cope with are not especially unusual. His life has been divided between 32 years in New York and 31 earlier years in his native Poland. Then there is a stereotypical cultural exile to match. The son and grandson of rabbis, Singer remains skeptical toward both theological and political formulas.

What is unusual is the way he has managed by a kind of spiritual thrift to save something from all the elements that have made up his inheritance and experience. His "alienation" has enriched rather than impoverished him. He has retained no one great ball of twine to lead him out of the labyrinth, but does he ever have a marvelous pocketful of bits and pieces of string!

What a strange amalgam Singer is! Hunched over a 32-year-old Yiddish typewriter in New York City, in 1967, he writes of the Polish past—of dybbuks he does not believe in and of shtetls (East European Jewish villages) long disappeared. By his own admission he writes "as if none of the terrible things that have happened to the Jewish people during the last two decades really did occur."

Irving Howe has spelled out his odd predicament: "Singer writes in Yiddish, a language that no amount of energy or affection seems likely to save from extinction. He writes about a world that is gone, destroyed by brutality beyond historical comparison. . . . And he does all this without a sigh or apology, without so much as a Jewish groan. It strikes one as a kind of inspired madness. . . ."

Even the dwindling remnant of the Yiddish community, as Howe emphasizes, is "more than a little dubious about his purpose and stress"—sensing that nearly every sentence, despite the subject matter, carries the whiff of the 20th-century: an unmistakable brand of wry self-knowledge, an undisguisable witness's air of having looked over the abyss.

Singer himself says: "When I sit down to write I have a feeling that I'm talking maybe to millions or maybe to nobody."

Permanently exiled between cultures and between times, Singer is an updated version of the Wandering Jew. But in a curious way his very isolation has become the common experience he can communicate—and by communicating, transcend. He evidently brings something to more and more readers as a fellow-modern who has learned, without tricks or self-deceptions, to balance the seeming incompatibilities of the past and the present—writing out of both the heart and the whirlwind of change.

Now quite possibly on the edge of a breakthrough to a popular audience, Singer lives quietly in an airy, spacious apartment on the upper West side. In a corner of his well-lighted living room, where copies of the *Jewish Daily Forward* and *Esquire* share table space, stands his desk. Final drafts may pass through his ancient Yiddish portable, but he usually writes in longhand, from about 9 to 12 in morning, allowing an hour's time out for telephone interruptions.

He gives off an almost spellbound air of concentration which makes it possible to believe him when he says that these interruptions don't break up the flow. He can write quite successfully, he says, on the trains that take him on lecture tours.

A dapper, hyper-alert man, Singer sits in a winged armchair near his desk and speaks to an interviewer rapidly and animatedly but in a surprisingly gentle voice.

Question: You have been called a Yiddish "modernist," which is an ambiguous phrase. Just how do you connect to your tradition?

Answer: A writer must have roots. But no writer sits down with a notion of continuing a tradition. I write about what I know. Every writer must do that. I don't write in a Yiddish tradition. What is thought of as the Yiddish writer's tradition is a sentimental and a radical tradition. He is always wanting to make the world better and complaining about the lot of the Jews. I am neither a sentimentalist nor a radical.

Question: Then you are saying that all novelists need some sort of tradition—a frame to refer to or at least react against?

Answer: You can't avoid tradition. It lingers on long after it has ceased to dominate. Every idea is a remnant of some tradition. You can't write just about people—or yourself—though novelists still try.

Never have so many novels been written in the first person. Modern literature gives off the smell of confession. The novel has become a couch.

The first-person novel isn't an outpouring of the soul or a profound description of character, as some pretend. It's a game of no-secrets—of telling everything. The trouble is, these are secrets that everybody knows.

I'm against censorship, but I'm for auto-censorship. It's part of the writer's craft.

Question: Is this being old-fashioned?

Answer: It may become very fashionable to be old-fashioned. If a man has character, he doesn't care. Ten years from now the "new" things will seem the most old-fashioned.

This silly fuss about novelty and about youth! As if youth were a high virtue—as if you should get a Nobel prize for being young.

My old-fashioned aim is to entertain. I avoid gimmicks. I try to avoid page after page of repeating, of blowing up the smallest detail. That awful "modern" garrulousness—it's a result of the writer's futile desire to teach, to explain, to change society.

Actually, the force of the novelist and poet is a force without direction. It stirs the soul, but it doesn't lead to action.

Question: Do you regard entertainment as the novelist's primary obligation?

Answer: The oldest purpose of art has been to entertain. A good writer entertains a good reader. Literature has never accomplished more than that.

Nowadays we've confused excitement with entertainment. We go to a new film, and we don't say, "It's entertaining." We praise it by saying: "It's exciting."

It's part of the same cliche as the rebel. The rebel is "exciting"— and we don't worry whether he's rebelling against evil or good. Actually, the writer is neither rebel nor revolutionary. He can never be more than a storyteller. Whenever he tries to be more than a storyteller, he becomes less.

Question: But isn't the modern writer, if nothing else, concerned with evil?

Answer: The typical modern writer describes a lot of evil—evil is "exciting." But he often wants to prove that murder, for instance, is perfectly natural. He doesn't believe in free choice. In a way, modern writing tries not only to describe evil but to justify it from a sociological or psychological point of view.

Question: How does writing in Yiddish affect the stories most of us have to read in English?

Answer: I work with my translators. To that extent, the translation becomes a final draft, with the translator acting as editor.

I sometimes like the overstatement. In Yiddish you can make it. In English, not so well. English is a language of understatement. Gogol is a great overstater who suffers in English translation.

Irony and humor are hard to translate. They never come out exactly the same. There is usually something that goes wrong.

I haven't written any of my stories in English. We're never quite at home in a language we learn second. I think this is why in Conrad the sea seems real in a way the people don't. With Nabokov, the criticism is that he writes too well in English. You pay a price in self-consciousness.

Question: To conclude on one of your main themes: Traditions are ending—and have ended—all around us. Do you believe the tradition of having a tradition is itself at an end?

Answer: Nature creates new soil after the old soil is eroded. Our soil is being destroyed—this we can see. New traditions are being created before our very eyes. But this we can't see.

An Interview with Isaac Bashevis Singer

Harold Flender/1968

From the *National Jewish Monthly,* 82 (March 1968), 18, 19, 78,
79 and (April 1968), 14–16. Reprinted by permission from *B'nai
B'rith International Jewish Monthly.* A version of this interview
also appeared in the *Paris Review* (Fall 1968).

I

Q: How would you define a Jewish writer as opposed to a writer
who happens to be Jewish?

A: To me there are only Yiddish writers, Hebrew writers, English
writers, Spanish writers. The whole idea of a Jewish writer, a Catholic
writer, is kind of farfetched to me. But if you force me to admit that
there is such a thing as a Jewish writer, I would say that he is a man
who is really immersed in Jewishness, who knows Hebrew, Yiddish,
the Talmud, the Midrash, the Hassidic literature, the Cabbala, and so
forth. And if he writes, in addition, about Jews and Jewish history
and Jewish life, we can call him a Jewish writer. We can also call him
just a writer. But a writer who happens to be Jewish and writes in
English, is an English writer; if he writes in Spanish, he's a Spanish
writer; or in French, a French writer.

Q: I guess you would call your father a Jewish writer, because he
wrote religious tracts.

A: My father was a real Jewish writer, because he wrote all the time
about the Jewish religion, naturally.

Q: Was your father an influence in your decision to become a
writer?

A: Well, he didn't encourage me to become a secular writer, but
he always spoke about writing, because even in religious writing
there is such a thing as criticism, good writing and bad writing. I have
heard about these things all my life. So in a way I would say writing
is in my blood.

Q: Many writers, when they start out, have other writers they use
as models. When you began to write, were there any writers you
used as models?

A: Well, my model was my older brother, I. J. Singer, who wrote *The Brothers Ashkenazi*. In later years, before I began to publish, he gave me a number of rules about writing which seem to me still sacred. Not that these rules cannot be broken once in a while, but it's good to remember them. One was that facts never become obsolete or stale. Commentaries always become obsolete and stale. When a writer tries to explain too much, to psychologize, he's already out of date when he begins. If Homer had tried to explain the deeds of his heroes according to the old Greek philosophy or psychology of his time, if such a thing existed—it really didn't exist—nobody could read Homer any more. Homer just gave us the images and the facts, and because of this, the *Iliad* and the *Odyssey* are fresh in our times. And I think this is true about all writers. Once a writer tries to explain the hero's motives from a psychological point of view, he has already lost. This doesn't mean I am against the psychological novel. There are some masters who have done it well. But I don't think it is a good thing for a writer, especially a young writer, to imitate them.

Q: You once told me that the first piece of fiction you ever read was *The Adventures of Sherlock Holmes*.

A: I read those things when I was a boy of 10 or 11, and to me they looked so sublime, so wonderful, that until today I don't dare to read Sherlock Holmes again, because I am afraid I may be a little disappointed.

Q: Do you think that the author of *Sherlock Holmes,* A. Conan Doyle, influenced you in any way?

A: Not any real influence. But I will say one thing. I loved from childhood the tension in a story. There should be a beginning and an end. And to this rule I keep today. I don't believe in a story where the reader knows already when he begins it what will be the end. I think that storytelling has become in this age almost a forgotten art.

Q: Besides your brother, what other authors would you say influenced you?

A: I would say that almost all authors influenced me. Whenever I read a book and there is something good in it, I am interested in it and I think about it and there may be some influence. I loved Knut Hamsun when I was a young man. I read his books many times and still think they are marvelous. I read Tolstoy, Dostoyevsky and Gogol, naturally. A year or two ago I had to write a review about Gogol's stories. And when I read them I was astonished. I said to myself, who stole from whom? It's not really that I stole from him, but a lot of my stories have the same kind of feeling and the same kinds of moods as Gogol's.

Q: Do you know of any authors whom you have influenced?

A: I don't think that I have influenced any author. Maybe there are authors who think I have influenced them, but this whole business of influence is not of great importance. If a writer is a writer he will always be himself, even if he has read a million books. And if he isn't . . . if he's an imitator, he will be an imitator even if he has read only a single book, because the imitation is in his character.

Q: Isaac, you write in Yiddish, which is a language very few people can read today. Your books have been translated into 58 different languages. Are you bothered by the fact that the vast majority of your readers have to read you in translation, that very few can read you in Yiddish? Do you feel that a lot is lost in translation?

A: The fact that I don't have as many readers in Yiddish as I would like, this bothers me. I think it's not good that a language is in a way going downhill instead of up. I would like Yiddish to bloom and flower just as the Yiddishists say it does. But so far as translation is concerned, naturally every writer loses in translation, and poets and humorists are the greatest losers. Also authors whose writing is tightly connected to folklore are heavy losers. In my own case, I think I am a heavy loser, but since I have recently been assisting in the translation of my works, I know the problem, and take care that I don't lose too much. It's very hard to find a perfect equivalent for an idiom in another language. But it's also a fact that we all learned our literature through translation. Most people have studied the Bible only in translation, have read Homer in translation, and all the classics. It seems that translation, although it does damage, cannot kill an author. If he's really good, he will come through even in translation. I have seen it in my own case. Also translation helps me in a way. I go through my writings again and again while I edit the translation and work with the translator, and I see all the defects of my writing while I am doing this. So I would say that in many cases, translation has helped me to avoid many pitfalls.

Q: Is it true that for five years you stopped writing entirely, because you felt there was nobody to write for?

A: When I came to this country I stopped writing for a number of years. I don't know exactly if it was because I thought there were no readers. There were many readers. Coming from one country to another, immigrating, is a kind of crisis. I had a feeling that my language was so lost. My images were not any more. Things . . . I saw thousands of objects for which I had no name in Yiddish in Poland. Take such a thing as the subway . . . we didn't have a subway in Poland. Suddenly my feeling was that I had lost my language, and also my feeling about the things which surrounded me. For a number of years I couldn't write.

Q: Do you think Yiddish has any future at all, or that very soon it will be a dead language?

A: It won't be a dead language, because Yiddish is connected with 500 or 600 years of Jewish history . . . of important Jewish history. And whoever will want to study this history will have to study Yiddish. Not only this, but modern Hebrew literature is a product of Yiddish literature. One almost cannot understand modern Hebrew literature if one doesn't know Yiddish. Jews are, as a rule, not a people who easily forget. Yiddish will not be forgotten. Take such a language as Aramaic. It's already 2,000 years since the Jews used Aramaic, and the language is still here. It has now become a part of Hebrew. Aramaic is used now in certificates and in divorce papers. Jews never really forget anything, especially a language which has created so much and has played such a part as Yiddish.

Q: When one thinks of contemporary Yiddish writers, one thinks immediately of you. But then it is hard to come up with any other names. Are there any Yiddish writers whom you consider highly?

A: Yes. A. Zeitlin. He's really a great poet. I consider his writing of the same value as the poetry of Thomas Hardy, and I have a high opinion of Thomas Hardy. There are a number of others, some of them well known, like Sholem Asch. There was David Bergson. There was one Polish writer called A. M. Fuchs who was really a strong writer, but he wrote always on the same topic, with a million variations. But there is something about Yiddish writing which is very old-fashioned, because the modern Yiddish writer does not write about real Jewish things. He is the product of the enlightenment. He was brought up with the idea that one should get away from Jewishness and become universal. And because they tried so hard to

become universal, they became very provincial. This is the tragedy—
not of the whole of Yiddish writing, but of a lot of it. And thank God,
when I began to write I avoided this misfortune, even though I was
discouraged all the time. They told me, "Why do you write about
devils and imps? Why don't you write about the situation of the
Jews, about Zionism, about Socialism, about the unions and about
how the tailors must get a raise," and so on and so on. But something in me refused to do this. They complained to me that I was
obsolete. That I went back to the generations which have already
vanished. That I was almost a reactionary. But young writers are
sometimes very stubborn, and I was later glad that I had the character not to do what they wanted me to do. That type of writing has
become obsolete and stale.

Q: When you say "that type of writing," you mean the writings
about unions and . . .

A: About unions, about immigration, about progress, about anti-
Semitism. About all this journalistic kind of writing, which had one
desire to create what they call a better world, to make the Jewish
situation better. This kind of writing was very much in fashion in the
twenties, and I would say that the Yiddish writers never got out of it,
really.

Q: Don't you believe in a better world?

A: Yes, but I don't think that a fiction writer who sits down to write
a novel to make a better world can achieve anything. The better
world will be made by many people, by the politicians, by the states-
men, by the sociologists. One thing I am sure is that the novelists will
not do it. Let them rather create a better novel. This is enough.

Q: I notice that the supernatural keeps cropping up in practically
everything you write, particularly your short stories. Why this strong
concern with the supernatural? Do you personally believe in the
supernatural?

A: Absolutely. The reason why it always comes up is that it is
always on my mind. I don't know if I should call myself a mystic, but
I feel always that we are surrounded by mysterious powers, which
play a great part in everything we are doing. I would say that
telepathy and clairvoyance play a part in every love story, in every
business, in everything human beings are doing. I always say that for
thousands of years people used to wear woolen clothes, and when

they took them off at night, they saw sparks. And many people must have been afraid to talk about these sparks lest they should be suspected of being sorcerers and witches. We know now that they were real, and that behind these sparks there was real power, the electricity which today drives our industry. And I say that we, too, in each generation, see such sparks which we ignore just because they don't fit into our picture of science or knowledge. And I think it is the writer's duty as well as pleasure and function, to bring out these sparks. To me, clairvoyance and telepathy and . . .

Q: And devils?

A: And devils and imps . . . and ghosts . . . all these things which people today call superstition are the very sparks which we are ignoring in our day.

Q: Do you think they will be able to be explained scientifically, the way the sparks can be explained today as electricity?

A: I think that the notion of science, what is scientific and what is not, will change in time. Not every scientific fact must be repeated in a laboratory. There are many facts which cannot be worked out in a laboratory and still they are facts. You cannot show in a laboratory that there ever was a Napoleon, but still we believe that there was a Napoleon, even though it cannot be proved as clearly as, let's say, an electric current. What we call today ghosts and spirits and clairvoyance, is also the type of facts which you cannot make experiments with. But this doesn't mean that they are not true. Let's take such a thing as talent. You cannot put a talent into a laboratory and say "Now write a good poem." But we still know that talent does exist. If something is true it is scientific, no matter if it can be reproduced in a laboratory or not. And I believe that the world in the future will have to pay attention to these truths.

Q: How about the devil? In many of your writings the devil is the main character.

A: Naturally, I use the devil and the imps as literary symbols. The reason I use them is that I have a feeling for them. I still live with this idea that we are surrounded by all kinds of powers. When I am in a dark room at night, I am afraid, just as I was when I was seven or eight years old. I have spoken to many rationalists who boast about how logical they are, and when I ask them if they would consent to sleep through a winter night in a room where a corpse is, they shivered. It seems that the fear of the supernatural is in everybody. There is no reason why we shouldn't make use of it. Because if you are afraid of something, it means you have admitted that it exists. We aren't afraid of something which doesn't exist.

Q: But you are the only Jewish writer I know of who writes about the devil. Even Hebrew literature has avoided the theme of the diabolical.

A: Yiddish and Hebrew literature are both under the influence of the Enlightenment. Modern authors think modern literature should be rational and logical, should deal with the real world. To them, when I began to write, I seemed a most reactionary writer, one who went back to the dark ages. They all condemned me for it. But today, since this kind of writing has a certain degree of success, they begin somehow to make peace with it.

Q: What seems peculiar to me is how many young people are interested in your writing. Not only Jewish students, but students whose backgrounds have nothing in common with the things you write about.

A: A reader does not expect the writer to tell him something he already knows. If a man has talent, no matter what the topic is, he will always find readers. And I would also say that the problems I think about today, even though they looked very obsolete to the Yiddish writers and critics are, in a way, very modern. People nowadays are more disappointed in science than they have ever been. No matter how science will go on progressing, the mystery of life and being will not become less; it may even grow stronger. We may reach the moon or go to the planet Mars, but the vast sky with its billions of galaxies will still remain a secret. We will never reach the center of the earth, and because of this, mysticism is nowadays stronger than it was, say, 200 years ago, when people thought that with the microscope and the telescope, they would discover all the secrets of heaven and earth.

II

Q: The hero of most Western writing is the Superman, the Prometheus character. The hero of Yiddish fiction seems to be the little man. He's poor but proud, always struggling against high personal, financial, and political odds to maintain his dignity and status. Sholom Aleichem's Tevye is an example of what I mean by the little man. Peretz's Buntsche Schweig is another. And your own classic example of the little man would be Gimpel the Fool. How do you account for the fact that in so much of Yiddish fiction the hero is the little man?

A: Well, there were very few heroes in the Jewish ghettoes—very few knights and counts and people who fought duels and so on. In my own case, I don't think I write in the tradition of the Yiddish writers with the little man. Their little man is a victim of anti-Semitism, the economic situation, and so on. My people are not big men in the sense that they play a big part in the world, but in their own fashion they are men of character, men of thought, men of great suffering. It is true that Gimpel the Fool is a little man, but he's not the same kind of little man as Sholom Aleichem's Tevye, because Tevye is a little man with little desires, and with little prejudice. All he needed was to make a living. Their tragedies are different. Gimpel was a fool, but he wasn't little. The tradition of the little man is something I have avoided in my writing.

Q: I can't help but get the feeling from your writing that you have grave doubts about the sufficiency of knowledge, or even wisdom.

A: In a way it is true. Yiddish writing was built on the ideas of the Enlightenment, and I am against the idea that the Enlightenment can save us. Enlightenment, no matter how far it goes, will not bring redemption. I never believed that socialism or any other "ism" is going to redeem humanity and create what they call the New Man. When I began to write, people really believed that once the means of production would belong to the government, new men would come up. I was clever enough, or maybe foolish enough and skeptical enough, to know that this was a lot of nonsense, that no matter who owns the railroads or the factories, men will remain the same. And since I also believe in the hidden powers and what you call the supernatural, there is certainly not much belief in me in progress, especially that kind of cheap progress where you invent a machine and suddenly you change the whole face of humanity.

Q: What do you think will save humanity?

A: Nothing will save us. We will make a lot of progress, but we will keep on suffering, and there will never be an end to it. We will always invent new sources of pain. The idea that man is going to be saved is a completely religious idea, and the religious leaders never said we would be saved on this earth. They believed that the soul is saved in another world. In other words, if we behave well here, there is a hope that our soul will go to paradise. The idea of creating here on this earth a paradise is not Jewish and certainly not Christian, but a kind of Greek or pagan idea. As the Jews say, from a pig's tail you cannot make a silk purse. You cannot take life and suddenly turn it into one great delight, an ocean of pleasure. I admit that conditions can improve, and I hope we will do away with wars, but there will be enough sickness and all kinds of tragedies so that humanity will keep on suffering more or less in the same way as it always has. Being a pessimist to me means to be a realist.

Q: You don't think man can attain paradise in heaven?

A: In heaven, perhaps yes. I don't know, because I never have been in heaven.

Q: Many readers, Isaac, look upon you as a master storyteller. Others feel that you have a far more significant purpose in your writing than merely to tell stories.

A: I think that to write a story well is the duty of a storyteller. I try with all my might that a story should come out right. What I call right is that the construction should be right, the description right, that there should be equilibrium between the form and content, and so on. But this is not everything. In each story I try to say something, and what I try to say is more or less connected with my ideas that this world and this life are not everything, and there is a soul and there is a God and there may be life after death. I always come back to these religious truths, although I am not religious in the sense of dogma. I don't keep all the rules of organized religion. But the basic truths of religion are dear to me. I would consider myself more of a Jewish writer than most of the Yiddish writers, because I am more a believer in the Jewish truths than they. Most of them believe in progress. Progress has become their idol. They believe that people will progress to such a degree that the Jews will be treated well, they will be able to assimilate, mix with the Gentiles, get good jobs, and perhaps be President one day. To me, all these hopes are obsolete and petty. I feel that our real great hope lies in the soul and not in the body. Thus, I consider myself a religious writer.

Q: Sometimes, reading you, I can't help but think of certain Far

Eastern philosophers I have read, such as the Indian philosopher Krishnamurthi. Were you at all influenced by Buddhist or Hindu writings?

A: I read these writers too late to have been really influenced by them. But when I read them in my later years, a short time ago, I said to myself that I thought the same thoughts. It seems that the so-called Eternal Truths may be eternal. They are in our blood and in our very essence.

Q: In oriental writings the emphasis is often on the negative, whereas in your writing, there is always a reverence for life and a reaffirmation of the possibilities for life that remain after failure and despair have come and gone.

A: I feel that in spite of all our sufferings, in spite of the fact that life will never bring the paradise we want it to bring, it is still worth living. I would say that the greatest gift which humanity has gotten is free choice. It is true that we are limited in spite of that free choice, but it is such a great gift, and it has so much potentiality. The modern writer as a rule avoids the idea of free choice. He is a fatalist, and I think this is wrong. Whatever we have reached until now is because of free will, not because conditions have changed, as the Marxists believe. Naturally, conditions also play a part.

Q: In trying to get at your philosophy from your writings, I notice in your novel, *The Slave,* two conflicting points of view. You describe your main character, the slave Jacob, as follows—and I quote from the novel: "He lamented the injustice visited on all living things— Jews, Gentiles, animals, even the flies and gnats crawling on the hips of the cattle." Now this is certainly a moving description of a compassionate and I would even say saintly soul. On the other hand, elsewhere in the novel, this same character says: "No matter what one does, one stumbles into sin. Touch something and you hurt someone." So we have here a noble, idealistic attitude and a completely cynical attitude, both possessed by the same character.

A: I don't agree that this is cynical. The fact that we stumble into sin doesn't mean that Jacob was delighted about the fact. Just the opposite. He deplored the fact that no matter how good you want to be, you fall into a pitfall just the same. For example, you are going to give charity to a poor man, and while you do this, you step on a little frog or on a worm which you kill. In other words, he deplored the fact that while we do good, we also do evil. But this is not cynical. It is the sentiment of a man who really likes to do good, but who sees that life on this earth is not made for it. The cynic is the person who makes peace with evil, who says that since evil rules in this world, let's adjust ourselves to it, and get all the pleasure we can get from it.

Q: Most of your writing deals with a people without power, without land, without statehood, political organization, or even a choice of occupation. In other words, you write about Jewish people when they were restricted, deprived, and perhaps even maimed. Yet these people had a great moral response and an intensity of faith. Are you, in effect, saying that the Jews were better off when they were restricted and discriminated against?

A: I think there is no question about it—that power is a great temptation, and those who have power will sooner or later stumble into injustice. It was the good fortune of the Jewish people that for 2,000 years they didn't have any power. Because of this our sins were never as great as those who really had power over the life and death of other people. But I bring this up not in order to preach. Although I am a mystic, I am also a realist, and many mystics are realists. And since this was the actual situation of Jewish people in Poland or in Russia—they had no power—I had to describe such people. I never really knew people who had a lot of power, except Poles, or once in a while a rich man, whose power was in his money.

Q: Let's get back to the business of writing. Some commentators on the current scene, notably Marshall McLuhan, the Canadian writer and philosopher, feel that literature as we have known it for hundreds of years is an anachronism. They say it's on the way out, because of electronic entertainment, radio, television, films, stereophonic records, and magnetic tapes, and other mechanical means of communication yet to be invented. Do you believe this to be true?

A: It will be true if our writers are not good writers. But if we have people who have the power to tell a story, there will always be readers. I don't think human nature is going to change to such a degree that people will stop being interested in a work of imagination. Naturally, facts are very interesting. Already today non-fiction plays a very big part. But there is no machine and no kind of reporting and no kind of film that can do what a Tolstoy or a Dostoyevsky or a Gogol did. It is true that poetry has suffered a great blow in our times—not because of television or other things, but because poetry itself became bad. But I don't think that good literature has anything to fear from technology. The very opposite. The more technology, the more people will be interested in what the human mind can produce without the help of electronics.

Q: Would you encourage young people today to think of serious writing as a way of life? Do you really feel there is a future for them in this age when the vast majority of people would rather snap on the TV set than curl up with a good book?

A: When it comes to business, to finances, I really don't know. It may be that a time will come when the novelist will get such small royalties that he will not be able to make a living. But if a young man would come to me and I would see that he has talent and he would ask me if he should write, I would say go on and write, and don't be afraid of any inventions and of any kind of progress. Progress never can kill literature, as it cannot kill religion.

Q: In addition to writing stories and novels, you spent many years of your life in journalism. You still work as a journalist for *The Forward.*

A: Yes. I am a journalist. But journalism in Yiddish is quite different from journalism in other languages, especially English. In America, a journalist is a man who deals with facts, or he is a commentator on the political situation. A Yiddish newspaper, even if it's a daily, is actually a magazine. I can write an article in *The Forward* on whether life makes sense and why you shouldn't commit suicide, or if there are imps and devils. Our reader is accustomed to get the news mostly from the radio and television, or from his English newspaper. When he buys his Yiddish paper, he wants to read articles.

Q: Many contemporary writers are affiliated with universities. What do you think of teaching as a way of making a living while writing?

A: I think journalism is a healthier occupation for a writer than teaching, especially if he teaches literature. By teaching literature, the writer gets accustomed to analyzing literature all the time. Then when he sits down to write, he writes and analyzes at the same time. One man, a critic, said to me: "I could never write anything, because the moment I write the first line, I am already writing an essay about it. I am already criticizing my own writing."

Q: Could you tell me something about the way you work? Do you work every day, seven days a week?

A: Well, when I get up in the morning, I always have the desire to sit down to write. And most of the days I do write something. I do not always succeed. I get telephone calls, and sometimes I have to write an article for *The Forward*. And once in a while I have to write a review. I am interviewed, and otherwise interrupted. But somehow I manage to keep on writing. I don't have to run away. Some writers say they can write only if they go to a far-off island. I think that being disturbed is part of life, and sometimes it's useful to be disturbed because while you are busy with something else, your perspective changes or the horizon widens. All I can say about myself is that I have never written in peace, as some writers say they have.

Q: It's hard to keep from noticing that among the most widely read and respected authors in the United States today, a large percentage are Jews—yourself, Saul Bellow, Philip Roth, Henry Roth, Bernard Malamud. Even non-Jewish writers are writing on Jewish themes and producing best sellers. How do you account for the post-World War II popularity of Jewish writers and Jewish themes?

A: I think that for many centuries the Jew was completely ignored in literature. Authors wrote about Jews always in cliches. Either the Jew was a usurer, a bad man, a Shylock, or he was a poor man, a victim of anti-Semitism. In other words, they either scolded him or pitied him. And because of this, the Jew's way of life, his way of love, was a secret to humanity. It's only a short time ago that Jewish writers began to write about Jews the same way as Americans write about Americans and English writers about Englishmen. They tell everything about them, the good and the evil. They don't try to apologize for them. They don't try to scold them. And I would say that since there was a lot of curiosity about Jewish life, I am not astonished that Jewish literature is now in vogue. This doesn't mean that it is always going to be so. I believe that sooner or later things will even out, and there will be as much curiosity about the Jews as about any other people. How many Jews are good writers or bad writers I don't know. I don't think we are producing as many good writers as people think. We have a lot of able, gifted writers, and able people, but I see very few great writers among us, as there are very few great writers among other people. There are few great writers anywhere.

Isaac Bashevis Singer: An Interview
Cyrena Pondrom/1969

From *Contemporary Literature*, 10, nos. 1 & 2 (1969), 1–38, 332–351. Reprinted by permission from the University of Wisconsin Press.

The interview was edited from transcriptions of extended tape-recorded conversations with Mr. Singer on March 29, April 9, and April 12, 1968. All were held in Madison, Wisconsin, with L. S. Dembo participating on March 29. Part I is chiefly drawn from the first recorded conversation. Part II combines the second and third sessions. Mr. Singer has read the text to verify accuracy of transcription.

Q: Mr. Singer, since you've been in this country you've published *The Family Moskat, The Magician of Lublin, The Slave,* a number of collections of stories, and *The Manor,* which is your latest novel to appear in English. And isn't there supposed to be a sequel to *The Manor?*

A: It's a part of two books but I don't know how to call two books a duality? There will be a second part.

Q: Is the other book written?

A: Written, and also already translated, but I work on the translation and I work on the book itself. It happens often with me, working on the translation and working on the book itself go together, because when it's being translated I see some of the defects and I work on them—so in a way the English translation is sometimes almost a second original. I cut while I translate and I add sometimes.

Q: What kinds of thing do you usually change?

A: Oh, sometimes I may find a chapter that is not good enough; I think it needs some more description or dialogue, or sometimes I find the opposite: there is too much of it, it should be cut. I am not faithful to the original, because why should I be?—since the author is here, he can do whatever he pleases to correct things. So because of this, if there will ever be a student—or an amateur or whatever—who will compare things, one will be surprised to see what divergences, what differences, there are between the translation and the Yiddish original.

Q: Do you prefer that the English translation be treated as the primary text?

A: It's not a question "if I prefer," but it's treated that way anyhow, because all the translations into other languages are made from the English translation and I'm cautious. In some cases I'm pleased with it and in some cases I'm displeased, but it doesn't help me any.

Q: I remember you told me several weeks ago that when a German translation of—was it, *The Magician . . . ?*

A: Yes, that they went back to the Yiddish, and they found things which I have cut—I don't know why I cut them.

Q: Were you pleased that they restored them?

A: In this case I was pleased, because I really found that by restoring the original they have improved the translation. But in other cases I would be in despair if they would restore what was in Yiddish because in Yiddish you can use a lot of overstatement, but you cannot use it in English. What seems to be quite all right in one language, looks sometimes very silly in another language.

Q: Well, Yiddish is a language of overstatement in general.

A: Yes, yes, Yiddish is a language of overstatement and English of understatement, so because of this I have had in many cases to cut. Perhaps if I could find the most wonderful translator who could make these overstatements into understatements it would be all right, but in some cases it is so difficult that I'd rather cut than leave it there.

Q: What sorts of things do you add when you translate? I noticed at one point in *Satan in Goray* what seemed to be some explanatory phrases for Gentiles. Do you ever add this kind of thing?

A: I don't think that I did this. I think that this was done by my editor, Cecil Hemley. As a rule, I don't like to explain. I say that the reader can always find a dictionary or an encyclopedia.

Q: Well, I only noticed a few such. I know you have worked with a lot of different translators. Do you always supervise the translation extremely closely?

A: Lately, yes. In the beginning when *The Family Moskat* was translated, I didn't do it, because my knowledge of English was less than today, and also it was done by a very experienced translator; he wouldn't have even allowed me to interfere with him. But since then I have to do all this; the translators I know well and they will let me do many things; they'll work together with me.

Q: Do you think you're virtually capable of being your own translator now?

A: Almost. Almost but not completely. Since I am a foreigner, sometimes when I dictate to the translator for a half an hour I will keep on and speak good English, and then I will make a mistake of a man who came yesterday from the old country, because a foreigner is never sure of himself in another language.

Q: Some of the short stories you sign along with the translator, as translator. Does this mean that you have done substantially more of the translation?

A: I can explain to you. In some cases, the translator does not know Yiddish, so I sit down with the translator and I dictate to him my translation and then he reworks the English and sees to it that it sounds better. And because of this, I sign my name. But if the translator would work from the Yiddish I wouldn't sign my name. When my name is signed it means that the rough translation was done by me, and he worked on the style.

Q: Turning to a cultural question for a minute, do you actually still consider yourself a foreigner in America?

A: Well, actually not. Certainly not from a legal point of view. If you ask me from an *emotional* point of view, I don't feel myself a foreigner because I love America and I love the American people, and I don't say this because I want to flatter anybody—I have no reason for it; it so happens. If you love somebody you don't feel as a stranger to him. And since my own country, Poland, where I was born, almost does not exist as far as I am concerned—it's a different world there—the U.S. is my real home now. So just as English has become to me a second original, America is to me my real country.

Q: If we can continue just a few minutes more on technical questions, one of the things that I noticed about the short stories is that collections do not seem to reflect chronology.

A: Yes, yes, I mix them up always, and I don't really write down the date when they were written, so because of this there is a real mix-up. In other words, when you read a collection of short stories of mine one story might have been written twenty years ago and the other, four weeks ago.

Q: That's what I thought. Then, as a rule, you are not aiming at a central theme or development in a collection?

A: No. I just take a number of stories which I think could be published and I publish them. In my new collection, *The Séance,* I have some stories which are very new, and there is I believe one story called "Two Corpses Go Dancing," which I wrote twenty-five years ago. I must one day take all my stories and give the real dates when they were written, or the approximate dates because in some cases I don't know myself any more. Dates could be verified also from the Yiddish—those which appeared in Yiddish newspapers or magazines, because in Yiddish they appeared mostly as soon as they were written.

Q: To turn to questions having more to do with your basic techniques, one of the things that caught my attention in both *The Slave* and *The Magician of Lublin* is your use of Biblical analogues.

A: It is true, it is true. And I would say this is true almost about all my writing; you will find it even in *Satan in Goray.* I was brought up on the Bible. Whenever there is an opportunity I will compare something to some Biblical event, a Biblical name, or something.

Q: How does the process begin? Do such allusions present themselves as you go along? Or do you think sometimes in terms of an overall pattern?

A: No. I don't, because if this would be true I would know about it—as a matter of fact, you say that I use a lot of Biblical allusions; I recognize that it's true, but only after you told it to me . . . I myself do not realize it.

Q: It emerges from the text rather than your having a prior pattern in your mind.

A: Exactly.

Q: So actually it's more accidental than deliberate.

A: I wouldn't call it accidental, but it's also not deliberate. It is just in me.

Q: Do you sometimes use names themselves to suggest the allusion deliberately?

A: I think that in *The Slave,* I called my hero Jacob just because I needed a name. Why I called him Jacob, I don't know myself. But then since his name was already Jacob, the allusion to Jacob was a natural thing, and when I got the opportunity to compare him to his Biblical namesake, I did it.

Q: Yes. It seems to me that your novels differ quite a lot in structure, in plan.

A: Generally, I have two kinds of novels, the one, the so-called realistic novels or chronicles, like *The Family Moskat* and *The Manor,* which are more or less realistic novels, stories about families, the development of families, where I use very little of the supernatural. They are constructed in the way large novels should be constructed, according to my opinion. I don't tell the story straightly but I skip time and I go from one person to another; I leave one event and I go to another one and then I return to this event again, almost in the tradition of the Russian novels. And then there is the short novel, which is built around one person; it has one central hero and everything turns around him and the story goes a straight way; I keep on telling the story from the beginning to the end without interruptions.

Q: *The Magician of Lublin* would be an example of this.

A: *The Magician of Lublin,* even *The Slave* is a story like this. I tell this Jacob's story from the beginning to the end. Jacob is in every chapter.

Q: *Satan in Goray* falls somewhere between the two?

A: Yes. *Satan in Goray,* even though it's a small novel, actually tells the story not of a man but of a whole milieu. It's a small novel which should have been a large novel, but the way I wrote it demanded that it should be short, because you cannot write about hysteria and the supernatural long. . . . It's a strange thing: you can write about the supernatural a novel of 150 pages; if you will make it 800 pages there is already a contradiction, because life itself is not so full of the supernatural that you can go on for 800 pages. It would be a great disproportion.

Q: Does the supernatural actually appear, or is it really a part of the psychology of the characters that you're developing?

A: It is not just a method. Somehow, whenever I sit down to write a short story—not always, but in many cases—the supernatural will pop up, almost by itself, because I'm deeply interested in it.

Q: Yes, I understand this, but take one of the stories that I felt was really electrifying, "The Black Wedding." What was happening there seemed to me a clue to what was happening with many of your other characters. It seemed to me that the girl here was really obsessed with the fact that this man was a devil, whereas whether he *really* was or not was not the point of the story; the point was what was happening inside of her mind. And many of your characters seem to have this obsessive quality.

A: Yes, this is true. Obsession is really a very important theme of mind and this is the reason that I would write about dybbuks. I like a person who is obsessed by some mania or a single idea, a fixed idea, and everything turns around this idea. I think that this kind of literature is very important to me because not many writers wrote in this way. I'm glad that you mentioned "The Black Wedding" because it was not recognized by many writers as one of my best stories, but I do recognize it as such. It was also published lately in a collection of stories, psychiatric stories. In this story the woman is not only obsessed, you can call her insane.

Q: Psychopathic.

A: She is really psychopathic, to a high degree. But from her point of view, she's right. Assuming that all the things that happen are devilish, she's right in her behavior and everything is becoming consistent in a mad way.

Q: But isn't it extremely important that the "devilishness" of things is an assumption? What is the reality of the obsessions of the characters?

A: Since we don't know really what reality is, whatever we are obsessed with becomes our reality. Let's say a man who is obsessed by the idea of making money: money becomes to him of such importance that he really measures everything with money. He thinks he can buy everything with money and sell everything; and from his point of view he becomes right—everything has a price. Some men say every woman has a price, every man has a price, he can buy the Pope, he can. . . . This is the way they feel. And so with people who are obsessed by sex, or politics or many other things. In a way I would say we are all obsessed, but some more and some less.

Q: This also seems to me to be the center of *The Magician of Lublin*.

A: Yes. Here was a man who was really obsessed by women and by living in danger.

Q: He was obsessed by the idea of being Jewish, too, and what constituted a Jew.

A: Not really so much, in the beginning. I think in the beginning, the Jewish question existed for him, as much as being Jewish disturbs his obsession, because he felt guilty in a way, but at the end when he is disappointed in the worldly pleasures, he returns to Jewishness.

Q: Do you think this is a form of salvation for him or is that an unfair question?

A: If it was a salvation then how long it lasted I cannot tell you. I don't know really. First of all, I indicate in this book that, while he's already there in this little hut without a door to get out, he's still the magician of Lublin, and he still dreams about women. In one case he imagines that Emilia has a tunnel, and she comes to him right there where he repents, which shows how the mind works; he cannot really escape from anything. Any escape, wherever there is an escape, there's always a hole in it. . . .

Q: But even his playing the role of a thaumaturgic rabbi is also a form of obsession for him, wouldn't you say?

A: Yes. He's trying . . . yes, he becomes obsessed with the idea of the opposite of what he was, let's say, like a Communist may become sometimes an anti-Communist—this happens all the time.

Q: But what about his motives for building that hut and putting himself inside? Aren't the motives essentially mistaken?

A: Well, you can call them by all kinds of names—but I will tell you what his motives are. He has come to the conclusion that if there is temptation he will surrender. He cannot withstand temptation; in other words, if he would be in a house with a married woman, he would sin against God, he would break the Ten Commandments. And since he has convinced himself—or at least tried to convince himself—that this is bad, a man like him must run away from temptation. The only way the magician could run away from temptation would be to immure himself, because there was no other way.

Q: Is this then to say that the rabbi's comment is correct, that this is really an abdication of free will?

A: It is, absolutely . . . it is true, yes. In other words if you take the Ten Commandments seriously, and if you think that the Ten Commandments are the very essence of our life, and if you think that if we break the Ten Commandments we are broken too, then we have to take all the measures not to break them. And while it looks to some people like an easy thing, it's actually the most difficult thing, especially to people like Yasha of *The Magician of Lublin.* For him not to commit adultery was the most difficult thing, so he had really to use all the means. If a person has a terrible sickness, a cancer, if he would be told that by not eating certain foods and keeping away from certain spheres and certain people he would be cured, he would naturally do everything to be cured. So it is with pious men. They will do everything possible not to break the Ten Commandments or the other commandments which God has given.

Q: You don't legislate the norms of the story yourself though.

A: I don't tell the reader what I think, or what he should do. I say, assuming that we have such a hero and he had such experience, and he has such a character, he may come to such a conclusion.

Q: Yes. That's a very important *if,* that *if* it is true that you're completely immured in the Ten Commandments, *then* it is necessary for a man like Yasha to do this.

A: Exactly.

Q: But, there was an "if" on it.

A: Yes.

Q: Now, is Yasha abandoning some of the higher challenges to humanity in order to protect himself this way?

A: In a way he does, because according to Jewish religion this is not the way of salvaging your soul, because running away is not such a wonderful thing. A real man must be able to fight temptation and not to surrender to it. But in the same way, it is so and it's not so, because the Talmud has given men scores of ways to avoid temptation. That is, according to Jewish religion, if you are tempted, then you have to withstand temptation, but don't look for temptation. If you look for temptation, this means already that you want to surrender. In other words, if you happen to go on a dark street and you are attacked by somebody, naturally you will defend yourself, but if you are a cautious man you will just try not to go on dark streets to be attacked. Because how many times can a man beat the attacker; sometimes the attacker may beat the man. In life we avoid danger. And since sin is a danger to these people, they actually deal with sin the way we deal with danger: avoid it as much as possible and if you cannot avoid it, fight it.

Q: But still, when you say "these people," you're still suggesting that you are the observer, the spectator, and you are just recording . . .

A: Yes, but I don't tell people what is good and what is bad. This I keep to myself.

Q: That's what I thought. Therefore, Yasha's sin, the depth of his sin, is a product of his own imagination. He sins deeply because he *thinks* he is sinning deeply.

A: Yes, but I may also agree with him; even if I *would* agree I would not put in my point of view there. It's enough for me if I give his story and his point of view, but naturally you can ask yourself, "Why does this writer . . . why is he interested in such a man like Yasha, why is he interested in the problem of sin?" So most probably, I myself am also interested in these things; I wouldn't just write about a thing which is strange to me and where I am not interested.

Q: Nonetheless, is there a point in your deliberately withholding an authorial judgment? In other words, are you saying something about the way you understand the world to work?

A: I would say that I was saying in this book, if I would have Yasha's courage I would do as he did—in a certain period of my life, at least in the time that I wrote this. As a matter of fact, all my life I dreamt about running away; this is always my dream, and not into a hut, although I thought about this also, but somewhere to an island. It is this idea somehow that bothers me. One day, I actually will be running away. . . .

Q: But not to Italy?

A: Italy?

Q: That's where Yasha wanted to run away to. . . .

A: Not Italy, not Italy. One day I tried to run away to Patchogue. This is one of the most ridiculous stories of my life. I had hay fever. It was a strange kind of summer: to tell you the story would last too long. And I said to myself, since it's already time for me to do something and not just to talk, let me go away to some little village and stay there. Since I have hay fever I went to my doctor and I said, "Where could I go?" So he said, "Do you know there is a town not far from here called Patchogue, somewhere out on Long Island." He said: "I have a feeling that there you will suffer less from hay fever because it's near the sea." So I said to myself, "Maybe this is my opportunity. Maybe I will go away for my hay fever, and I am going to stay there in Patchogue, running away from civilization." Well, what kind of a running away this was! I went into some noisy hotel— it was the very opposite of running away. I stayed there not more than three or four days. Really, if I will ever write this story, it will be a funny story.

Q: Patchogue. I know the village and I can think of it as the wrong place to run away to.

A: The wrong place, yes. I think that wherever a man runs away is always the wrong place—even this famous painter about whom Somerset Maugham wrote . . . Gauguin.

Q: But getting back to Yasha, judged objectively, one might say that Yasha's sin is really no great sin, except that he thinks it's so. For example, the letter that Emilia sends him at the end of the novel shows that she in her own way is culpable; she has sinned in her own way, looking at him the way she has [Singer: This is true.] and that he has not committed any serious crime against her.

A: Not against her. His real sin was that he wanted to steal—also stealing. And then he considered himself a murderer, that he caused the death of this woman called Magda.

Q: But did he really cause her death?

A: He really did. I mean, her suicide was caused by his behavior.

Q: But wasn't her suicide caused by her own obsession about what she thought he was?

A: Yes, this is always the case. Because, he made her believe that he really loved her—which he did —this is the eternal problem of humanity: a woman cannot really understand that a man can love many women. They just cannot, they refuse to understand it. I don't know why, maybe because women cannot love at the same time many men. Anyhow, this Magda felt that if he loves the other one, he doesn't love her, which in a way is true and in a way is false. The novel has not yet been written about a man who loves truly a few women. Why the writers wait with this novel I will never know. But why isn't there a novel written about a man who loves dearly three or four women at the same time?[1]

---

[1]In an unrecorded comment Singer returned to the topic: "When one tries to write such a novel, people refuse to interpret it that way. If you show a man who loves one woman 150 percent, another 110 percent, another 90 percent, people say he only loves the first one—the others he doesn't really love."

Q: You've continually said "she felt" that he could not have loved her, or "he felt" that the theft would be the great sin, now . . .

A: How do *I* feel, this is what you want to ask me? I can tell you how I feel; I feel that if we break the Ten Commandments, we are really in great trouble. If people make up their minds that in certain cases you're allowed to kill, or to steal, or to be a false witness (like these revolutionaries who would say, "for the revolution you may kill, for the revolution you may bear false witness") or also to live with another man's wife, to fool people somehow—once we allow ourselves to go on this way, we are in the open, like a man who goes out in the cold winter night in a light suit with all the winds and all the snow blowing; he must get pneumonia sooner or later. I think that the Ten Commandments contain the greatest human wisdom; the question is only how to keep them. And also the question is, is it possible to keep them?—because while Moses said, "Thou shalt not kill, thou shalt not steal, thou shalt not commit adultery," he did not tell us the details, how to avoid doing these things. And all this—our theological laws and everything which we think about today is really to find ways and means how to keep the Ten Commandments. If it's impossible, if one day we were to learn that it's impossible completely, as we say today about the Sermon on the Mount, then our despair would be limitless. If men and women are allowed to fool one another, this means that the whole institution of marriage is a joke. And if you are allowed to kill and steal, then naturally you cannot complain when somebody kills you or steals from you. Most peculiar, those people who break the Ten Commandments and say that there's nothing to it, they themselves, if somebody breaks the Ten Commandments to their damage, are in a terrible rage. In other words, the same Don Juan for whom it's nothing to live with another man's wife—God forbid if somebody will do it to him. Or the same man who will steal, if somebody steals from him he's in a rage and he calls the police and he says, "See what happened to me." As a matter of fact, I have a story which will come out in my next collection where I describe a thief who convinces himself that his wife is also a thief and he is enraged because he wanted to live with an honest woman, not with another thief. In other words, we all believe in the Ten Commandments as far as we are concerned, for *our good*. We stop believing in them when we think that they have hindered us from enjoying life.

Q: But what about what you said just a moment ago—a man naturally can love, constitutionally can love, two or three women at the same time?

A: As a reader, when I read *The Magician of Lublin,* although I haven't read it since it came out, my feeling was that he really loved all these women. He loved his wife and he loved Magda and he loved Emilia. The solution to his problem would have been if he could have taken them all in the same house and lived with them, and if they would let him have some other affairs in addition. If we could create such a society, it would be very convenient for Yasha, but it wouldn't have been convenient for other people. Tolstoy was the only writer who thought about these things in a very serious way, both in his creations and also in a philosophical way. He saw the problem but he certainly did not know how to solve it.

Q: So far you've been speaking ethically; let's shift now to a metaphysical standpoint. I know in *In My Father's Court* you commented upon your early scepticism, and all through the novels there are references—Asa Heshel, Yasha, Jacob even—to . . .

A: They all doubt.

Q: Right, to the problem of doubt.

A: And so do I. I doubt. While I speak about the Ten Commandments, some voice asks, "Who made the Ten Commandments, just a man like you, and why take it so seriously?" It's my deepest conviction that it's man-made, not God-made. I don't believe that God came down on Mount Sinai. But even though they are man-made, they just express the principles of the divine, because there is nothing, nothing . . . You cannot correct it, you can only interpret it.

Q: Even if they're man-made, it really doesn't matter, does it?

A: It matters as much as if you would say $2 + 2 = 4$ is man-made. It is true they are man-made, but they are true just the same. Or if you say that the sum of a triangle is 180 degrees, naturally the 180 and the word *triangle* are man-made. But it's a truth which will remain as long as humanity. The same thing is true with the Ten Commandments.

Q: Does the very fact that you withhold authorial judgment in the novels enable you to convey your view that this may be something man-made, even if something absolutely necessary?

A: Yes, because I made Yasha say to himself, "How do I know that this particular faith is the truth? There are other faiths and other books, other sacred books." And so I express also the doubt.

Q: And you express all of this strictly through Yasha's point of view?

A: Yes, the only thing which I don't do, I don't say, "And because of this I think, dear reader, you should do this and this." This I avoid because—I *cannot* do this.

Q: But we are left unsure whether or not Yasha is doing the right thing or whether or not he's imagining, and this, in fact, corresponds very closely with your own interpretation. . . .

A: Yes, because we don't know really if he succeeded there. Maybe after a while he left—since he was such a magician, he could very well break the door or go out through the window. It's very easy to.

Q: Now, what are you saying about human responsibility? You said that Magda's suicide is his fault.

A: In a way it is, because if he would have behaved in the way that religion tells us to behave, she wouldn't have committed suicide.

Q: But can anyone really be responsible for what another person chooses to do with his life, even to take it?

A: Well, in some cases one person can be the cause of another person's death, either by just taking out a gun and shooting him, or by leading him into an abyss of such despair that nothing is left. One of the common causes is lying to a person, which we all do. At least men do. You lie to a person, and the reason that a man lies is that he cannot speak to the woman in his language. Because they really have two languages: not word languages, but emotional languages.

Q: Is it even possible to speak at all without lying?

A: Very difficult, very difficult. The very act of speaking contains already the grain of a lie. Whatever you say is a lie; if you meet a person and you say, "Pleased to meet you," it's already sometimes a lie, you may not be pleased. Or whatever—exaggerations. Language itself is full of exaggerations and little lies. But still, one can live with those little lies, but if you go on lying to a person, day after day and week after week and year after year, which many do, it can cause a great tragedy in that other person's life. But how to avoid it—again, the whole institution of marriage—is a great problem. Because the man who said, "Thou shalt not commit adultery" should have said, "Don't get married" (so there wouldn't be any adultery because, from a Jewish point of view, you don't commit adultery if you don't live with a married woman). In other words, the question is, "Can a man make a contract with a woman for life?" Can he write in this contract: "From now on until the end of my life, I will love only you and nobody else"? Isn't such a contract a lie from the very beginning? Those who said that you should not commit adultery assumed that this is possible.

Q: So then in a sense man's condition is hopeless?

A: It's not hopeless, but it's so entangled that we can never get out. It's becoming more so instead of less.

Q: But he must have the Ten Commandments in order not to suffer moral and ethical collapse, and yet, if he obeys the Ten Commandments, he's going against his own nature.

A: Yes, no question about it. At least in some cases. In my case, let's say, or in many of our cases, "Thou shalt not kill" is not a problem. We don't feel like killing. Although sometimes, when you get angry, you even think about this, but I think we have been brought up enough . . . and also, there is a punishment. Society punishes for killing, and we are afraid of doing it, while society does not punish for adultery—although in the old times it did, but it doesn't do it any more.

Q: Are you saying then that this is really the primary ethical problem?

A: I would say that in this book *The Magician of Lublin,* although it tells the story about the magician, it's our, it's everybody's problem. The emotions are an ocean and an abyss. There are so many and so contradictory and so strange that learning swimming in this ocean is an art which one can never learn completely. It's a real abyss.

Q: It's an ocean in which all men drown, in other words.

A: They drown or they choke in them. There is also a lot of enjoyment in them.

Q: For you, then, it's paradoxical. All through your books you're affirming life and yet saying that there is really no way around the kind of suffering and injury. . . .

A: No question about it. Everyday life shows this. Naturally, it's wonderful to be here and to see you and to sit with you quietly, but suddenly some robber or somebody could come in with two guns and try to shoot us, or rob us, or rape, or whatever he would do—life can become miserable in five minutes . . . in two minutes. It's always a stepping on a little bridge which can collapse any second. So it is with our health, so it is morally, and so it is with our abilities. And so it is with writing. You can write ten good novels and then write a very bad one, as if you would be the worst beginner, and we have seen it in many great writers who suddenly come out with the most terrible stuff. So it is with your friends, so it is with your marriage; one day it's wonderful, the next day you are going to divorce. And so on and so on.

Q: How does this relate to what seems to me a similarly paradoxical view of free will and determinism? Let me read a very brief selection from *The Slave* to you and get you to comment on it. Jacob is speaking: "Everything was pre-ordained. True, the will was free, but heaven also made its ordinances. He had been driven, he knew, by powers stronger than himself. How else could he have found his way back from Josefov to the mountain village?"

A: Our philosophers and sages always said that this problem of free will and determinism is something which cannot be solved. It's just like the question of the squaring of the circle—you cannot solve it—you cannot find out what is the square of the circle. It *is* a contradiction, because if everything is determined there is no free will, and if there is no free will, there cannot be determinism. But experience shows us that both of them exist, and we live in this paradox all our lives. If you walk down the street and a car is coming, crossing, you will not say, "If I am determined to die, I will die, and if I am determined to live, I will live." You'll run for your dear life, knowing somehow that if you will not run, the car will hit you. At the same time we also have a feeling that things are determined, and everything just happens according to a plan and according to causes and so on and so on. We are both driven and we have the feeling of free will. There may be some answer, but the answer is not in this world, not in this little marrow which we call brain. Maybe some higher brain or a higher spirit could explain it. To us it will remain a contradiction forever.

Q: So from the sensation of free will comes the knowledge of responsibility.

A: Yes, since we believe that we are free, we also believe that we have responsibility.

Q: And the sensation of determinism, of things being foreordained, somehow does not wipe out that responsibility?

A: It does not. It could be explained like a man who's in prison; naturally he's not a free man, he's in prison. But still he's free enough to behave badly or in a good way. Many prisoners are let out because they behaved well in prison. In a way this seems to be also our life. While we are basically in prison—we cannot do many things, we are pushed around just like a prisoner—there is still left freedom enough for us to behave badly or to behave in a good way. But this answer is not really a complete answer; it's nothing but a saying, an approximation, just like squaring the circle—while you cannot square it completely you can go on squaring it to a very high degree.

Q: What are these powers: "He had been driven he knew by powers stronger than himself." Yasha, too, feels that powers have led him "straight to Zaruski's hoard," and Asa Heshel also feels that he's being *led* back to Warsaw and other places as he goes. What do you mean by these powers?

A: I really mean powers. It's not for me just a phrase or a literary way of saying things. I believe that powers which we don't know take a great part in our life. After all, we have lived for thousands of years—or God knows how long humanity's old—without knowing about electricity. But still, electric power was here; the lightning and thunder was electricity, and then, when you combed your hair at night you saw sparks. . . . There are millions and millions of powers, even now, of which we have no idea, which take part in our life, push us or pull us or do all kinds of things with us. It is true I don't know what these powers are. They may be divine powers or other kinds of powers, but I will always have this feeling, and this is the reason that I write about the supernatural. The supernatural for me is not really supernatural; it's powers which we don't know. It's clear for everybody that five hundred years from now, the children who will go to school will know thousands and thousands of things which we don't know, and they will be even astonished that their great grandparents didn't know of these things, which will look to them so simple. In a thousand years from now, they will know things which these children will not know, and so on and so on. Nature is a well without a bottom. And because of this, whatever we know is only a little, little on the surface, while below us, and above us, and on all sides, there are powers of which we have no inkling. This is what I mean by powers.

Q: But there is a difference between natural powers and, say, demonic powers.

A: I don't know. No, there may not be a difference. For example, a man who took off his wool jacket five hundred years ago at night and saw sparks might have thought that these sparks are supernatural; because there was no reason for him to think that a wool sweater should produce sparks. But we now know that they are . . . we call them natural, although we don't know what electricity is until today. We call light natural, although we don't know what light is. So most probably there is no such thing as two natures. There is one nature, but it is large and deep. The things we know we call nature and what we don't know we call supernatural.

Q: Here you may be alluding to your interest in psychic research.

A: I certainly am. I am astonished why other people are not. I think that everybody really is.

Q: Are you suggesting that it's possible to shortcut man's ignorance by mystical experience?

A: Not really, no. I wish it would—I would be very happy if this would be true, but I don't think so. With mystical experience we will never reach the moon, or we will never cross the ocean. You need an airplane, a jet plane. You need all these things. Science—I'm not against science and logic. I don't say throw away your laboratories and go into a little room and make dark and God will reveal to you things. I don't believe in this. The only thing I believe is that we should not belittle our mystical experience either. We should not say that the sparks which we don't understand are nothing just because we don't understand them. Pay attention to the things which don't fit into your sum of knowledge, because they may fit a little later.

Q: But in your novels, demons or forces always manifest themselves in psychological terms, as psychological forces, so that, say, for the reader who would not respond to supernaturalism you would still offer an insight into human nature.

A: Yes. In writing you have to find a way to say these things or hint them. I found that folklore is the best way of expressing these feelings, because folklore has already expressed them, has already given clothes to these ideas. By really calling demons names and by assigning to them certain functions, it makes it more concrete and in writing you have to be concrete; if not it becomes philosophy or brooding. But basically behind all these names and all these functions is the idea that powers exist—of which we really don't know.

Q: What about this comment of Jacob's—again going back to *The Slave?* It's just the moment very shortly before his death: "They were debating something among themselves, but without hostility. . . . Both sides were in their own way right, and . . . he was amazed. If only men could apprehend these things while they were still strong. . . . They would serve the Lord differently."

A: It seems that before he died, he had a feeling of revelation, that he had learned something. How do I know that it was so? I don't know. But I assume that it's possible, because people, before they are dead, have sometimes seen things. There are cases where people before they died said, "Here is father, here is mother." They even knew of people who died, although they didn't know it with real knowledge. Naturally, I use my imagination. A writer can do it—a fiction writer. If it really happens, I don't know. I always try to hint at these powers, but I am also a sceptic—in other words I don't say to you there are so many powers and here they exist and this is what they're doing. No. If I call them names, it's only because from a literary point of view, it's good. But behind all this is this feeling that maybe someday we learn the truth, like why did we die; maybe after our death or . . .

Q: Or maybe not at all.

A: Perhaps as you say, perhaps never. I even admit this kind of thought.

Q: Would you say that Spinoza has had a strong influence on your thinking?

A: In the beginning he had an influence. I have a story called "The Spinoza of Market Street." Actually Spinoza preached the very opposite of what I think.

Q: It wasn't scepticism in any case, was it?

A: No, he considered himself a rationalist, but like all rationalists he became mystical against his will. Because, according to Spinoza, substance has an endless number of attributes and we only know two of them, thought and extension. So by giving substance an endless number of attributes he has already called millions and trillions of powers which we don't know. What are the other attributes of God? If we don't know them—and we will never know them according to him—they may be mercy, and they may be *anything*. So many of the rationalists talk so long, they talk themselves out of business.

Q: Would you agree with Rabbi Benish in *Satan in Goray* that it's a sin to delve too deeply into things that were really meant to be hidden?

A: Well, in a way yes and a way no, because this Rabbi Benish was a leader of his community, and he knew that these people have weak little brains, and if they go into mysticism, it will only bring evil, which it really did in this particular case. If mysticism becomes a mass movement, it's always bad, because it's not for the masses, it's not for many. It should be an esoteric thing.

Q: Do you believe that there are absolute limits on what a man can know?

A: No question about it. Not only are they there, but they are very near to us. Wherever we go we touch these limits. However, I would say that men can a little bit stretch these limits, and whatever stretching he does is already a great gain. We know that man has stretched his limits in science to a great extent. We have learned in the last two hundred years things which humanity hasn't grasped in a hundred thousand. Perhaps we can also stretch the limits of our psychic knowledge, psychic powers, which are even stiffer limits and not so easy to push. But at least there is the desire in some of us to try.

Q: But this is still knowledge, within thought and extension, isn't it? This is not knowledge of all the myriad attributes that are possible?

A: No. I have a hope some way that perhaps you can find a third attribute if you try very hard. That is, it's not written in any book that these are all—although Spinoza said that these are the two, actually they are arbitrary. You could call them by different names. I'm sure that man knows more than what Spinoza said we are able to know.

Q: Can fiction help to stretch the limits?

A: Real fiction, or at least I would say the type of fiction which I like.

Q: And you write . . .

A: . . . this kind of fiction, I hope. The kind of fiction that is written today by some writers, you know, who try to become sociologists in their writing—this is not the kind of writing which will push these particular limits. Maybe they will push other limits, social limits, I don't know.

Q: How does it push the limit? This is, I take it, visionary writing. Maybe this is not something that can be formulated.

A: No, no—it can be formulated. I would say that if a man really thinks about these things, he indulges in these problems, and also if he will live a better life, a life without guilt, without too many contradictions, he may, by this very fact, push a little bit the limits. Because we know that a man like Swedenborg really had a kind of knowledge that was to our minds supernatural. And you will be surprised that Immanuel Kant, the great philosopher, has written almost a whole book about Swedenborg—this is not known, this book; it is not well known because people just ignore it. Kant tells the miracles which Swedenborg has shown and believes that they are very possible, because according to Kant's philosophy we never see the thing-in-itself, only the phenomenon. Behind all the phenomena there is a great mystery which Kant calls the "thing-in-itself." And since we don't know anything of this mystery, we don't know the powers which may be concealed there. So Kant believed really that Swedenborg was an unusual man.

Q: Does Kant believe that Swedenborg actually penetrated into the thing-in-itself?

A: He doesn't say that he penetrated the thing-in-itself, but he tells in a very serious way the miracles which Swedenborg worked and he comments about them. So this great philosopher was able to believe that some men can have certain powers which we don't all have. As a matter of fact, we see these powers in many other ways. A talented man can do more than a man without talent—he has a certain power. It's also a power. Naturally it doesn't look supernatural to us because there are many writers and many painters. We call nature things which we see often; things which we see seldom, we call supernatural. But in a way nobody can really explain a man like Shakespeare or Dostoevsky. Even though there are thousands of books about Shakespeare, none of them explains why Shakespeare was Shakespeare, what he did or how he did it.

Q: The essence of Shakespeare, in other words, remains impenetrable.

A: Yes, the essence. So we see these prodigies, these very gifted children—a child of five, three years, who will do calculations which only a computer can do. These things appear from time to time to give us a hint of the possibilities of human life in some cases.

Q: You mentioned Kant, and some of the things you say make me think of Kierkegaard. Do you know Kierkegaard?

A: Not really. . . . I stopped my study of philosophy with Schopenhauer and Nietzsche and somehow I never went further. I convinced myself that philosophy can never reveal anything. It can tell us what we cannot do, but it can never tell us what we can do. I began to read mostly books which are connected with psychic research, because these people at least try to give us something positive, although most of it is straw and lies and chaff.

Q: What have you read in particular? Have you gone back to the Kabala at all?

A: Oh, yes. I studied the Kabala when I was still young, and once in a while I will go back to it. I have even written a speech which I call "Kabala and Modern Man." I read Hasidic books, and a lot of books about the occult, about psychic research, like *The Phantasms of the Living,* and many others. I also read a lot of magazines, and I'm especially interested in the letters which readers write to these magazines, because these naive letters sometimes discover to me whole worlds. Not discover, they give *hints* of hidden things. To me a writer must be interested in the mystery of life. A writer who says to me that he's a complete realist, to me he's not a writer anymore.

Q: And yet your own work often uses extremely detailed . . .

A: Yes, realism—because the so-called real world itself is a great secret, a great mystery. Also, I don't like writers who write about great miracles and mysteries without even describing the background. In other words, a miracle must be invented amid realism because, if it's one miracle after the other and there's no realism, the miracle itself becomes nothing.

Q: All great literature begins in realism then?

A: I think, yes. Once a man brought me a story which began with a cut-off head which spoke. And I said to the man, "Isn't it miracle enough that a head which is not chopped off can talk?"

Q: Do you turn again to some of the things you read as a child and as a young man? I think you've mentioned Dostoevsky to me before.

A: Yes, once in a while I will open up a book and read, not from

beginning to end, but a page in the middle or so. I read a lot of books
in this way where I sit down sometimes near my bookcase, take out
a book, and read a page inside.

Q: You know, we were talking earlier about Dostoevsky and the
realistic setting and after I left you that day I began to reflect that,
after all, many of the settings that you describe are actually places on
a map of Poland.

A: Oh, surely. Whatever can be real, I make real. In other words, I
don't believe in distortion—like Pinter who will distort the facts just
to fit his purpose; I don't believe in this. Be as real as possible. But if
you want to tell about a miracle, about a mystical experience, bring it
into the milieu of realism. If not, it becomes nothing.

Q: Do you go to any lengths to establish this realism? I remember
James Joyce used to write back to Dublin and ask for locations to be
verified.

A: Well, in my case I don't need it, because I always write about a
few little towns. I always come back to the same. I don't venture to
go out too far, like a little child—her mother told her don't go out to
the other side of the street. . . . I think that whatever I need to tell
about, I can tell about the places which I know best, like Warsaw,
or Bilgoray, or Frampol—because why couldn't these things have
happened there? Why do I have to go into other places? But since
I am already in this country over thirty years, I begin now to write
about New York, about things which happen in this country.

Q: Only recently, though?

A: Only recently, but always with people who come from the other
side. I would never dare to write, almost never, about a person born
here because I know that I don't know him enough.

Q: Do you see a significant difference then between Jewish life,
let's say in Poland, and Jewish life in the United States as you've
lived it?

A: Oh, there's no question. There's always a difference even
between Jewish life in one little town and another; there is some
difference. There is individuality in everything. There's no question
that there are many differences. But at the same time, there are also
many similarities . . . naturally, the life of my father as a Jew and my
life is as far as heaven from earth, but still we are alike in many ways,
too. This is what literature is: to describe individuality, all these dif-

ferences. All the novels we read are basically love stories. Still, why do we read many novels?—because we want to see the difference between one love story and the other. And this is true about every-thing. History never repeats itself, and no human emotion is the same, no conditions are the same. Always, there's always a dif-ference.

Q: I know a number of the reviews and comments on your work, especially on *The Manor,* have suggested that you were interested in the problem of Jewish identity. But I noticed that you brushed the question off about Yasha. Is it fairer to say that you're most interested in human identity?

A: Well, in Jewish identity, human identity, *ethical* identity, human responsibility—can man really serve God? And how should he serve God? And is there a God to serve?

Q: I imagine you must have read some writers in what is called the modern Jewish Renaissance, the American Jewish writers such as Bellow, Malamud, and Roth.

A: I read them a little, but I don't pay too much attention to these young modern writers. I mean, if I would find there great brilliancy I would be impressed; I have a feeling that modern young writers don't reveal much which is new to me. Maybe I am mistaken. Most probably I am mistaken, because all elderly people have this feeling, that whatever there is to know, they know already.

Q: Bellow has translated a story of yours, I think.

A: Yes, he did, he did. He translated "Gimpel the Fool" and I am grateful to him for doing this. They are talented people, but, you know, at may age, you want to read only the masters. You don't want to spend your time with reading anything which isn't first-class. So if I want to read fiction, I always go back to Tolstoy or Dostoevsky or Gogol. If I find something good in other writing I certainly am very happy, but I seldom find things which make me enthusiastic. I must confess this.

Q: If not the contemporary American Jewish Renaissance, what about the Yiddish culture in New York when you first came?

A: It was on the decline even then. And I'll tell you, Yiddish culture and I are two different things. Though I love Yiddish, I'm not a Yid-dishist, because these people really have a kind of social ideology. They want to create a movement. They always talk about a movement—the Jewish literature, the Jewish theater, or the Yiddish theater. I'm not a man of movements at all. In other words, they considered me, in a way, selfish. They said, "You only think about your own work, about your own talent. You forget us, the movement." But I'm disappointed in movements. I know that movements and mediocrity always go together. Whatever becomes a mass movement—even if mysticism were to become a mass movement—would be bad. So, from a literary point of view, I went my own way. Also, these people were all on the socialistic side. They always thought about creating a better world. And, because of this, they were sentimental, which is not my way; I would also like to see a better world, but I don't think, really, that men can create it.

Q: You can't be a sceptic and a socialist at the same time, in other words?

A: Yes. They can make an effort, you know. But we cannot create a different society. We cannot do all these things which these people preach. And I have seen what happened to Russia, how they had the Revolution; they spoke about a new man and a new way of life and actually it's the old men and the old way of life, a little changed.

Q: You go back to the masters—would you be willing to talk at all about the writers who've meant the most to you?

A: Well, I would say that Tolstoy, Dostoevsky, and Gogol meant the most to me. And also I have great respect for Flaubert, although he's not one hundred percent my kind of writer. I loved Edgar Allan Poe, although I read him in translation and I see that in this country there's a great tendency to belittle him. But I don't agree with this. It is true that I haven't read him for a long time. But my feeling is that the man was a genius, no matter what they say. And someday in the future, he will be again fashionable, they will again praise him. He is one of these writers whom I've never forgotten.

Q: What is there in Polish literature that you particularly like?

A: Oh, in Polish there is a great literary masterpiece: *Pan Tadeusz* by Adam Mickiewicz. Mickiewicz was a genius of the same kind as Byron and Pushkin and such people. The book was translated into many languages, also into English; it was translated into English only a short time ago, again. But poetry cannot be translated and he is one of those who lost a lot in translation. Another good writer among the Poles was Slenkewicz, the one who wrote *Quo Vadis,* but he is not of the size of Mickiewicz. They have a poet called Slowacki, and Bennett. But the real genius there was Mickiewicz.

Q: How about the Yiddish tradition in Poland?

A: Well, Yiddish literature in Poland is not very old. I mean the modern literature, because before this there were mostly Biblical things and religious books. But secular literature in Yiddish is not even a hundred years old. They have done quite well in a hundred years, but there is no reason for too much satisfaction.

Q: The form of your stories and some of your novels, plus the Biblical allusions, has led a number of people to talk of you as writing fable or parable.

A: Well, people always need a name for things, so whatever you will write or whatever you will do, they like to put you into a certain category. Even if you would be new, they would like to feel that a name is already prepared for you in advance. Which is not really true. I don't call myself a fabulist; I hope that one day somebody will find a new name for me, not use the old names.

Q: Have you read any Kafka? Do you like Kafka?

A: Yes, I like him, but one Kafka in a century is enough. It's not good to have whole armies, whole multitudes, of Kafkas. He's not the kind of writer whom one should imitate or even emulate. There could have been only one Kafka, like one Joyce and one Proust. While there could have been another Tolstoy—it couldn't do any damage if you would have a hundred Tolstoys; but a hundred Kafkas wouldn't be good. He's a unique case.

Q: Why wouldn't it be good?

A: It wouldn't be good because it's description of dreams, *completely* so. Kafka is not enough embedded in life—his miracles are too arbitrary to create the kind of literature that could last forever. The reader gets very tired if life is distorted, or too much invented, completely defying the order of things. In other words, the real mystic should describe life as it is, and then bring out the other side. But when you begin immediately with symbolism or with distortions, you create a kind of literature which even if it is unique, you cannot have too much of it. Like with food, you can eat a lot of bread, a lot of potatoes, a lot of vegetables, you cannot eat a lot of mustard. You can only have a little bit of it. And this is true even about spiritual things.

Q: Then you wouldn't put Kafka in the same category as you put Tolstoy or Gogol?

A: No, no, not at all.

Q: What about James Joyce?

A: Also not . . . also not.

Q: Would you emphasize the significance of a narrative event, of plot over symbol, from what you've just said?

A: Well, to my mind, the symbol should be the climax of a work, the result of a whole work. You cannot begin immediately with the symbol and go on this way. Because if you heap one symbol upon the other, it very often happens that one symbol neutralizes the other or cancels the other.

Q: It's like the Biblical analogue—it's got to emerge from the work; it can't be imposed on it from without.

A: Exactly, exactly. It's peculiar—I wanted to say the same thing. When you read the Bible, you get the story and you get description, but somehow the story is also symbolic.

Q: And that's perhaps the reason why the symbol and the central figure in your novels very often coincide: the magician in *The Magician of Lublin.* . . .

A: I hope so. If you look deep into reality, reality itself is very symbolic. As I said before about a man who began his story with a cut-off head: it is true, from a symbolical point of view you can make a cut-off head talk, but you cannot write a whole play with a cut-off head because we need to step on a more familiar ground, to be able to go into what is not familiar.

Q: And Kafka writes of people with their heads cut off, who speak?

A: Exactly, quite often he does this.

Q: You said reality itself is very symbolic. At this point I'd like to come back to the question, "What is real? What is reality?"

A: We don't know; Kant and other philosophers like David Hume and John Locke or Berkeley and others have already taught us that there is no real way of defining reality. In a way we can say that reality is what is real to us. But still we *assume* reality is not an assumption, that there is something behind our feelings and our senses. What we call reality is the things to which we are accustomed. If you see a table every day, a table looks to you real. If you would see a table for the first time in your life, you would most probably

feel that it's something not real. Or if you try to think about what
a table is, you know that a table contains millions and trillions of
molecules. Each molecule contains many, many atoms, and each
atom contains protons and electrons; then the table stops being the
table, it becomes an amalgamation of miracles. So actually what we
call reality are things to which we are accustomed. The everyday
things we call reality. But if you want to go into something which is
not everyday, the best thing is to begin with everyday and go from
there. If you begin immediately with the miracles, with the unusual,
you cannot go far from a literary point of view.

Q: To go back to Berkeley then, there's a sense in which the
contents of a literary work are as real as anything.

A: Surely, according to Berkeley, the whole world is ideas in God.
So since literature's full of ideas and images, it is just as real as anything.

Q: Do you think of literature as having a purpose, a function to
serve?

A: Not the kind of function which many younger people think—
a sociological function, a function to build a better society and so on.
I don't believe that literature has this power. I say that literature is a
force without direction. What I mean by this is: it moves one way
and another way; it doesn't go straight from one point to another.
Literature will never, can never, enhance the revolution, can never
enhance social reforms. And if it does, it is in a very small way, because literature has to give many points of view: the point of view not
only of the oppressed but also of the oppressor, not only of the one
who is wronged but also of the one who is doing wrong. I say if
literature is a force, it's a vector which goes not straight but around
and around—like the waves of the oceans, they keep on going, but
they go nowhere. Literature stirs the mind; it makes you think about
a million things, but it does not lead you. So the basic function of
literature, as far as I can say, is to entertain the spirit in a very big
way. I mean small literature entertains small spirits and great literature
entertains greater spirits. But it's basically an entertainment and it has
only qualities of entertainment—which means, if you are not entertained while you read a book, there is no other reward for you. While
you read, let's say, mathematics, you can say, "I'm bored now, but it
will be useful to me to build a bridge or to build a house." In litera-

ture, if you don't enjoy it while you read, the purpose is lost. It has to be enjoyed; like all the good things of life, it's a kind of luxury, rather than a thing with a function.

Q: How does one enjoy literature, what does one respond to in a piece of fiction?

A: Well, if you enjoy something, you don't really have to ask your self *why* you enjoy. Naturally, professors like to analyze. But the reader does not always need this analysis. It's only in the later years that people began to analyze every kind of enjoyment. People don't really have to analyze the pleasure which they get out of love or sex, they enjoy it and that's it. I would say that it doesn't do any damage if you do analyze it but neither do we bring more enjoyment by the analysis. If there wouldn't have been a single book about Shakespeare, Shakespeare would still be as good as he is. And the same thing is true about all the writers. However, it seems to me that we are reaching a point where analysis itself becomes a pleasure to some people. And if it is a pleasure, I say more power to them. Why not? If you enjoy it, and others do too, keep on analyzing.

Q: I was really driving at something a little different: the matter of aesthetic response, the way one responds to the formal elements in a work, as one might respond to the formal elements in a painting. What is your relationship to a work that you create, from this standpoint?

A: I would say that in my own small way, I'm a perfectionist. I like perfection, I like to think that I have written something which is in my way perfect—which means the construction is right, the description is right, the dialogue is right. I have not done too much or too little, everything is in its place. And this kind of enjoyment is shared by a painter or even a housewife when she thinks that she has done a good job in cleaning the house or preparing a supper. This feeling of doing a thing right is a human instinct as much as any other instinct which we have.

Q: You say that "everything is in its right place." How do you go about laying out a novel? Is it purely instinct or do you work from a plan?

A: Well, when it comes to a novel, no matter how much you plan, you can never act according to plan, because once you have written the first chapter, even the first page, you are not anymore the complete owner of the thing. The heroes themselves, the situation itself, bid for consequences and so on. In a short story, it's easier to have a complete plan and write according to it, but even in a short story you cannot do just what you please. Also there, the heroes, the characters, have their own lives and their own logic, and you have to act accordingly. But still, the very idea that you have done something right (let's say you have written an essay or a story and you read it and you think, "It is exactly what I wanted to do") is a pleasure which I cannot define, and it doesn't even have to be defined. It's as basic as any other emotion.

Q: This might sound like a cliché, but what you're saying is that the mystery in the creation of literature is as great as the mystery in the response to life.

A: No question about it. Surely, because literature is a part of life. If you go out and you see a girl and you like her, you really don't have to analyze why you like her. You don't need to measure her nose and her face and so on and so on. It's enough if you like her. By measuring, you cannot spoil it, unless your measurements are wrong, and they may hypnotize you in the wrong way. The reason we love a beautiful woman or a beautiful building or anything is that we have an instinct for proportion that we cannot explain. We will say that one nose is better looking than the other. And if you ask yourself, "What is your point of view, how do you know how a nose should be?" the only answer could be that we—Plato's explanation—that we have seen somewhere a nose above, before we came to this earth, and we know exactly what it is. But whatever the answer, there is in all human beings a feeling of how things should be and how they shouldn't be. We call a freak a freak not from any other point of view but from *our* point of view, from what we are accustomed to, from what we consider right.

Q: This will get back to the idea of analysis and analysis being a pleasure in itself. Could you say that in certain types of people the instinct for analysis is almost an aesthetic instinct—the instinct for seeing relationships within the work or in life?

A: Yes, yes, that may be true, because actually analysis itself is a form of creation. It is true that some people have it more and some people have it less. But there is such a thing. We like to analyze things; and in the sciences, analysis has accomplished much; the whole of science is really built on logic and analysis. In art, it hasn't done as much, but still, I'm not against literary criticism—far from it. But I'm against it when the writer himself is his own critic, while he writes. For example, sometimes in *Pale Fire,* as Nabokov writes, he says, "I could have written it so." He writes essays about his heroes. And I think this is not the right way of mixing analysis and giving images. To me this looks unaesthetic.

Q: What do you think of Nabokov in general, since you mentioned him?

A: Well, he's a good writer, but I would say he's not *my* writer.

Q: Are you suggesting that the writer loses the right to define what the work is, as soon as he finishes the work?

A: No, he doesn't lose, he has the same rights as anybody else, but not more.

Q: And he cannot define the work while he's writing it himself either, because this would be an act of literary criticism.

A: No, it's not really good. Let's imagine if a man would stand on his knees and declare his love to a girl. He would say, "I love you dearly, I cannot live without you," and then he would try to explain: "The reason why I love you dearly is . . ." We feel that he would spoil his love declaration; he would become really ridiculous. It's not necessary in this case. And the same thing is true when we tell a story. Most stories are love stories also. In some way, a story is always kind of a love declaration—near to it; and explaining and using all these foreign words and saying what I *could* have done is not the right way. I don't believe the writer should interpret, just as I feel it would be a very bad thing if a rose would explain exactly what colors it used and how it is to become a rose. The beauty of the rose is its silence, its *being* a rose. And I think this is really what Gertrude Stein meant when she said, "A rose is a rose is a rose." It meant that you cannot say more.

Q: In other words, the writer creates a coherent and self-sustaining illusion.

A: Exactly.

Q: And this is perhaps the reason that your work relies as heavily as it does on irony?

A: There may be irony, but the irony should never be outspoken, not clearly. When you go into a store there's a sign which says there are shoes and so on. But literature doesn't need any signs; go into the store and see the merchandise by itself.

Q: Perhaps the word should be paradox, not irony. Paradox certainly exists in the world.

A: All over. Everything to me, everything is a paradox. The very existence of things is a paradox.

II

Q: Mr. Singer, if we may, I would like to discuss the short stories, since in the last interview we chiefly considered your novels. One of the things that struck me in the *Short Friday* collection is the presence of some stories in which you've assumed the point of view of a demon or a magical creature. If I remember correctly, we have spoken about demons sometimes being a manifestation of a man's inner feelings and obsessions. Is this true in a story like "The Last Demon," for example, which is written completely from the point of view of the demon?

A: Well, I think I told you that I really believe in demons. To me they are alive. If a voice from God would come out and would say, "There are no demons," there would still remain something of my way of thinking. At least to me, demons exist, just as God exists. I assume that there are intelligent powers not connected with a body, or not with a human body or with an animal body. And these powers still work, so for me they exist. About the story of "The Last Demon": I imagine that there is a demon in this little village, but since I don't know anything about demons, I always make the demon behave as if it would be a human being. In other words, he has the mind of a human being without the body of a human being.

Q: Would this make the story an allegory or fable?

A: I wouldn't really call it an allegory. When I write about a demon, I go, so to say, into *his* point of view. I assume that he exists not only as a fable. . . . Our human existences may also be a fable or an allegory, but it's also existence: you have to eat, you have to sleep. I don't know anything about demons, so whatever existence I give them must be a kind of human existence. But still I try to find some individuality in them, taken from folklore, from stories. In other words, to me a demon is not only a fable or an allegory—he's like some separate creature which lives by its own right and by its own laws. A demon may have different laws, different ambitions, but he has to be human, not because I want to make him human to teach something about humanity, but because I have no *other* experience. I can give him, once in a while, also the powers of an animal, but anyhow, it's all taken from experience or from folklore, which is a kind of experience. And from imagination, which is also a form of experience.

Q: Let's take up a possibly related question. In "Yentl the Yeshiva Boy" you said, "Though their bodies were different, their souls were of one kind." Are you using "soul" to indicate something like human nature? What do you mean by "soul"?

A: In this case I meant really human nature, because the soul expresses human nature. When we say the soul or the spirit, we mean actually the man, because we don't know if the soul and the body are two sides of the same coin, as Spinoza says, or if they can be separated. In this case what I meant is that they have kindred spirits: whatever it means. But I may also use the word "soul" in a different way.

Q: That's what I was thinking. Now when you use it in the different way, do you in any sense imply the notion of *fixed* human nature?

A: No, I don't believe in a fixed human nature, because I believe in free choice, so it cannot be completely fixed. But naturally, it has its inclinations, there's no question about it. For example, in the story you mentioned, "Yentl the Yeshiva Boy," we have to do with homo-sexual people. This is *their* inclination. Free choice does not really deny human nature, nor does human nature deny free choice. These two can live together. Like in a prison—although you are impris-oned, you have some freedom; some prisoners get out for good behavior, and some prisoners stay longer because of bad behavior. In the prison itself there is a choice.

Q: Would you link the soul to the part of the person that is en-gaged in free choice?

A: No, I would link the soul to everything: to sin and to virtue, to passion and to insanity, to everything.

Q: So along with Spinoza you would not necessarily mean to take the soul as the opposite of body at all?

A: In some cases, I would—say, when I speak about a hereafter.

Then the body has decayed and I assume that the soul remains. In literature the writer does not have to be completely consistent. He can use a term once so, in another time so. You are completely free because it's playing around. The writer plays around with words and also with ideas. Especially, when you write about demons, you are playing all the time. And since you are playing, you can change your point of view, you can change everything. Still there is a certain consistency which is connected with the writer himself. No matter how he plays, you see what is behind the play: how he reacts, how *he* plays. As a matter of fact, when we study actors, we know that they are themselves in every part. The same thing is true with writers.

Q: To go back to the story we started with, "The Last Demon": although it seems to be about a demon, there actually is in it a strong current, it seems to me, about the possibly corrupting power of literature.

A: Yes, absolutely so. In other words, this story belittles the writers.

Q: What were you doing here? The quotation that I noted was, "Satan has cooked up a new dish of kasha. The Jews have now developed writers. Yiddish ones, Hebrew ones, and they have taken over our trade. . . . They know all our tricks—mockery, piety. They have a hundred reasons why a rat must be kosher. All that they want to do is redeem the world."

A: Exactly. Actually I am chiding here not only the writers, but the whole Enlightenment. The Jewish Enlightenment is a kind of rationalism which came very late, a hundred years later than rationalism came to Europe. It was obsolete to begin with. And because it was obsolete, it was old-fashioned and silly. So our kind of Enlightenment, which we call the Haskalah, is something which I often chide, because Yiddish literature and Hebrew literature is always under its influence. All the writers are writers of the Enlightenment—and I would say that I am almost an exception. Maybe there is another exception, but they're very few.

In some sense I am saying that the writers actually are small assistants of Satan. They help him . . . they help the imps. In other words, what the devil did in the old time himself, now the writers have taken over.

Q: All right, that quickly brings us to the question, if these writers are doing the wrong thing, what should a writer be doing?

A: Well, I never say what he should be doing because I myself am in a way a split personality. If I would be a very religious man I would say that the writer should write about religion, like my father did, but this, as you know, I cannot do. I can make fun of the Enlightenment but at the same time I cannot give anything which should take the place of the Enlightenment. However, I have my kind of philosophy, which is expressed in my writings—not that I practice it one hundred percent, but at least I believe in it. What I believe is this: we don't know what God wants from us and there is no chance *ever* to know. Revelation is always dubious; we don't know if God has *ever* revealed Himself, or if He has ever told a man how we should behave, or if revelation is the *nature* of God—we know nothing. So our best guess is to behave in a right way towards other human beings and also towards the animals. Not that we are sure that this is going to be rewarded and that this is God's will, but this is our best bet, as gamblers will say. Since we don't know which horse will reach the aim, let's bet on the horse that looks the strongest; let's not build our fortune on other people's misfortune. And I think that this is to what all philosophers came—religious philosophers and actually all philosophers, no matter if rationalists or mystics. Somehow, if you read the history of philosophy and the history of religions, they all came to the same conclusion, because this is how far human thought, human philosophy, can reach. So let's assume that God does not want me to stab my fellow man, to gossip about him, to denounce him, and so on and so on—that God does not want us to be bad to one another. Comparing God to our father, us to the children, our father's real desire is that his children should not do damage one to the other. This is to me nothing but an assumption because, as I say, I don't know. There are many arguments which can prove that the opposite is true: God has given us power to do damage to one another, which means He does not mind. However, since we cannot go further, we have to rest here and say this is it. If we made a mistake, so still it's better to be good than to be bad.

Q: When you use the words "good" and "bad," you're really using them on the basis of revelation, are you not?

A: No, on the basis of human needs. I mean, you are a good man if you don't make people suffer. This is the only measure; there is no other measure. The Ten Commandments and all the commandments in the world are built on this.

Q: On something which is fundamentally experience . . .

A: Fundamentally experience, and in us, Kant calls it the categorical imperative. There are all kinds of names for it, but we all know exactly what it means.

Q: Do you see a human being as fundamentally, in part, evil?

A: Well, I don't belong to those who say men are born good, only that civilization spoils them. This to me is completely silly. Man is born bad, with a certain goodness in him, which he can enhance and which he can completely destroy, or almost completely destroy, as we see from experience.

Q: It seemed to me in the *Short Friday* collection that one of your concerns was a description of the nature of evil. In fact, that collection, I think, contains some of the most grotesque or horrifying of the stories you've written. I'm thinking particularly of the stories "Blood" and "Under the Knife," although there are others similar in the same collection. To begin with, in "Under the Knife" did you view Leib as a psychotic, and does this have something to do with the nature of evil?

A: The man who murders two innocent women, because he wants to take revenge on the woman who rejected him.

Q: Yes; he kills one woman who befriends him (the streetwalker) and the elder sister of the woman he loved. It seems to me that there are a number of possibilities here. One of them is that this is the study of a man who is totally obsessed and as a result psychotic.

A: It is actually another story of obsession. I don't like to write about people who are indifferent, or who are only mildly interested in a thing. I think that literature can serve us best when it will write about obsessed characters, because here you can see the human being with all his qualities, good or bad. Here is a man who is obsessed by revenge, although there was no reason for him to kill this woman. (She might have loved him once and now she doesn't love him; she wants to live her own life, and she's entitled to it.) But to him, she is evil, although he's actually evil. I'm concerned with the idea that he revenges himself on people who are completely innocent. This is what happened really with Hitler; he was angry with a few Jews, a few journalists whom he considered evil. And he took revenge on people who had nothing to do with journalism, most innocent victims. This is what happens in every war; whenever people fight for something, the victim always is not the one whom they fight, but people who have nothing to do with him. For example, when we fight now in Viet Nam we are not killing the leaders of Communism, but innocent recruits. And they are not killing Rockefeller or Johnson, whom they consider evil, but again those who have nothing to do with these leaders.

Q: In other words, the most important thing about the story is the fact that the person whom he wanted to injure escaped untouched?

A: Yes, yes . . . and also, I make this Leib at the end sick. I show by this that nature itself takes revenge in its own way, that if you wait a little, everything is revenged anyhow, everything is in a way straightened out by nature itself. I remember that I once went in a bus and a number of people were quarreling over a seat. They began a great quarrel, and I wanted to give them my seat, but they said, "No, no, we don't want your seat." I was reading the newspaper for a few minutes, and then I lifted my eyes; they were all gone. The whole quarrel was a quarrel about sitting two minutes on a bench. It wasn't worthwhile. And I think that all human fights, or almost all of them, are of the same kind. If we just would wait a little bit, the whole thing would be over.

Q: Are you saying something too about the randomness of suffering?

A: I don't know myself what I'm saying, all I know is that I just got this idea of this story. And the story, in a way, is a consistent story— I mean it works itself out from the beginning to the end. And once a story is right, is done right, you can find in it many, many things. It's not the writer's ability to know everything which the story may imply.

Q: What about "Blood" now?

A: Here is another obsession: people who are obsessed by blood. And I also tried to show in this the nature of sadism. In a way sadism is a kind of riddle; we have a word for sadism, but we seldom really know what it is. We say that the sadist enjoys bringing suffering to people, but here I made sadism clearer than it is when you just read the dictionary. Here you see people who enjoy killing animals and you infer from this that they might have enjoyed killing people too, if they would have gone a little further. And also you see it connected with sex. The shedding of blood arouses these people.

Q: Are you implying that there's something fundamentally associated between carnal lust and blood lust?

A: I think, yes. For example, men's obsession for thousands of years and until today to have a virgin is only this, that the first time a man lives with a virgin he makes her suffer a little bit, and he sees blood. And men were terribly obsessed with this; to marry a woman who was not a virgin was a great misfortune and a great shame. He had to get his pound of flesh from this woman. The woman herself, even though she's the victim, was sometimes very much excited by this, as I heard women tell me, exaggerating even their suffering— which is a kind of masochism. . . . Hunting is deeply connected with sex. If you will read the Bible or Homer, you will see that sometimes the woman asks her lover to give her a few heads or limbs of the enemy. The passion of the flesh is deeply connected with the flesh itself, with the blood of the flesh.

Q: In other words, would you suggest that all human drives, particularly sex, but all human drives, have a component which is destructive and consumptive?

A: There is no question about it. Passion, an immense desire for the female, is kind of a strange desire to revenge himself upon a person he loves. A man may be loving a woman very much, but he's little disturbed by the fact that this woman will get pregnant and she suffers while she gives birth. He takes it for granted; in a way, it's his privilege. He feels that this is the way he can rule her. Women enjoy the fact that men go to war—not all women, but more than we dare to know.

Q: In other words, you're placing sexuality very much at the root of most of experience. Is that a fair statement?

A: There is sexuality in everything. About this I have no quarrel with Freud. The only real quarrel with him which I have—although I'm not a specialist—is about his remedies. He believes that if things become clear to us, we stop being bothered by them. The first thing is, they never become clear, so this is not going to help any . . . and even if they would be clear, it would still not help because it is not a question of being clear or not clear. If a man has a passion for somebody, you cannot talk him out of it. If a father really would like to sleep with his daughter, no matter how much he will lie on the couch and talk about it, he will still have this desire.

Q: When I reflect on it, actually there are very few, perhaps no, portraits in your work of passion, a clear passion, that comes to a good end.

A: No, passion in itself can never bring any good end. It's only when we curb our passion. . . . By the way, there isn't such a thing as a good end; what is a good end? It does not exist. The only thing we call "a good end" is if a man lives without any passion. He doesn't strive to do anything and he goes on living a monotonous life, so he may continue for eighty years or so, being bored to death and boring other people; then he dies. While "the bad end" is that of a man who goes into things in a very hard way, lives only a few years longer, dies suddenly. Both ends are actually not so good.

Q: Then passion is its own reward?

A: It speeds up human life, it gives it more content, more intensity. Passion is bad when it brings suffering to other people. But even if you damage yourself, you are sinning, from an ethical point of view. Just as a father doesn't want one child to hit another, he doesn't want that child to do damage to itself.

Q: Well, once again you're caught then; the alternative is boredom.

A: I think so.

Q: But any kind of passion probably . . .

A: Yes, yes—it means suffering and causing people to suffer. At its best, it brings suffering to the owner, to the one who has the passion, and in most of the cases, it brings suffering to the man who has the passion and to his objects. If a man says, "I am passionately in love with a woman," it means that he suffers, and sooner or later the woman will also suffer, one way or another. If he will not marry her . . . she will suffer. If he marries her, he may be jealous, or he may cool off after a while, and get a passion for somebody else. Passion really is suffering. This, I will say, is part of my writing.

Q: But also a basis of meaning?

A: Surely, without it a man is a vegetable.

Q: So we're back again to the paradox, aren't we?

A: Yes, just as in a little village wherever you walk you come immediately into the fields, so it is in life, wherever you go you are immediately at a paradox, at a contradiction.

Q: There was another direction suggested in the story "Blood." After the sadism and the slaughtering, as a kind of culmination of evil, Risha turned deliberately to deceiving the community about the purity of the meat she sold. You wrote, "She got so much satisfaction from deceiving the community, that this soon became as powerful a passion with her as lechery and cruelty." Is the desire to deceive the community one of the basic or perhaps most serious expressions of evil?

A: You cannot live in passion, really, without deceiving. Every man who has a passion must lie, especially if the passion is connected with sex. The man has to lie to the woman or the woman has to lie to the man. For Risha, deceiving the community is actually a kind of culmination of deceiving; she has deceived her husband before. She began by deceiving one man, but she deceived all men.

Q: Is it the case then that passion always brings one into conflict with the community?

A: I would say yes, because the community is not a passionate institution. It's an institution of curbing. People create a community only because they curb their passions, because if every member of the community would go after his passion, the community would not exist. A collective is an institution where everybody curbs himself. A really passionate man does not belong. He's either a criminal, or he's crazy, or he's an outcast. He's never really a part of the community.

Q: Unless, of course, he buys membership in the community by deception?

A: Exactly. Yes, this is true. If he deceives the community he can for a while stay within it.

Q: This returns us to the conflict between human nature and the Ten Commandments that you discussed in the first interview, although in "Blood" it is the kosher laws that are being violated.

A: The same thing: it's always the same thing. This is also the Ten Commandments, because the Ten Commandments say you should not bear false witness; in other words, you should not deceive the community.

Q: Thus the religious laws are expressions of the community's desire to control.

A: Yes. The laws of the Torah and of all religious codes say you cannot give in to passion and still let others live. To give in to passion to the very end means that you should live, and the other one should die or should suffer the pangs of death. And the community is a kind of experiment to curb passion, and because of this to maintain life.

Q: All this discussion brings us back to the question you've treated again and again: the problem of will. To what extent are the people in the two stories we've discussed exercising free will? They are really driven people.

A: They don't. This Risha did not exercise free will at all. She has made up her mind, it seems, long ago that she has to have her way in everything. The man with whom she sins, this slaughterer, is a better person than she. He's a man who really would have been a part of the community, but she seduces him and brings out what is bad in him. At the end I make him repent. He dies in the poorhouse and confesses his sins. This woman becomes an animal at the end; she becomes a werewolf. In other words, if man completely stops curbing himself, he becomes a beast—in a negative way, because the beasts are curbed by nature, by higher powers, but when man becomes an animal, he becomes ten times worse than an animal.

Q: The situation of your characters in these two stories seems to be different from the situation of Cunegunde in the story very near the end of *Short Friday*. Now here is another woman who clearly is . . .

A: Possessed by fear. The fear of this Cunegunde turns into a destructive power; although she does not really destroy, she wants to destroy. In other words, even though witches may not exist, potential witches there are by the millions: people who would destroy if they could.

Q: Does it make a difference that in the "Cunegunde" story we are told of the disasters of her childhood, whereas we see Risha in "Blood" only at adulthood, making what seems to be an unmotivated choice?

A: It is true that I did not tell about Risha's childhood. I just avoided it. But certainly there must be a good reason. One of the reasons is always heredity, in which modern people don't believe, but I do believe. I know that in our time we always believe in circumstances. We say that circumstances made the person, which I believe. But I believe that the heredity is more important. We come already to this world laden with certain powers, with certain desires and passions. So not in every case where I describe a passion do I have to describe the circumstances, because not in every case do the circumstances play such a big part. In "Cunegunde" it was necessary to give the circumstances, because to become what she was you needed also unusual circumstances, while Risha's desire for blood might have been with her from her very childhood.

Q: Where is free will in all of this?

A: I believe, as I said before, man is in a prison. However, in the frame of the prison, there is still a little freedom left. In the frame of our prison, we have free will and this is a great gift—because the animals and the dead things don't have even this little freedom.

Q: Can man give away his freedom? Can he make a choice which means that from that point on he actually cannot act freely?

A: No, I don't believe this, but I can say he can neglect the little freedom he possesses. Once it is misused and neglected, it almost stops to exist. However, a spark is always left. No matter how low a person has fallen, some voice in him will always tell him he can repent, he can change. We all feel this.

Q: Do some people have a greater share of freedom than others?

A: I would say that people with great passion have more freedom than those who have no passion. It seems a paradox—but I believe in it. I will tell you why: the person who has very little passion lives according to a routine. And since a community means routine, he lives in peace with the community. Although he lives a moral life, it's not free will. The community itself becomes a prison to him. He's afraid of the rabbi, afraid of the priest, afraid of the elders, of his wife, of his mother-in-law. Although he behaves well, he's a prisoner. While a man with great passion—since he has learned to misbehave, since he's not a slave of the community, he can also become the opposite of evil. This is a paradox, but it makes sense just the same. Let's say that a man has decided that he's a lecher. He doesn't care about his wife, about the marriage institution; he'll just do what he wants. But since he has the courage to defy the community, he might have, in other circumstances, the courage even to defy himself and his passion and to become the very opposite. This is the reason why sinners sometimes become saints, and here we have something which is connected with Yasha the magician. Here is a man who has given in—given in to his passion, but he defied the community, because his

way of repenting is not the way the community dictated. He is again
a rebel. There is a deep connection between the saint and the sinner,
a fact which was known for generations.

Q: Then you would link the freedom a man possesses to courage
rather than to self-knowledge. Or what is the role of self-knowledge in
freedom?

A: I would say that the courage is more important than the self-
knowledge because a man really does not know himself enough, and
even if he knows himself, this is not always a reason for curbing
himself. He may know what is right and not be able to do it. It's the
kind of courage, almost a physical courage which *is* in such men—
because a man of great passion is a man of great vitality. If he has
great vitality, everything in him is greater, even his free will. Or it
might be greater.

Q: Possibly there's another story which suggests that there are
some limits upon what even the most courageous man can do in
trying to control his own drives. I'm thinking of "The Fast" in *Short
Friday*. To quote a line from it: "In time opposing this lusting creature
becomes a habit." Then as the hero, Itche Nokhum, continues to
mortify the flesh, to fast, to sleep on the bench, the specter of his
former wife rises before him and he sees it as primeval substance,
and it dissolves in blood spatters on the floor. The scene ends with his
statement that he *cannot* forget her, and her lament that she is in his
power. Does this suggest a qualification on what you've just said?

A: Yes. When two persons really have a great desire for one
another—which people call love, or passion, or let's call it as we
want—this may become that strong. In this story I almost make the
passion itself become a body. The woman whom he sees there was
created by him. She's not there, but his desire for her is so great that
he has given her a body, if only for a short while.

Q: Turning to another sort of question—one of the stories in *Short
Friday* fascinates me because it seems to me that the I-figure may
be your own persona as well as a fictional narrator. This is the story
"Alone."

A: It's true that I went to Miami Beach; I go there sometimes in the
summer because I suffer from hay fever. It is true that I was in a hotel
in which suddenly for no reason—or we didn't know the reasons—
they told us to leave and to go to other hotels. I have never experi-

enced anything like it, that a hundred or two hundred guests should be told to leave. It is true that I got into another hotel, that I was there alone. The storm did not take place then, but I combined the moving with the storm. And there was a Cuban girl also, though she was not a hunchback.

Q: The story interested me in part because it seemed to concern the nature of perception. At the first, for example, the problem was lack of understanding, as you point out; in fact the whole framework of the story . . .

A: . . . is subjective. Yes. It is subjective because it's written in the first person, which I used not to do in the old times. Only a few years ago I decided that one may once in a while write in the first person.

Q: Are you trying when you use first person to write as much as possible in your own voice, or are you writing in the voice of a character who views the scene?

A: Well, I would say it's a combination of both. As much as I can give of myself I give of myself. There's no reason why not. And when I have to hide something, I let the character speak.

Q: It seemed to me also that the main character may have seen more clearly than usual. He says, "Through the heavenly channels, which, says the Cabala, control the flow of Divine Mercy, came truths impossible to grasp in a northern climate." And further, "At the same time the eternal questions tapped in my brain: Who is behind the world of appearance? Is it Substance with its Infinite Attributes? Is it the Monad of all Monads? Is it the Absolute, Blind Will, the Unconscious?" Is this sense of truth the illusion of a character in special circumstances, or is this a penetration to reality by a character who would otherwise not be able to see so clearly?

A: I gave in this story my own feelings, but the feelings in a special case, because when one is alone, one is more inclined really to philosophize than when one is in company and everything is in order. When you are alone, contact with other people is broken, and you begin to brood about something higher or lower. I mentioned here, actually, a number of philosophers, although not by name. The Substance with Infinite Attributes is Spinoza; the Monad of all Monads is Leibnitz. The Absolute can be Schelling or Fichte. Blind Will is Schopenhauer, and the Unconscious is von Hartmann. And the question, who is *behind* the world of appearance: this can be Plato, and Kant—and anything. Naturally I mentioned only the idealistic philosophers. I did not mention, let's say, Feuerbach, or others. I don't even have the feeling that I have to dispute with them. I don't believe in materialism.

Q: Thus in this section you simply indicate the spread of idealistic philosophy rather than suggest a position. Do you, yourself, ever adopt a position discriminating between the world as a conception of the mind and the world as a poor imitation of an absolute form?

A: I feel, like the most idealistic philosophers and actually like everybody else, that what we see here is only kind of an image, a picture, which is fitted to our power of conception. To me, and I think to many others, we are living in a kind of a dream, even when we are awake. The only difference is that this dream seems to have a certain consistency. If you dream at night that you have a house, you wake up in the morning and there is no house, but your dream of a house in the day as a rule goes on day after day. So it is a consistent dream; a dream behind which there is a reality. But what reality is, we don't know and we will *never* know. The thing-in-itself will always be a puzzle to every human being. And when a person is alone, he's brooding, he feels these things even more than when he is with people, where the illusion of reality is a little stronger.

Q: Interpreting the story "Alone," do you think a man gets closer to intuition of the *Ding-an-sich* when he is alone and brooding?

A: Very much so. He has no choice, because when a person is completely alone for a time, he feels that the day is almost as dreamy as the night. Things become almost without substance. This feeling that things lose their substance is very strong when a person is alone, or in times of tragedy, in times of great confusion. And also when you come to a strange city you already feel that there is something wrong with your conception of reality, because here are people living without knowing you. You don't exist for them, and they almost don't exist for you either. The feeling of reality is actually strongest when a man sits in one place among his family or among his friends, among the things he is used to. The more you move away from your things—you don't have to be Immanuel Kant to feel that things just melt between your fingers.

Q: The discussion of idealism leads me to an historical question. In your memoir, *In My Father's Court,* you comment that you are now "familiar with all the defects and hiatuses of Spinozaism. But at that time I was under a spell which lasted many years." How long did the spell last?

A: Really many years. I used to carry around Spinoza's *Ethics* wherever I went. But later on I began to see that Spinoza is in his own way a realist, which I did not like too much. After I read David Hume, Kant, and others, I felt that something is wrong with Spinoza's belief in reality, because to him what we see is real. And then there is his rationalism and his idea that God has no will and no purpose. I did not like that. As I became older I became more inclined to mysticism and to religion, and I felt that to say that the universe is nothing but a huge machine with no will or no purpose is minimizing creation. I will take from Spinoza his pantheism; I believe like Spinoza that everything is God. But to be sure that God has only these two attributes which we know (though he says He has endless attributes) and that He has no will and has no purpose is wrong; it is to be too sure about things where men cannot be sure. I could just as well say that will and purpose are also attributes of God—and so is beauty, and so is, maybe, morality. The Cabala has both sides: it has all the good sides of Spinoza and all the good sides of Plato. This is the reason I admire so much the Cabala.

Q: In other words, your dispute with Spinoza really turns on this question of the ideal versus the real?

A: Exactly. And about the question of free will and purpose. Once we assume that God has will and purpose, then there is no limitation to what God can do with His creation; it may have the most wonderful purpose and the most wonderful direction. Spinoza was actually a materialist. He called matter God, because he also says that matter (extension) and thinking are two sides of the same coin, which means to him there is nothing but matter, that matter itself thinks. Since I moved away from materialism, I began also to move away from Spinoza, although he fascinates me just the same. He was a great and a deep thinker in his own terms.

Q: Did you begin to move away from Spinoza before you came to this country or later?

A: Before.

Q: That means that most of what you have written was written after you became critical of some of his basic thinking.

A: Yes, I would say so—even the story "The Spinoza of Market Street" is a Spinoza story I have written in later years. At the end the main character (who has finally married) says, "Divine Spinoza, forgive me. I have become a fool." Well, I don't believe that a man who lives with a woman is a fool. Spinoza compares people who love to the insane. He did not believe in love; at least he *says* so.

Q: Thus, as it seems, the whole story is extremely ironic.

A: It is in a way. First I describe this man who is—even though he is a Spinozaist—a deep thinker. But what I wanted to say is that if you are a human being, if you are alive, you cannot live according to Spinoza. And another thing: Spinoza belittles very much the emotions. To him the emotions are very negative. His ideal man must get rid of his emotions, at least as much as possible. Only then could he be a real thinker, and could he have what he calls the *amor dei intellectualis*—the intellectual love for God. I dispute this. I consider the human emotions a great treasure—not only a material treasure, but also a great treasure of revelation, because our emotions reveal to us things which we cannot grasp with our intellect. The only thing is that the emotions, because they are so many and because they are so intense, can also be very dangerous. They are a weapon which can be used in many ways. Man can kill himself with emotions, kill others with emotions, so he has to control them, to curb them—but not to get rid of them, not really to dismiss them, as Spinoza says.

Q: So in "The Spinoza of Market Street" the emotions really conquered the intellect and the man was better off, or wiser.

A: Yes. I think so, although he says he became a fool, I think he became wiser—that he had sense enough in his old age to get a woman, even though she was such a woman. To his heart, she was a vulgar piece, but still he had somebody.

Q: Now what about the Cabala: this was also something which you studied as a boy, wasn't it? At about the time you discovered Spinoza?

A: Almost in the same time or a little earlier—although one is not allowed to study the Cabala, from a Jewish point of view, before one is thirty years old, because it's esoteric and dangerous, according to tradition. But I stole these books from my father's bookcase and I studied them. Spinoza was not in my father's library, but I once heard my father curse Spinoza. He said he was a heretic, a disbeliever, and

I became curious. My father even mentioned that what he said was also said in a different way by the famous saint, Baal Shem. Baal Shem said the world is God and God is the world. From these words I got a notion what Spinoza is. In my kind of education, in my kind of circumstances, we had to learn things very quickly and from hints. In the time when I heard the name, there wasn't anything about Spinoza in Yiddish—and also, my father forbade me to read worldly books, secular books. If my father would have caught me reading Spinoza, I don't know what would have happened in our house; there would have been a scandal. We had to steal ideas, steal emotions.

Q: About what time did you begin, then, to get rather widely acquainted with secular books?

A: Not until I left really my father's house, although I read a lot while I was in my father's house. But I had always to hide, to go up to an attic, or to the fields somewhere. Reading was an illegal business, except reading holy books. Only when I went to Warsaw to live with my brother in the early 'twenties could I study. But since I had then all the books which I wanted, my desire to read became smaller, you know how it is. But still, I read. Then I read Kant and Schopenhauer and Nietzsche and David Hume, whom I admire very much.

Q: During this time you must have been in your late teens and in your twenties. [Singer: Yes.] Did you stay with your brother then?

A: My brother was there, but I had a furnished room. I didn't live with my brother, but we were attached. I saw him all the time. There was a Warsaw writers' club, and at this writers' club they all came, the painters and even the actors and naturally the writers. I even met there a number of European writers, including Galsworthy.

Q: What other contact did you have with English literature at this time?

A: Not much, except that I read Dickens. I loved very much Oscar Wilde—not his plays, but *The Picture of Dorian Gray*. I read that the first time in Hebrew, and in Hebrew it was even more beautiful than in English. Hebrew is just made for this kind of writing. I also read *De Profundis*.

Q: How important was the Yiddish literary tradition to you then?

A: It was important, but not really very important. In the same time I began to read European literature in translation, and even though I was young I immediately saw that the great European writers are better than our Yiddish writers.

Q: Whom did you read?

A: Maupassant, Victor Hugo, Flaubert; and Dostoevsky, Tolstoy, Knut Hamsun, and Turgenev.

Q: So Hamsun would rate alongside the Russian realists as an important figure for you?

A: Yes. . . . Dostoevsky is not a realist. And even Tolstoy I wouldn't call a complete realist, but I loved Hamsun. There was a time when I was really drunk with Hamsun. Later on he became a realist, and when he became a realist, he became almost nothing. He lost himself; but his great works are *Pan* and *Hunger.* There he is the real Hamsun. I also translated from German *The Magic Mountain.*

Q: What is your attitude towards Mann?

A: He is, there is no question, a highly talented writer, but I like better his *Buddenbrooks* than *Der Zauberberg.* I feel that modern writers began to write essays about literature instead of telling stories. I call this modern kind of writing the epoch of the essay; they write disguised essays which they call stories. And I think that *The Magic Mountain* is such a disguised essay. I still believe in the old-fashioned storytelling; the writer should tell a story and the essays should be written by the critics.

Q: During these Warsaw years a socialist point of view was dominant among literary men, wasn't it?

A: Very dominant and very much in fashion. I never believed in it—because the first thing is, they were materialists and I was against materialism. And also I was a pessimist; I didn't believe that we can really change the human condition by changing the regime. Not that I was antagonistic, but I was sceptical about the whole thing. Today, to say that I'm sceptical about this isn't a great prowess, but in my time you had to have a lot of character, because everybody fell into this kind of faith. They all believed a new time is coming. There will be new people and a new nature . . . a new man. And it will all be brought by Karl Marx and his disciples. And even though I wasn't highly educated and I was young, I said, "I don't believe it." So I had to be for the second time a disbeliever. First I was a disbeliever in our dogma, where people screamed at me and scolded. Then I became a disbeliever for the second time, in Karl Marx.

Q: Your scepticism about Judaism began when you were very young, didn't it?

A: I always loved Judaism and I always believed in God, but as far as dogma is concerned, doubt began very early. Because I saw that these dogmas are man-made things: I did not believe that God told Moses, let's say, not to touch money on the Sabbath, or not to write on the Sabbath. They have millions and millions of little laws. They made from one law fifty, and then from the fifty a thousand, and so on. Every generation added something new.

Q: These two kinds of scepticism then meant that from the time you were very young you were really separated from the society around you? There must have been considerable controversy with your family.

A: With my family, with friends, with writers, with critics. I was really surrounded, so to say, with a hostile milieu.

Q: And of course you did not go through what has become almost a cliché about writers in the century, the period of disillusionment following the German-Russian Pact.

A: No, I never believed in them and I wasn't disillusioned; to me, Stalin and Hitler were made of the same stuff.

Q: In a real sense then you've stood quite outside the fashions in writing.

A: Yes, as a matter of fact, I still am outside. I'm far from being an insider even today.

Isaac Bashevis Singer:
Conversations in California

David M. Andersen/1970

From *Modern Fiction Studies*, 16 (1970), 423–39. Reprinted by permission.

The distinguished novelist and short story writer Isaac Bashevis Singer was a guest of the Department of English at San Fernando Valley State College for the week of February 16–20, 1970. During his stay Mr. Singer read two of his stories, lectured on his concept of the Jewish writer, and answered many questions about his life and work. Fortunately, much of the discussion was recorded, and the transcript represented here preserves many of Mr. Singer's thoughts and reminiscences.

Isaac Singer was born in Radzymin, Poland, in 1904. The son and grandson of Hasidic rabbis, he was raised in the Orthodox tradition. The *shtetl* life of his early years, his family's influence on him, and the rich Yiddish tradition in which he was nurtured are recorded in his delightful memoir *In My Father's Court*. At about the age of nineteen he became a part of Warsaw's literary scene and began his career as a writer with the Yiddish magazine *Literarishe Bletter*. As his reading and circle of friends grew larger, he became skeptical of Jewish Orthodoxy and started what he calls a "life-long quarrel with the Almighty."

Since coming to America in 1935, Mr. Singer has lived in New York City and contributed, as he still does, under a variety of pseudonyms to the Yiddish-language newspaper the *Jewish Daily Forward*. He has witnessed a steady and saddening decline of his Yiddish readers, an audience so immediate that they often called him at home to talk about his latest story, but with the publication in English of *The Family Moskat* by Knopf (1950) and *Satan in Goray* (1955) has come an enormous, new audience. In a sense, Mr. Singer's trip to California reflects the growing interest of this new readership.

A month after his visit to Northridge, Mr. Singer received the

National Book Award for children's literature. His literary reputation
is beginning to catch up with his brilliance as a storyteller. Literary
quarterlies frequently publish critical articles on his novels and short
stories; his works are being reprinted in paperback; many of his
stories have been anthologized in college readers; almost every
month one of his pieces appears in such magazines as *The New
Yorker, Esquire, Playboy,* and *Harper's;* and his fiction, as Singer
wryly notes, is probably already grist for dissertation mills.

He strikes one as being a very frail man, yet when he joins in on a
conversation he reveals a remarkable vigor and enthusiasm for life.
He is a man who listens carefully, and when he speaks, invariably
he says something worth remembering. And occasionally, he is frank
to admit, "If I can't answer the question you ask, I'll give you the
answer to another question." The conversations which follow range
over a host of topics from the writer's personal convictions about his
art to comments on the condition of modern society. As you listen to
him, you realize that he is not only a consummate storyteller but a
man who has important things to say about human existence as well.

This transcript complements a number of other published interviews which the reader will find of interest: *Commentary* (February
1965), *Paris Review* (Fall 1968), and *Contemporary Literature* (Winter, Summer 1969).

The first part of the transcript contains questions from the audiences that came to hear Mr. Singer on the 18th and 20th of February,
1970. The second part was recorded on the 20th of February, 1970,
with four members of the English Department, Robert Chianese,
Julian Rice, Arthur Lane, and David Andersen. We are grateful to Mr.
Singer for kindly consenting to check the manuscript for accuracy.

I

*Of all the places in the United States I can't really imagine a writer
living in the middle of Manhattan. Why do you live in that spot?*
There are two reasons for this. The first reason is I have a few
thousand books and to move them—many of these books are so old
that in the process of moving they would fall to pieces. The second
reason is that I myself would fall to pieces in the process. The third
reason is that Manhattan is just as good a place as Brooklyn or

Queens. And I can give you still a fourth reason. There are two ordeals in a man's life: this is when he paints his house and when he's moving. And why should I move, and then when I move to a new apartment I have to paint it in addition. But to be serious, many of my readers live in Manhattan, at least the Yiddish readers. My newspaper *The Jewish Daily Forward* where I still contribute is in Manhattan, and many of my readers when they read a story of mine like to lift up the telephone and call me, and here they can call me— they don't have to make a long distance. For all these reasons I decided to live in Manhattan as long as it's possible.

After reading In My Father's Court, *I wondered how and when you became so funny? Your family didn't seem to be the kind to nourish humor unless it was your older brother.*

Well, I will tell you; there was humor in my family. My mother had a great sense of humor. My father, although he was a rabbi and a very serious man, still he was able to make a joke. As a matter of fact, there are even jokes in the *Talmud*. The only book which contains almost no jokes is the *Old Testament,* and I think maybe the *New Testament*. The *Bible* does not contain any jokes, but there is a half a joke in the *Old Testament,* although the scholars are not sure if it's a joke, if it's irony, if it's satire. But I would say if I have some sense of humor, it's not mine; I took it from my parents—I inherited it.

Mr. Singer, you bring us some very moving pictures of nature in your books. At what point did you begin to enjoy and understand nature?

I will tell you. I was brought up in Warsaw, and until I was about thirteen years I never really saw fields or forests—to such a degree that I once found in our courtyard a few blades of grass, somewhere in a nook they grew up, and I was so delighted I used to bring out every few minutes a glass of water and help them grow. But when I was about fourteen years, this was the time when the Germans invaded Warsaw, my mother took me to a *shtetl,* a little village, which was surrounded by forests and fields, and I stayed there about four or five years. And this was the first time that I really came in contact with nature. You were very kind to say that I understand nature. The truth is that no one understands nature, but everyone admires nature, and I think this is enough.

Since you choose to write in Yiddish, can you speak about the future of the Yiddish language?

Yiddish is a sick language because the young people don't speak it. And many consider it a dead language. But in our history between being sick and dying is a long way.

You mentioned Poe and Shakespeare in your speech. What other writers in the English language have you read and enjoyed who might have influenced you?

When I was a boy I read Dickens. As a matter of fact—*The Pickwick Club* I read in Hebrew. I until today don't know how it sounds in English. It sounded good in Hebrew, believe it or not. I also read *The Picture of Dorian Gray* in Hebrew, and Tolstoy and Dostoevski I read either in Hebrew, in Polish, in German. Edgar Allan Poe I read in Polish. And Shakespeare, "enlarged and improved," I read in Yiddish. It's only in my later years that I had to read Shakespeare without "improvement." I was wondering why this man had to improve him—to make the effort—but this was how the situation was.

Are there any other American writers today that you might be interested in?

Well, I looked into books of Saul Bellow. I tried to read *Portnoy's Complaint.* I admired very much Conrad Richter who has a trilogy called *The Trees, The Fields,* and *The Town.* He is not very much known although he got a Pulitzer Prize and the National Book Award. But I consider his first volume, *The Trees,* a real American masterpiece. And I'm astonished that so few intellectuals I meet know about him. I read with pleasure the books of Marchette Chute. She wrote about Chaucer and Shakespeare; as a matter of fact, I know her personally. I do read, but not enough. This is the real truth.

Were you influenced at all by the works of Sholom Aleichem?

I would say that all writers are influenced by everything they read and see. We're influenced by life. But I would not say that Sholom Aleichem was a special influence on me. I was influenced more by Gogol than Sholom Aleichem. About two years ago they gave me to write a review about a collection of Gogol, a new translation. And when I read these stories I said to myself, "How is it possible that this man who has lived a hundred years before me has stolen so many of my stories."

When you write a story or a novel, is it based on people you know?

It is true I always rather take as a model a person whom I know. But it is never the same person because I combine all kinds of things. Sometimes I make from three people one person. Sometimes I take a person whom I met on Madison Avenue and decide he would fit very much to be in Lublin or Frampol. Because of this it happened to me that after the story was written I forgot who the model was. By the way, Frampol is a very small village in Poland. I remember that once a man came over to me and said to me, "You can bluff the whole world but not me." I said, "What is the matter?" He said, "I am from Frampol. You write always about sex and devils. I haven't see neither sex nor devils in Frampol."

If a person was to write a short story of Yiddish content, where is the best place to publish it?

A short time ago I published two very Jewish stories in two Catholic magazines. It seems that real editors don't care if the story is Jewish or Gentile. If they like the story, they will publish it.

But your name is known, you see—that's the difference.

You are right that my name is a little bit known, but I had to sell stories to be known. So I had to make my way one way or another. Which reminds me we had a magazine in Warsaw which was called the *Literarishe Bletter,* a Yiddish magazine, and once we got a story, a very bad story from a man. And the editor sent it back. So the man wrote a letter; he said, "I know why you don't publish my story— because I have no talent. If I would have been Romain Rolland or Sholem Asch or Tolstoy, I'm sure you would have published it, but because God has wronged me, he has not given me any talent, this is the way you treat me." I understand that from a humanistic point of view, but you know that editors are not lovers of humanity; they have to publish what they think is good.

Which of your own works pleases you most?

This question was asked here some time ago, and I said to the man, "How many children do you have? If you tell me what child you love best, I will tell you what book I like best." He said, "The youngest." So I said to him, "Then you have given my answer." Not that the youngest is always the best, but somehow we have a sentiment for our latest effort. But actually it's very hard for a writer to say what he likes best. Actually if I had the time I would like to rewrite many of them.

II

Mr. Chianese: Since many of your stories are involved with your personal life, I'd like to ask if you are keeping a writer's notebook or any kind of diary that may record further personal incidents?

Mr. Singer: Well, Mr. Chianese, I used to have a diary. Lately I don't. But I have always with me a notebook. Besides topics which I write down there all the time, I also write down programs which I never keep. For forty years I keep on writing a program where I say: you get up 7 o'clock; 8 o'clock breakfast; 9 o'clock you sit down to work; you work until 1; then you go to sleep 11 o'clock. But for forty years I was trying to keep it, and I never kept it. But I still hope. When I see a new notebook somewhere at Woolworth's, I always buy it, and I say: this time it's going to be a real program. But somehow Satan does not allow me to keep what I promised myself. So I have a lot of such booklets lying around, witnesses of my weak will.

Mr. Rice: You mentioned Satan, and I think many contemporary readers of your work wonder to what extent devils and demons should be taken literally or symbolically as a means of character revelation.

Mr. Singer: In my case they should be taken both symbolically and literally. Naturally, I use them as literary symbols, and they are very useful. They constitute a kind of literary stenography. Where you say "Satan" it means many things, and the reader understands what they mean. But, in addition to it, I also believed from my childhood, and I still do, that we are surrounded by powers of which we have no inkling and who play a big part in our life. Naturally, I don't know if they are imps or demons, these are nothing but names taken from folklore, but the belief is there. And, as a matter of fact, I think that many people who say that they don't believe in such things, "do" believe in them. Once I had a kind of debate with a rationalist, and he said to me, "How can you speak about corpses and demons? Children believe in such things." And I said to him, "How's about staying over a winter night in a dark room with a corpse? Would you like to do this?" The man shuddered; he said, "I would die!" So I said, "Do you know why you would die? Because you're afraid that there is something about it." It is in every human being, and it comes out especially in a crisis. A man who will say "I don't believe in luck," if things begin to go badly with him he will suddenly say, "I have bad luck." Sometimes the opposite, good luck. I think that the belief in beings of which we don't know and who surround us is deeply rooted in every human soul.

Mr. Rice: What is the nature of these beings? Are some evil and some good?

Mr. Singer: Naturally, some of them are evil, some of them may be good, some of them may be neutral. The truth is I don't know. Since I am a skeptic, I'm even a skeptic about these things. I said to an audience: if a voice would come from heaven and would say, "There are no demons," I would not commit suicide. If there are no demons, there are no demons. But I believe there must be demons since humanity is believing in them already since many ages, and there is not really a tribe or a country or a group of people where this belief does not exist. There are millions of witnesses who say that they have seen some. In my own case, I have really no axe to grind; I have seen nothing. My life is going in a very "natural" way. But by talking to people I have convinced myself that cases of telepathy, clairvoyance, and premonitions are as often as cases of the flu in the time of an epidemic. Almost everybody has had such experience, but people are ashamed to admit that they have had them. It's not fashionable; it sounds superstitious. But I think that a writer should be the last man to deny what "he" thinks is reality whether it is fashionable or not. Also, fashions do change. Maybe I will create a new fashion. You can never tell.

Mr. Rice: Why have you chosen to set some of your most power-ful and effective works like *The Slave* and *Satan in Goray* in the seventeenth century? And how did you get them to have such imme-diacy? Did you do research?

Mr. Singer: Well, the story of the false Messiah, Sabbatai Zevi, delighted me because it's always an interesting story when people begin to believe in something which isn't there. And it was connected with mass hysteria because I believe that in the case of hysteria the real subconscious comes to expression. Then people really say what they want to say. Since Sabbatai Zevi lived in the seventeenth century, I had to write about the seventeenth century. As far as "knowing" the seventeenth century: first of all, I did research—or I would say that my life itself was research in this direction because I studied the old books. I read these Hebrew books which were printed in these times, and also I lived in a *shtetl,* a little town, and this little town was in the twentieth century almost as it was in the seventeenth century. No great changes have taken place. In addition, I did read history. When I began to write *Satan in Goray,* I understood that psychiatry is also necessary to write about these things. Hysteria is a mental sickness. So, because of this I did as much study as it was necessary. This was in the case of *Satan in Goray* which I wrote when I was still in Poland. When I wrote *The Slave* I didn't have to do a lot of research anymore because the research was already done before. However, I got new books, and I did some research. But I'm not the kind of a writer who will sit down for years and do research. I once read that before Flaubert wrote *Salammbô* he made thousands and thousands of notes. I wouldn't have the patience to do this. But Flaubert was a great writer, and what he did was good.

Mr. Rice: The movement after Sabbatai Zevi, the people who followed him on such a mass level, suggests to many modern readers analogies to modern revolutionary or Messianic ideas.

Mr. Singer: Revolutionary, yes. As a matter of fact, the Sabbatai Zevi movement went on maybe 200 years or 150 years after Sabbatai Zevi was converted. And everybody knew already that he was, so to say, a fake. But not everybody. Some people who live in the Turkish countryside or Greece still believe in Sabbatai Zevi. They believe that he went up to heaven, and he will one day appear, and they go out every Friday to meet him in case he decides to come. The belief in false Messiahs is very old and very young. What was Stalin if not a false Messiah? And what was Hitler if not a false Messiah? I would say that there are false Messiahs in every generation, and they always create havoc with people.

Mr. Rice: Is the desire for perfection sometimes very close to the will of Satan—to make the world perfect, since it so often begets its opposite?

Mr. Singer: I would say that many of the believers in false Messiahs are also perfectionists. They think, "Here is a man who's going to bring perfection." And they always bring the opposite. Hysteria is a sickness which hasn't been investigated enough. Hysteria really is an exaggeration of the emotions. And sometimes also an exaggeration of language—they go together. If a man says, "I am dying to eat lunch now," he's already exaggerating. And this exaggeration is a hint of hysteria. So we are exaggerating in language, and we are also exaggerating in our emotions. When we read the *Bible* or other old books we see that in the old times people did not exaggerate as much in language as they do today. I think that the exaggeration in language is bound to create hysteria and vice-versa—hysteria is creating exaggeration in language. Exactness is the very opposite of hysteria.

Mr. Chianese: You seem to be able to look at hysteria or mass-movements fairly objectively. But do you think if you were an adolescent or a young man now that you would be a rebel?

Mr. Singer: I am a rebel but a different kind of rebel. Most of the people are rebelling against a social system, against a government, against a regime. My quarrel is always with the Almighty, with God. I say to Him, "If You wouldn't have created the world the way as it is, we wouldn't have all these troubles." In other words, I don't believe that we can change things by having another dictator, another president, another king. It's He who has caused all these troubles, and I often rebel against Him. But the fact that I rebel against Him shows that I believe in Him and I really do. When I read in the *Bible* and God says, I created this world for my honor and for my glory, I say to Him, "Is it worth that for Your glory little children should be burned as they are so often in the old slums in Brooklyn and so on and so on?" Rebelling against a man is not in my nature because I know how helpless men are. The fact that a man is a king or a president does not mean really that he has power. They have no power. Let's take a president of the United States. First he has to fight for years until he's nominated and then until he's elected. The moment he's elected he has already to worry about the next nomination. And then he has a staff of millions of people. How can he know what's going on? So he's a helpless man; he cannot do much. What he does is, more or less, what he can do. And because of this, to rebel against Nixon or Johnson is not in my nature because I know how helpless they are. But the Almighty, since He calls himself "the *Almighty*," invites rebellion. So I rebel. And He doesn't mind it too much it seems. He says, "I've heard all this talk," and "Let me do things the way I do."

Mr. Rice: You were speaking before of the similarity between the exaggerations of language and the exaggerations of emotion. And this suggests some parallel between your philosophy of æsthetics and your philosophy of being—that is, that they are very closely related.

Mr. Singer: Clichés are not only bad from an æsthetic point of view but also from a sociological and from a point of view of human health. The person who exaggerates is already a hysteric person.

Mr. Andersen: In your story "A Friend of Kafka" there is a character who says that he can't understand Kafka's *The Castle*. He says it's too long to be a dream and not short enough to be an allegory. Then he makes a comment about the strictures a writer has to follow and as an example of such a stricture he says, "No novel should be longer than *War and Peace*." In your writing do you feel there are strictures imposed from outside?

Mr. Singer: Well, I think that this is true about every writer, since I believe that writing is connected in a great way with entertaining. We have to entertain the reader. We can't just let go completely. In other words, if I feel like writing a novel of 15,000 pages—even though if I would manage to write 15,000 good pages—it would still be a bore and unbearable to the reader, and a writer has to remember that. Shakespeare has never written a play of 800 pages because he knew the theatre, and he knew that a man who goes to the theatre has only two hours maximum. He cannot sit there in the theatre three days and nights. The same thing is true about novels and about poems and so on and so on. We are in contact with the one who consumes the art, and we must remember it. When a writer decides "to hell with the reader"—"I write for my own drawer"—he ends up by writing for his drawer. The length of a novel is not a stricture. It's in the nature of things. You are not going to make a chair tall to the ceiling or a table which will hang on the wall. It has to be used. The same thing is true about literature and about all arts. If you cannot make use of it, it stops being art and it's nothing but a game you play with.

Mr. Chianese: The problem of the writer as entertainer intrigues me because your stories seem to be stories that one would be entertained with even after a dinner, and I'm curious about the concept of the writer as the entertainer of small audiences, or of the kind of writer whose stories can be heard and entertain. Do you think that this tradition, sort of the bard, the court entertainer, or the person who just tells the good tale, do you think this has died out? Has it been because of print or don't people have the time to listen to story-tellers any more?

Mr. Singer: Well, people listen to a lot of stories on the radio and television. I was reading today a story to maybe 200 people, and they listened. The fact that people like to listen to a story proves that this old art of telling a story is far from being dead. Even when people "read" a story, they actually "listen" to a story. As far as entertainment is concerned, I would say that the ambition of a writer should be to entertain the best people of his generation. A great writer is one who can entertain great people. A small writer is a writer who can only entertain the mob. In the time of Shakespeare the people who went to the Theatre Globe were the nobility, the educated people, and because of this he really could say the things he wanted to say. He entertained the best people of his time, and because of this he entertained the best people of all times. If he would have thought that *Hamlet* would be boring, he wouldn't have written it. And it's true really about all good writers. They always have a feeling that the reader is present. They have respect for the reader, and do not ignore him completely.

Mr. Rice: Someone asked about *The Magician of Lublin*—the ending—the other night. It has an ending which is both realistic, since men did actually immure themselves in that way, and it's also symbolic or at least it suggests the symbolic. Now what I'd like to ask you is: how conscious should a writer be in the use of symbols in his work? Is it just talent that acounts for the kind of skill which you have in being able to blend symbolism and realism so that one doesn't become too labored or too obvious? Does it come spontaneously?

Mr. Singer: If a writer has a story to tell, if it's a good story, and he has a passion to write the story, he does not have to worry too much about the symbolism because a good story is always symbolic. When we read the stories in the *Bible* we feel that the writer did not try really to create symbolic stories. He just told a story about Adam and Eve and about Jacob and Rachel, and somehow they're all symbolic. But when a writer sits down with the idea of "writing symbolism," he will fail. Symbols often cancel out one another. If you will write ten symbols, one symbol will defy the other, and the net result may be nothing. So the best thing is: you tell a story or write a play and the symbol will be there anyhow. Or if you don't find it yourself, there will always be a critic who will find it. After I published *The Magician of Lublin,* I got a telephone call from a psychoanalyst, and he said, "I loved the way you made your hero go back to his mother's womb." It never occurred to me for a moment that the Magician of Lublin went back to his mother's womb, but I said to him, "Once a story is written it's not anymore my private property, and you are as entitled to find your interpretation as I am."

Mr. Lane: The character of "Gimpel the Fool" struck me—I read the story a couple of times—and it seemed that he was almost like the writer—not you—but a writer in that he took into himself, without questioning, what the world had to offer—as though he was made a fool of. He accepted as truth everything everybody said to him. But he became a storyteller, a wanderer, a teller of tales.

Mr. Singer: It is true at the end he becomes a storyteller, and even though I really did not intend to give him the qualities of a writer, you may be right. What you say now proves what I said just a minute before, that once you have written a story it's not any more your private property. You are really revealing something to me. In a way, this man became a writer, a storyteller; why I did it I don't know. I said some time ago to an audience that once I got an anthology, and in this anthology there was the story "Gimpel the Fool." So I was very happy that they put it in an anthology; it has been in many anthologies. At the end there were a number of questions about "Gimpel." And when I began to read them I said, "What a miracle that I'm not a student now! I wouldn't be able to answer half these questions!" When you ask a writer what he meant by his story it's like asking a chicken which lays an egg what chemicals did she use to lay this egg. The poor chicken has not studied chemistry. It just laid an egg. We don't know always what we are doing, and this is the reason why criticism, constructive criticism, is good and necessary. It sounds to me now peculiar that I made from this naive man Gimpel a storyteller. It seems that somehow in my subconscious was the idea that here is a man who had the qualities of becoming a writer or at

least a storyteller. We don't know what we are doing. It's the same
thing when you have a son. You don't know what your son is going
to do, whom he is going to marry, what kind of grandchildren you are
going to have. The same thing is true with our spiritual children; we
don't know what their part is going to be after they leave us.

Mr. Lane: But what you created, whether deliberately and consciously or not, was a man who didn't erect any barricades between
himself and the outside world. And so he was able to take into himself all of that, and ultimately become a storyteller.

Mr. Singer: Actually whatever we do is part of nature, and it is as
puzzling as nature. Let's say you say a few words. It is true that you
have said these words. But since you are yourself a part of nature,
and your tongue is a part of nature, and language is a part of nature,
there is more to these words than you intend.

Mr. Andersen: What does the literary critic do then? What is his
function? He doesn't write stories himself. Is he simply a voyeur who
looks in on someone else's creative work and parasitically lives off it?

Mr. Singer: No. I don't consider, Dr. Andersen, a critic a parasite.
A good critic is a man who takes the egg of the chicken, and he says,
"What chemicals did the chicken use?" It's true that the chicken does
not know chemistry, but the chemistry is there. So they find sociological truths, and psychological, and many other truths. Let's say we dig
in the earth, and we find a document, and this document, a clay
tablet four thousand years old, was written by a woman before she
gave out her linen to the laundress: so many shirts, so many under-
wear, and so on and so on. This woman certainly did not intend to
teach people an old language. She has just written down an order for
the laundry. But, at the same time, when the scholars find this note
they may learn about an old language and about the time and what
clothes people wore. They can study this laundry note for years. The
same thing is what we writers do. We write a little story, and then
other people in later years find in them many things which we did not
intend. There is not a writer in the world who can explain what he
does, all his intentions and everything which his work contains. This
is one function of the critic. The second function is a very important
one: to discern between what is good and what is bad. (A laundry bill
is always good. But in writing it may be very bad even though it
contains many elements.) Sometimes a chicken will lay an egg which

contains all the chemicals which another chicken has used; but one egg comes out good, another egg comes out bad. This is the duty of the critic to find out. Sometimes not only the reader learns from good criticism but also the writer. And I think that modern critics have neglected this part of criticism. They assume that if there are some elements of sociology and of psychology in a work it's already good. Sometimes it contains all the elements, and it's bad in addition.

Mr. Chianese: In the story "A Friend of Kafka" I noticed there was very very low comedy, almost slapstick—that kind of low comedy which is right next door to a grotesque idea of death and people falling apart. And I wonder if you see a natural connection between your attitude toward comedy and the grotesque?

Mr. Singer: The greatest trick of comedians is their telling the truth. The truth is very often terribly funny. When you read a story by Sholom Aleichem or Mark Twain or Gogol—especially Gogol— what he tells you there is the whole truth, but the whole truth makes you laugh. And this is, I would say, the case about this story ["A Friend of Kafka"]. I did nothing else but just tell the way Jacques Cohn, as I call him, spoke and the way he lived. But if you tell the whole truth it becomes sometimes either very tragic or very funny and sometimes a mixture of both of them. And I think all comedians know it.

Mr. Rice: Yes, you had mentioned that sometimes you will start out to write a serious story or a sad story and it will turn out funny. And again that suggests that parallelism between art and life.

Mr. Singer: There is no question about it. And since a writer cannot completely plan what he is going to do, he can never be sure if it's going to be a tragedy or a comedy. Although, when Gogol wrote *The Inspector General* he knew that it was going to be a comedy. But there are tragic elements in this comedy too. Actually all these divisions are very much artificial. In real writing they go together—comedy and tragedy, and sociology and psychology, and love and hatred. It's only that we use all kinds of divisions to be oriented.

Mr. Lane: One of the ways that you handle that so beautifully is— and it almost slips by the reader time and time again (it slipped by me until I began to think about it)—was that you pick the narrator very carefully, or maybe it's just subconsciously right on your part.

The narrator is always the framework, the man-through-whom; and sometimes it's a woman through whom the story comes. I wondered, have you in writing a story (since, I guess this is an artistic question) have you ever tried different narrators for the same story and then settled on one as being preferable, say Jacques in "A Friend of Kafka"?

Mr. Singer: I would say I use two kind of narrators. Either I am the narrator myself, or it's an old woman. Because when I want to tell stories connected with folklore, I always let an old woman tell the story. Why I like narrators? There is a good reason for that: because when I write a story without a narrator I have to describe things, while if the narrator is a woman she can tell many things almost in one sentence. Because in life when you sit down to tell a story you don't act like a writer. You don't describe too much. You jump, you digress and this gives to the story speed and drama.

Mr. Lane: That's why you get that beautifully ingratiating atmosphere in the story because it sounds like something being told around a fire late at night by an old person.

Mr. Singer: I do it often, and it comes out especially good when you let an old woman tell a story. In a moment she's here, and a moment she's there. And because of this you feel almost that a human being is talking to you, and you don't need the kind of description which you expect when the writer himself is telling the story.

Mr. Andersen: You mentioned the use of folklore in your stories, and, of course, old women would retain the folklore, but what do you think of the general movement away from folklore as a source of material for fiction, a movement which seems to have started with T. S. Eliot?

Mr. Singer: I think that it's a great tragedy that modern writing has divorced itself from folklore; because folklore is the best soil on which literature grows. Until about 50 years ago or so, literature was so deeply connected to folklore that we really didn't know where one ends and the other one begins. It's the modern writer who has decided that we have enough of the folklore. Actually we are living in folklore, and we are creating folklore. We don't realize, for example, that psychoanalysis is going to be folklore fifty years from now. They will say these old-fashioned people believed that if you lie down on a couch you are going to be cured of many other things. Or our sociology will be folklore. We are all the time creating folklore; and because of this, there is no sense for a writer to run from it. Eliot most probably thought that the epoch of folklore was finished, let's say, a hundred years ago. And now we are living in a world of reality and exact science. But it's far from it. An epoch which has created such people like Hitler and Stalin and all kinds of false prophets we have today is an epoch which is deeply sunk in folklore. There is no charm in literature without folklore. That fact that literature, the drama, has gone away from folklore is doing a lot of damage to modern art. This is my conviction. And I believe it is a gold mine which has never been exhausted and can never be exhausted.

Mr. Chianese: You said before that you don't feel that there are any particular strictures about how the writer should go about his task; but then you mentioned the problem of length, and I just remembered that Edgar Allan Poe also mentioned that length is a crucial element of writing. And it seems like a very foreign thing to sit down and say, "I'm going to write a short story; I'm going to write a short story; I'm going to write something short." But do you do this? Do you say, "This is going to be a short story or a very very short story?"

Mr. Singer: Absolutely, Mr. Chianese. When I sit down to write a short story I know that this is going to be a short story and not a novel, and I think I'm not an exception in this respect. Because you write differently when it's going to be a short story; you write differently when it's going to be a novel. And what this man in my story "A Friend of Kafka," Bamberg, said, that no novel should be longer than *War and Peace,* there is a lot of truth in it. Naturally, some genius could come out with a novel twice as long as *War and Peace,* and if every page would be interesting, we would not complain. We never complain if it's good and if it's interesting. But the chances are that such a long novel may be tedious and tire even the best readers. When you build a house for two people you don't build a mansion of two thousand rooms unless you are a dictator who can do anything. The measure, the length, and so on, these are very important things, just like a tailor will not make for you a jacket for a six foot man if you are only five feet. The same thing is true with a writer. He has to have, more or less, an idea of how much he wants to say. You cannot let your pen completely free, and this does not mean I am against freedom. You wouldn't say that a tailor who makes a suit to measure is a slave; he's bound by the object and so are we. We are not talking to the walls; we are talking to human beings, and we know there are limits to their patience.

Mr. Rice: You willingly and gladly accept the confinement or the restraint of form in literature. And this seems to be a major idea not only in terms of art but in terms of philosophy. A novel with the title *The Slave* suggests an interesting concept of human bondage and freedom. There are limits and so on to real freedom.

Mr. Singer: Dr. Rice, there is somewhere an expression, I don't know who said it, that in the limitations we recognize the master. The fact is that a master always knows his limitations. It is the dilettante who thinks that he can work on all sides. For example, a real story-teller, a real writer, will not write a novel which will be a morality sermon, a lecture in sociology, a lecture in psychology; he will not do these things. He says to himself, "I am only a storyteller, and I'm not going to compete with Freud or with some other scholar." It is the dilettante who tries to do everything together. The masters of litera-ture always know what they can do and what they cannot do.

Mr. Rice: Is it related to the idealism of mass hysteria, of political movements that are too idealistic—they think they can do anything?

Mr. Singer: Exactly. What is the false Messiah? The false Messiah is also a man who thinks that he can do anything with a few letters, and so on and so on. The real master always knows that he's only a human being and so are the people for whom he works. And he has to limit himself or go to pieces.

Mr. Lane: Could I go back to the point you were making, David [Andersen], about folklore and Eliot's objection to folklore. I think Eliot's point was a special pleading for his own kind of folklore which was a specifically non-pagan folklore. He objected to pagan folklore because it wasn't high Anglo-Catholic. And Eliot's whole point at that time seems to have been something like the politics of renunciation and suffering. And the other day you told this marvelous anecdote about suffering. I wondered if you could repeat that. It's a fine answer to Eliot.

Mr. Singer: I'm glad to do it. I once went to a tailor in Warsaw, and I asked him to make me a coat, and I said, "Make it with crooked pockets; I like crooked pockets." The man said to me, "If you know me, you should know that you don't have to say 'crooked pockets.' You can say 'straight pockets'; they would come out crooked anyhow." This is true in many cases. Here is a little story which is symbolic, you know. The man did not mean to be symbolic, but it is symbolic anyhow. We often ask for crooked pockets while they would have come out crooked anyhow. I told this story in con-nection with a man who said to me, "I don't suffer enough, and I think that this is the reason my writing does not come out well. What should I do to suffer more?" And I told him, "Don't do anything; you will suffer more than you expect."

Mr. Rice: You've been talking about some of the problems of the writer, and I wonder if you would have any advice to give the reader of your work—not necessarily the deeply critical reader—but should one approach your work in any special way?

Mr. Singer: The only advice I can give the reader is: never read a book because a critic told you to read it or because it's fashionable to read it. If you read a book and you don't like it, close it and forget about it. This is my advice to the reader. When a reader reads be-cause it's fashionable or because it was recommended, I call this forced reading—it's never good. And I think there is a great problem in the universities and in schools where people are forced to read. It does damage to the reader because he's getting accustomed to read—to eat, so to say—without an appetite. Eat as long as you are hungry. The moment you are filled, leave the food. The same thing is true in literature. Naturally, the professors cannot afford to do this because they have to—let's say, if they teach Shakespeare—the student has to read Shakespeare, often. If he says that he wants to study Shakespeare, he should read Shakespeare. But generally I think that free reading is the best kind of reading. In my own case I practice this. Sometimes a man will tell me, "This book is a must." And I say, "There isn't such a thing as a 'must' in literature." If I read two pages and I don't like them, I close the book, and I leave the "musts" to someone else. So this is my advice to the reader.

I. B. Singer, Storyteller

Herbert R. Lottman/1972

From *The New York Times Book Review* (25 June 1972), 5,
32–33. Copyright © 1972 by The New York Times Company.
Reprinted by permission of Herbert R. Lottman and The New
York Times Company.

You don't have to know Yiddish to translate Isaac Bashevis Singer.
In fact, better not to. Singer isn't always tolerant of other Yiddishists;
his remarks on his contemporaries, not to say his peers, are often
severe. I've helped Isaac Singer put some of his stories, essays and
a play into English in recent years, by which I mean that he read his
Yiddish manuscript aloud, translating freely into English as he went
along, and I copied it down, doing my best to preserve the author's
art while helping shape the best English-language expression of it.
Often this led to debate over a word, a phrase, a sentiment. Sometimes the conversation moved into philosophy of life as well as
art.

"It wasn't hard for me to become a storyteller," Singer says. "Both
my mother and my father told stories—he told miracle stories. I was
inventing my own at the age of 5 or 6. I became interested in the
supernatural, in which my parents were ardent believers. They often
told me stories of demons and dybbuks. I still believe in God, that
you can pray to Him and He can help you. In my writing, I always
want to show how the spirit works, influencing not only our own
bodies but other bodies.

"You write for your newspapers with facts. That's the way I write,
too. The reader gets the facts and draws his own conclusions. The
words which express emotions are few and poor in individuality.
They are miserable generalizations. I use few adjectives and a minimum of verbs, but a lot of nouns. Facts and nouns go together.

"I have to write in notebooks with lined paper, but without the
vertical red-line margin you find in so many notebooks, because I
write from right to left and the margin only confuses me. They don't

seem to make these any more," indicating notebooks he has brought
with him to Europe, "but I've hoarded a supply and I know that the
Kresge chain somehow still carries them. When I'm on a lecture tour
I always ask my hosts to take me to Kresge. I send the notebooks to
my newspaper to be set in type. Almost all my fiction appears first in
The Jewish Daily Forward. They also used to publish my articles, and
I wrote thousands of them—on philosophy, ethics, Jewish questions.
I am afraid someone will want to collect them someday, and already
I'm embarrassed.

"It takes me a few sittings to write a story. Sometimes, but not
always, I rewrite it. The inspiration comes from one of my small spiral
notebooks where I jot down ideas. If I hear a good one I keep it in
the notebook and then I may transpose it to a Polish village setting of
50 years ago. Usually I don't make use of the topic if I can't introduce
the supernatural."

Every word in a Singer text is weighed, even in the English translation, and what the reader has before him is not the work of a translator removed from the source but (increasingly in recent years, as
Singer becomes more confident in English) his own pondered judgment. He must go over the text again and again to smooth out the
language. He will not abide repetition of a word; he is Flaubertian in
his insistence on *le mot juste.* The morning after a session of translating, when I think that the manuscript is ready, he runs in for breakfast
with the word "yearning," which must go in. As for content, often he
doesn't know in advance what he will say. In a way, he feels he is
engaged in automatic writing.

Singer began to write a story while staying on our farm, to take
advantage of my being available to edit the translation. It was based
on an incident that had taken place on his ocean voyage to Portugal
a few weeks earlier. A ship's waiter had been nasty and immediately
was imagined as his persecutor. Coleridge would have made him
an albatross.

"I really didn't know how I would end it. I think that I was guided
by a ghost."

By the next day he had found a closing for the story, which turned
out to be its whole point. Yet if I had interceded during the editing
with a counter-suggestion, he would object with vehemence.

"I need three conditions to write a story. The first is that I have a topic or a theme, call it what you like, a story with a beginning, a middle and an end. I don't believe in the kind of writing where the writer cuts off a slice of life. While some great writers succeeded in making their slice of life tasty to the literary palate, most of these slices have no taste whatsoever and are a bore to the reader. Modern fiction almost despises storytelling. It is so interested in depicting the inner man that it forgets to tell how the outer man looks, who he is and what he is doing. The psychologizers and sociologizers of modern fiction have actually declared war on the story, which to them is an old fashioned institution. I still believe that the mission of literature is to tell a story, where there is tension and where the reader does not know at the beginning what the end will be.

"The second condition is that I must have a passion to write this story. Sometimes the topic is good but nevertheless I feel indifferent to it. Indifference and art never go together. The artists were always forced to do their work whether by the muse, a dybbuk or even the desire to make money.

"The third condition is the most important. I must have the conviction, or perhaps the illusion, that I am the only writer who could write this particular story. A real story could only be written by one man. No writer in all the world or in any generation could have written *The Death of Ivan Ilitch* but Tolstoy. If I could imagine for a second that a story of mine could be written by another person, this story would be out.

"People often bother me about the meaning of a story, its tendency, its moral. My answer is that if I have the three conditions just mentioned, I worry very little about the meaning of the story, whether it will help humanity or, God forbid, set back its progress. I really don't believe that literature can influence life to any great degree. Art is a force, but without a vector. Like the waves of the sea it flows forward and backward, but the net result is static. While I believe that fiction requires a story and should appear dynamic, it actually describes human character and personality, which remains almost constant.

"I'd say that art stirs the mind but never moves it far in one direction or another. Admirers of Dostoevsky and Goethe were Nazis who played with the skulls of children. The hope that great literature can bring peace or make the human race better is without basis. When readers ask me about the message of my works, I tell them that the greatest message we've got is the Ten Commandments. They are short, precise, clear. We don't need new messages, and they will certainly not be found in novels, good or bad."

Yiddish was spoken by 10 million souls before World War II; today the estimate is between four and five million. Singer was born in the *shtetl,* or village, of Leoncin on the Vistula, in July 1904; but, while still a child his parents took him to Warsaw. During World War I he spent four years in Bilgoray, where he was to acquire his real experience of small-town life, animals, agriculture, even demons. Then he settled in Warsaw until he emigrated to the United States in 1935, at the insistence of his older brother Israel Joshua. In New York he tried to exist as a freelance contributor to the *Forward.*

"When I was new in America I really depended on the money I could get from the Yiddish press. I had to live from one article to the next even if it wasn't published or paid for three or four weeks. Once I was in Coney Island with 50 cents in my pocket. I was in a cafeteria, and I hesitated before deciding to spend a dime to phone the editor to see if an article of mine would be accepted. I was afraid that I might put the coin in the telephone only to be told that the editor wasn't in, and so the call would be for nothing. Finally I decided that I'd have to invest money to make money, so I called the number, the editor got on the phone and said my article was already in type. When I hung up a handful of coins fell out of the phone. I knew that if I didn't take them, other people waiting to use the phone would, so I took them. I was so elated I walked out of the cafeteria without paying my check. When I was outside I realized what I had done and went back to tell the cashier. But the manager was standing nearby so the cashier shooed me away, not wanting the manager to know that he had missed me. So on the beach I tore the cafeteria check into tiny pieces. It is rare that a series of lucky events come together like that.

"Nothing worse could happen than to lose a cafeteria check. Then they'd always make you pay for more than you actually ate. There was one terrible cafeteria. The original of the character I wrote about in the story we just translated once said that if you lost your check there, the only solution would be suicide."

In Paris we replaced cafeterias with cafes. Sitting at a particularly noisy one near the Gare St. Lazare during the evening rush hour:

"When I was young the thought that I could be sitting in Paris among so many people would have been unbelievable. When I was 19 or 20 I found myself stuck in a small village in Poland where my parents had moved. There was nothing to do or to see; I had mud up to my knees even in summer. I dreamed of getting out of there to a city. Paris seemed a paradise." (Singer's wife says: "The people here would never have done anything for you. America gave you everything." To me she adds: "He doesn't even have time to look at the nice buildings on Park Avenue, he runs around so much.")

Living with Singer requires living with his vegetarianism, a particularly difficult problem in France, where there is a good deal more conformity, especially at the dinner table, than Frenchmen might like to admit. He wouldn't even allow us to kill a fly in his presence. (I thought of the poor man, Reb Chayim of In My Father's Court, who wouldn't chase a fly that had alighted on his nose: "Was he to presume to tell a fly where it was permitted to stand and where not?")

"I wasn't a vegetarian from childhood. It started some 10 years ago when a bird I was attached to fell into a narrow vase. He could have stayed afloat, I suppose, but I wasn't at home to help him get out. The effort and the despair must have killed him. I said to myself that now is the time or never."

During one dinner on my farm he comments, seeing the casserole my wife has just brought to the table:

"There's nothing like rice. If I just had a little rice I could be happy always."

But he is soon heard to say: "There is nothing like potatoes. You couldn't make me happier than to give me potatoes."

Later there is discussion about how argumentative he is. My wife says that he should try to win an argument against me sometime, but these words are lost. A moment later he brings up the subject again.

"I would never argue with a potato. If a potato argued with me, it would win."

Yet it was hard to win against him. Once on a drive along the Normandy coast we hesitated and then decided not to stop at a banal-looking cafe he seemed to favor at a traffic intersection in Deauville, but went on to a more interesting place on the Trouville harbor. Driving back we passed the sad cafe again and he said: "Look, we should have gone there. I see they have a dog." His wife Alma: "And what do you need a dog for?" He: "For an argument."

My wife remarked that butterflies are stupid, staying indoors to die rather than fly out the window we open for them.

"I don't know how much cleverer Nabokov is than a butterfly, but no matter how great his wisdom he doesn't have the moral right to enjoy himself by extinguishing the spark of life which God has given to these creatures for a day or two. All the babble about decency, mercy, culture and ethics looks silly coming from the mouths of people who kill innocent creatures, chase a tired fox with their hounds or even support bullfights and slaughterhouses. All the explanations that nature is cruel and therefore we are entitled to be cruel are hypocritical. There is no proof that man is more important to nature than a butterfly or a cow. I consider my vegetarianism the greatest achievement of my life. I don't fool myself that I save many animals from slaughter; but my not eating meat is an expression of protest against the cruelty of nature, of people and even of the Almighty Himself. Personally I believe that there will never be any peace in this world as long as animals are treated the way we treat them today."

My wife comments that she would like to be a mosquito in her next life all the same, to be able to sting all those she doesn't care for. She'd be a tiger, she adds, expect that they are easy marks for men.

"Better if you want to hurt your enemies not to be a tiny mosquito. You have to be a man like Stalin or Hitler."

In practical affairs his kindness becomes generosity, and he has to be restrained at tipping time. His haste to reimburse money spent on his behalf is disconcerting.

"I was always taught that other people's money is sacred.

"In Poland as a young man I stayed with a farm family who charged me one droschen for a meal. I said no, in Warsaw it would cost 40 droschen, so I must pay them at least 30. Would you believe that after a few days they said I wasn't paying enough—why should a meal cost less here than in Warsaw? Before I left I was spending more than at a first-class hotel. I had to tell them that I couldn't afford to stay there any more."

He extends no unnecessary charity to literature that he doesn't like, nor to its makers. He is quick to accuse them of charlatanism, or of following fashion. Among his favorite writers are Gogol, Dostoevsky, Tolstoy, Flaubert (he should be), Poe. Among later writers, Knut Hamsun, Conrad Richter, Henry Miller.

On Miller: "I have nothing against literature which describes sex, or might even be called pornographic. A writer must be his own censor. If he hates vulgarity, he won't use vulgar language. But I don't believe that governors, judges and police officers should have the right to censor literature. Henry Miller had the courage to fight for his literary convictions, and he paid a high price for it in money and prestige for many years. But I have no respect for those who jumped on the bandwagon after Miller emerged victorious. A generation can afford to have one Kafka, one Joyce, one Miller, but when we create whole armies of them something is wrong. Miller himself despises his imitators. His writing has passion and character. He raves about sex in his individual way. Those who imitate him are creating according to a recipe. They are cold-blooded pornographers."

Among poets, he mentions Mickiewicz, Pushkin, Byron, Verlaine, Baudelaire. Lately he has read little fiction ("You need an immensely rich fantasy to compete with life in our day.") He is difficult with his contemporaries and he feels that they are sometimes difficult with him.

"Let's not walk through the Jewish quarter of Paris. If the Yiddish writers see me, I'll be in all kinds of trouble. One of them is sure to say, 'The others say terrible things about you but I defend you.' I don't want to be defended.

"Not only does the writer deal with the unique but his whole situation is often unique. Mine is unique because while the Yiddish language is richer now than it ever was, the number of Yiddish-speaking people is dwindling from day to day. Also the writers who wrote in Yiddish didn't have a chance to make use of the great themes which were given to them. Now they are almost all very old, and new writers in Yiddish don't appear. I often feel like a man who was given many treasures but has neither the time nor the possibility of making use of them. The soil of Yiddish literature is still virgin. Very little has been written about the builders of Zion, the creators of the Yiddish brand of socialism, the Enlightenment, about our adventurists, converts, scientists, business tycoons; even about the Chassidim and the Kabbalists very little fiction has been written. The people who rebuilt Israel are almost all Yiddish-speaking. The story of Israel could only be written in that language, because they all think in Yiddish, even such adversaries of Yiddish as Ben-Gurion. Sometimes I feel that our people, the living and the dead, call me from all sides to do justice to their great lives and unusual deaths.

"If we reach the time when Yiddish and Yiddish customs and folklore are forgotten, Hitler will have succeeded not only physically but also spiritually. I get up every morning with the feeling of excitement of a man who must do more than is in his power. It is true that the human story can never be told, but the Jewish story must remain forever untold because there are so few who can tell it.

"But every man can only do as much as is in his power. Lately I have begun to write for children and I actually get letters from young people asking me to write about topics they choose. I wish Yiddish could be as alive today as when I was a child and that there were many young talents writing in Yiddish. I would not call myself the last Yiddish writer but I am certainly one of the last. It is both a tragedy and a responsibility."

Yiddish Tradition vs. Jewish Tradition, A Dialogue

Isaac Bashevis Singer and Irving Howe/1973

From *Midstream* (June/July 1973), 33–38. This conversation originally took place as a broadcast on Yale University Radio. Copyright © 1973 by Yale University. Reprinted by permission of Irving Howe and *Midstream*.

Irving Howe: I understand that a story of yours called "The Mirror" has just been made into a play and is being produced at Yale. This is something new in your career because as far as I know you have never written a play before or had a story of yours made into a play. How did you go about taking this sketch which doesn't have very much action in it and make it into a play?

Isaac Bashevis Singer: Some of my works were made into plays but I didn't do it. They were adapted by others. This is the first time that I wrote a play myself and I must say, it was not an easy job for me because I really didn't know what a play was until I began to work on it. The play, *The Mirror,* is a story about a girl who is enticed by a devil into a mirror. Then he takes her to Sodom. The idea of the story is this. In the little town, the shtetl in Poland, she was very bored, she was bored to death. Then she goes to Sodom and there the wickedness is so terrible that she cannot stand it. The end of the story is that she remains in the mirror. In other words, she is neither in Sodom nor in Krashnik (which is the name of the shtetl); she remains suspended between two worlds. The idea is more or less that we run away from boredom into wickedness and there is almost nothing between.

Howe: You have a sentence in the story which suggests that idea. The sentence reads, "Everything hidden must be revealed; each secret longs to be disclosed; each love yearns to be betrayed; everything sacred must be desecrated." And the girl in the story, her name is Zirel, acts according to this idea.

Singer: Naturally, this is what the devil says to her and he persuades her. This story is a kind of basis for the play. I couldn't have written the play without the story, but there is not, as you said, enough action in the story to make a play. When she comes to Sodom, Asmodeus, the King of Sodom, tells her that he brought her there because he misses natural love. He has so much perversion around him that he's yearning for some natural love. The only thing is that he wants it instantly. He says, "Give me natural love in five minutes because we in Sodom have no time."

Howe: That sounds like an American idea.

Singer: Yes, exactly, we have no time. And when she says that it has to take time he becomes very angry and he gives her a pill; they have special pills for natural love.

Howe: That's another American idea.

Singer: Yes, pills for natural love. So, in a way, it reflects our time.

Howe: What happens in the play afterwards? What's the climax?

Singer: The climax is that she cannot be in Sodom, she cannot go back to Krashnik, because once you cross the mirror you can never go back. There is a magician there who promised to rescue her, but he cannot bring her back to Krashnik, he makes her stay in the mirror. In other words, she becomes completely isolated. It's a way of dying.

Howe: And that's how the play ends.

Singer: That's how the play ends.

Howe: When I heard that you were doing this dramatization of a story a number of problems arose in my mind. One of them is this: Those of us who have the privilege of being able to read your stories in Yiddish know that one of the great strengths and virtues of the stories is the language, the expository prose which is very concentrated and crisp and vivid. To take a story in which one of the great strengths is the language of the author's voice and then to put that into a drama where the author doesn't speak in his own voice, only the characters speak, must present a whole new kind of problem.

Singer: It is a problem, but since I make the devil speak (and the devil does not have to speak in a natural kind of a language, he can speak devilish language), I try in my own way to give him strong language.

Howe: By now you have become an expert in devilish language.

Singer: Well, I should be already. I feel sometimes I am half a devil myself.

Howe: That has been suggested by some people. There's another question that interested me very much in regard to the adaptation. You surely know better than I that there is a certain tradition in the Yiddish stage for non-realistic or stylized kinds of production and dramas. The Yiddish stage at its best, some decades ago, always had a great ability to present imaginative kinds of non-realistic plays. I was wondering, when you did this play, whether anything of the tradition of the Yiddish stage, something like An-Sky's *The Dybbuk* was in the back of your mind.

Singer: The truth is that the Yiddishists don't consider me a writer who writes in their tradition. Neither do I consider myself a writer in their tradition. I consider myself a writer in the Jewish tradition but not exactly the Yiddish tradition. It is true that I have seen An-Sky's *The Dybbuk* many years ago, but whatever influence he might have had on me I don't really know. I am more influenced by the cabalists, by the older writers, than by the modern writers.

Howe: It would be worth taking a minute to explain what the distinction is in your mind between being in the Yiddish tradition on the one hand and in the Jewish tradition on the other hand.

Singer: The Yiddish tradition, in my mind, is a tradition of sentimentality and of social justice. These are the two pillars, so to speak, of the Yiddish kind of emotions. They are always for the underdog, very much so, and they are always sentimental. When I began to write I already felt that this kind of tradition is not in my character. I am not a sentimental person by nature. By sentimental, I mean really sentimental, let's call it schmaltz as it should be called. Neither is it my nature to fight for social justice although I am for social justice. But since I'm a pessimist and I believe that no matter what people are going to do it will always be wrong and there will never be any justice in this world, I have in my own way given up. And because of this I had to create my own kind of tradition.

Howe: So that, in creating your own tradition, you feel that you went back to sources in Jewish lore and in Jewish thought which precede historically the rise of Yiddish literature.

Singer: This is exactly how I feel because according to the Bible and even the Talmud, God really resented that He created man. The

Bible keeps on repeating that one can expect very little from a
human being, he is only blood and flesh and even if he tries to do
good sometimes, it comes out wrong. I felt this way all my life.

Howe: This certainly comes through in a good many of your
stories. Yet the story of yours which perhaps is best known in America, "Gimpel the Fool," certainly can be seen as connected with parts
of the Yiddish tradition. That story has a feeling for the underdog, for
social justice, and there is also in that story the figure of "the sacred
fool" who has appeared in the writings of a good many Yiddish
writers like Peretz and others. Don't you think that that story has
some connection?

Singer: I think so, you may be right. I think the reason for its
special success may also be this, that it has the minimum schmaltz
which some of our people demand.

I want to say, by the way, that I am not against social justice. I
think day and night about how we could have a better world. The
only thing is I could never come to any conclusion because I see
that no matter what people try to do, it always . . . I just read the
memoirs of Yakir, the son of this general whom the Russians killed.
When you read such a book you fall into such despair that you really
lose hope.

Howe: You mentioned earlier that you felt your work was influenced by the Cabala. I don't think there are too many readers of the
Cabala in America these days. Maybe you could tell us a little something about that.

Singer: The Cabala is pantheistic. It says that everything is from
God. In other words, the table here and the chair in which we sit and
you yourself and I are all part of the Godhead. Since we are part of
the Godhead, all our mistakes in a way are the mistakes of God. The
Cabala teaches us that to be able to create, God in a way had to dim
His light, to extinguish part of His being to create a vacuum, and
because of this, He could create. If He didn't dim His light, His
radiance would have filled the cosmos to such a degree that creation
would be impossible. In other words, the Cabala teaches us that
Satan makes possible creation, that without him this could not have
happened.

Howe: That Satan is, so to speak, God's first mistake.

Singer: Not really a mistake. To be able to create He had to have

Satan because if Satan wouldn't have been there, everything would
be divinity, everything would be great and radiant . . .

Howe: . . . and boring . . .

Singer: . . . and there would be no place for individuality, for free
choice.

Howe: Had the thought *ever* occurred to you that this is very
similar to certain early Christian heresies such as the Manichaean
outlook?

Singer: Some critics told me that I am influenced by them
although I read very little. After they told me I tried to read.

Howe: I can understand that, yes.

Singer: Just as they told me once about Freud. When I wrote
Satan in Goray, they told me this is a Freudian work. I was then 28
years old, I had barely heard the name Freud. I didn't read him. But
a number of people come to the same conclusion.

Howe: After they told you, you made the proof.

Singer: Well, I looked into it, I read a little bit of Freud.

Howe: He was a great pessimist, too.

Singer: He was.

Howe: On your general work as a Yiddish writer: the tradition that
I myself have seen at work is a kind of underground tradition in the
Jewish experience of the last few centuries, and that's the tradition
which you struggle with and partly reject but it fascinates you. It's the
tradition of false Messianism, the Sabbatean tradition, the tradition of
Sabbatai Zevi which leads people to fanaticism, to hysteria, to disin-
tegration, to explosion. *Satan in Goray* is very much concerned with
this kind of tradition. It even comes through in some of your other
stories less directly.

Singer: To me, Sabbatai Zevi was the symbol of the man who
tries to do good and comes out bad. In other words, for me Sabbatai
Zevi is in a way Stalin and all these people who tried so hard to
create a better world and who ended up by creating the greatest
misery. Naturally, Sabbatai Zevi couldn't have created as much
misery as Stalin, he didn't have the power.

Howe: So that the whole tradition of Sabbatai Zevi is one which
you see as part of the Faustian impulse of human beings to be active,
to do things and then, afterwards, misery follows.

Singer: To fail, yes.

Howe: But that leads to the possibility that people would accuse you (and maybe some critics have) of a form of quietism, of believing that the best thing is to remain still in the world, not to act.

Singer: In a way, I'm not far from the Buddhist and the Indian way of thinking that the best thing you can do is run away from evil, not fight it, because the moment you begin to fight evil, you become a part of evil yourself.

Howe: That's the most interesting thing that's come out in a long time in regard to your own views. It certainly makes clear, although you write in Yiddish and have a marvelous Yiddish style, why the Yiddishist writers feel that in some ways you are a stranger in their midst.

Singer: It is true. Yiddishism was very much influenced by socialism, Yiddishism is actually a very young movement. It's only about 70 or 80 years old. It was influenced by Karl Marx and by all the so-called social dogooders. Somehow, when I was young, I already saw the bad results of all these good deeds. I have seen young people go to Soviet Russia and disappear there. All these illusions and all these vain hopes. I compared them to the people who believed in Sabbatai Zevi, they were just as honest in their own way, just as zealous, and just as disappointed.

Howe: So it looks in a paradoxical way, although you write in Yiddish and I write in English, that I am closer to the Yiddishist tradition than you are, even though you were brought up in that world and I was not.

Singer: I think so because you write your articles in *Dissent*, you still have hope that by your dissent and by the dissent of some other people like you, you can change things. I have lost this illusion.

Howe: I don't *always* have that hope, I have it sometimes.

Singer: Yes, but sometimes.

Howe: Let's turn to something else. What kind of work are you doing now? You have published a whole group of novels and before that there was a group of stories. What comes next?

Singer: My latest novel was *Enemies, A Love Story*, which was about refugees in this country. I dare to write about refugees in this country, but they always have to be people from the other side. In about a year or so, next fall, I hope to bring out a book of short stories. Many of these stories were published in *The New Yorker*, others were published in other magazines and some will be new ones. At the moment I am writing a novel about the old country, and the tentative name is *The Godseeker.* It is about a man who was seeking God. I have taken as a prototype my grandfather although it's not the story of my grandfather.

Howe: Your work has become famous in America. I think I know exactly when that began. In fact, I remember the occasion.

Singer: You took part in it, you helped me.

Howe: I took a little part. When Eliezer Greenberg and I were doing our *A Treasury of Yiddish Stories,* I remember that he said he had a special present for me and the present consisted of his reading to me, in Yiddish, "Gimpel the Fool." In Yiddish, of course, it reads wonderfully well, very strong and vivid prose. Then the story was printed in *Partisan Review.* I even remember sending it to them.

Singer: It was translated by Saul Bellow.

Howe: A fine translation. Then things began to move after that and by now, in some curious way, you have become part of American literature even though you don't write in English. It's clear that you have begun to influence (for good or bad, I don't know) American writers. What is your sense of your relationship to contemporary American writers? Do you see any grandchildren, any half-grandchildren there that you want to acknowledge?

Singer: I really don't see any grandchildren and I don't think that any writer really has grandchildren. A real writer is never a grandchild. It's only the epigones who become children and grandchildren.

Howe: You mean a real writer is like a mule, without offspring.

Singer: He's always first.

Howe: First and last.

Singer: First and last, yes. So the idea of having literary grandchildren does not appeal to me too much.

Howe: There's been a good deal of writing lately, so-called American-Jewish writing, about Jewish subjects in the English language. Do you have any sense of relationship there to you or do you have a sense of distance?

Singer: When I read what they call a Jewish novel, I don't look for the Jewishness, I look for good writing. I am not happy with bad writing which tries to cover up its bad writing with being Jewish; neither am I happy with bad writers who call themselves *avant-garde* and think that if they call themselves by this name their bad writing will be forgiven. I still demand that a writer should write clearly, should have a story to tell, should write it well, that his people, his heroes should be alive and that the story should be more or less convincing in its own terms. In other words, I'm not fooled by all these coverups. Because of this I don't feel that we are too successful in American literature or any other literature. The number of real talents is very small in every generation and it is as small today as it was in any other century. Calling oneself names and giving oneself fancy titles will not change this fact.

Howe: I tend to agree with you. I remember a little incident that occurred a few years ago. There was a wonderful dairy restaurant called Steinberg's on Broadway and 81st Street.

Singer: Surely; we used to meet there.

Howe: Unfortunately, they closed the store. But I remember once we were talking and you said to me, about a certain American writer who shall remain nameless, that he had a very fancy attic, he had a good second story, not such a bad first floor, but there were no foundations so there was nothing the building could rest on. You really feel that a story has to have the traditional element of narrative, of event and interest.

Singer: I call it an address. It must have an address.

Howe: You must know where you are going so if you mail a letter it will get there.

Singer: Exactly. It has to be unique as an address should be.

Seeing and Blindness: A Conversation with Isaac Bashevis Singer

Grace Farrell/1976

From *Novel: A Forum on Fiction*, 9, no. 2 (Winter 1976), 151–164. Reprinted by permission.

F: Last year at a literary convention in Chicago Irving Howe implied that the works of Jewish writers cannot be fully appreciated either intellectually or emotionally by a non-Jew. Mr. Singer, do you write only, or primarily, for Jewish readers?

S: I think it is completely false. It's as if you would say that a French writer cannot be appreciated by the English. In a way it is true that a people of your nationality, of your group, understand you a little better. If you mention a town, they might have been in the town; your language is their language. But just the same the great writers are understood by all people all over the world. Isn't it a fact that Dostoyevsky is admired all over the world, yet the whole world does not consist of Russians or of people who speak only Russian. It is not true at all. This was Irving Howe's way of apologizing for why we have so many bad writers. But every group has many bad writers. If a writer really has something to say then he will be understood by all people all over the world. I myself read translations from Japanese or from Chinese or from Indian, Hindu or whatever, and if there is something good, I understand it and I appreciate it even though I don't know their way of living. In other words I deny that this is true.

F: In the memoirs of your childhood, *In My Father's Court*, there is a story called "Old Jewishness" which ends during a great cholera epidemic which destroyed lives and filled mankind with sorrow and misery. You write, "The aged, the paralyzed, and the freakish were on display. Inside the synagogue stood worshippers in white linen robes and prayer shawls. A young man near the threshold lamented bitterly, having recently lost his father. Others said to him, 'May you have no more sorrow . . .' 'Oh Father, Father, why did you leave us?' he cried."

132

S: I remember this as if it happened yesterday. Yes.

F: The cry of that young man, "Father, Father, why did you leave us?" reminds me, as a reader who is also a Christian, of the cry of Christ on the cross.

S: Yes, *Eli, Eli lema sabachthani?* Why have you forsaken me? Yes. Actually this is the cry which we all cry when we are in trouble, whether one is a Jesus or just a simple person.

F: And it is perhaps what unites the Jewish and the non-Jewish reader of your fiction. We all partake of that anguish and we all question that abandonment.

S: Not only does it unite the Jewish and the non-Jewish, but the man and the animal. It does not express in words, but when an animal screams it is the same scream as that of a human being. The animal also asks God, why have you forsaken us.

F: We are all one.

S: Exactly. Made of the same stuff.

F: Your fiction maintains what I have called an uneasy coalescence of joy and pessimism, of humor and despair, of the old and the new, and more fundamentally perhaps of belief and skepticism. *In My Father's Court* reveals you to be the paradoxical result of two very different parents.

S: Yes. My mother was a skeptic and my father was a believer. But let me tell you, there is a believer in every skeptic and there is a doubter in every believer, because no matter how much you believe there is always a spark of doubt in you which asks how do you know this is true. And again the skeptic would not be a real skeptic if he were not a believer. If he did not believe in anything, I would not call him a skeptic. I would call him just a man who doesn't care. There are such people who really don't care one way or another, but such a person is not a skeptic. He just is ignorant or he knows the most unimportant things. Skeptics are people who would like to believe but they would like to get proof for their belief. And this proof can never be really obtained.

F: That's interesting because in "Why the Geese Shrieked," a story which dramatizes the skepticism of your mother and the faith of your father, you so much want to believe.

S: Yes, because it would be interesting really to see if some spirit has entered a goose. William James has written *The Will to Believe* where he maintains that the will to believe is in all of us. There is not much pleasure in being a skeptic. The real pleasure, the real fire, we get from believing, not from doubting.

F: If we did not have some basis for belief within us, then we would not even bother to ask those questions which the skeptic asks.

S: Exactly, exactly. Actually what we see—and I'm not speaking about those things which we cannot see—but what we see maintains already so much, tells us so much. You lift up your eyes and you look at the sky and see the stars, the same stars which people saw a half million years ago or which animals saw a billion years ago and which will be seen a billion years after we are gone. You see the earth, you see the sun, and you see all kinds of creatures and flowers, all these things are here. So even though we don't know the mysteries of the universe, what is revealed to us is already something of immense greatness.

F: *In My Father's Court* reveals your wonderment at the world about you, a wonderment which does become suppressed as you increasingly become witness to poverty and oppression. But still I see you as "the curious one," discovering a story each time you open your ears or look about at your world.

S: Actually wonderment and curiosity are made of the same stuff except that wonderment is about general things while curiosity is about specific things. This feeling of wonder is still with me today as it was when I was eight years old, or nine years old, and I think it is getting even stronger with the years instead of weaker. I'm still astonished when I open my eyes and I see the sky and the walls and things and human beings. It's a great mystery to me and the mystery really becomes more intense with age, because all the theories, and all the explanations, and all the books don't explain at all what is going on here before our very eyes. But we are what our passions are, what our despair is. Naturally I'm curious. As a matter of fact when a person comes to interview me I interview this person, because I'm just as curious about this person as this person is curious about me. I know that no matter how much we know of life, we know almost nothing and there is so much to learn. Whenever I think I know already, let's say about love or about sex or about human relations, I always keep on discovering new things.

F: Yet you have called yourself a pessimist.

S: Yes. I will tell you. I am a pessimist as far as human relations are concerned. If someone tells me that Socialism will bring eternal happiness or some League of Nations or the United Nations will end the wars, I say that this is nonsense. The human tragedy is going to last as long as humanity will last. If we will get peace in one way, we will have disturbances in another. But this does not mean that I'm a pessimist as far as God and the cosmos is concerned. Like the Cabalists I say that this is a terrible planet. I call this world hell or death. Here we were sent not to completely enjoy but to suffer and to go through all kinds of temptations, and God must have a good reason for this. But just the same this is not the very end. In other words, I'm an optimist as far as the kingdom of heaven is concerned, but as far as these kingdoms here are concerned, I'm a pessimist. Not that I believe that everything is hopeless. As a matter of fact even in this hell in which we live we have moments of joy and sometimes a larger part of joy according to one's fate and circumstances or to God's will. Jesus was not an optimist about life on earth. He said that the kingdom of heaven will give you some joy. But no man in his right mind unless he is a silly liberal believes that we can change the world.

F: In "The Secret" your father teaches you that even that which appears evil will eventually become good and in reality there is no evil. He compares the world to a fruit and its outer husk. The husk cannot be eaten, but it protects the fruit.

S: In a way I'm not so sure about things as my father. Because my father believed that everything that was written in the books is one hundred per cent true. I don't rely on any books. But I feel that the cosmos cannot be all evil, that the creator of all these galaxies could not just be an ice cold sadist who plays around with little creatures. There must be something great, good, eternal. But while he believed in it, I assume that it is so, or I like to think that it is so.

F: Back to "Why the Geese Shrieked." You want very much to believe.

S: Yes, I would like to believe. It is very hard to believe that the highest wisdom is also the lowest cruelty.

F: Do the Cabalists tell us why, if this world is hell or death, God bothered to create it?

S: Well, the Cabala says that God was before everything. Naturally

He was here always, and His radiance filled so to say the whole space. So there was no place for any other thing. I would say that God enjoyed Himself, studied Himself, developed Himself, but there was only God. But since one of God's attributes, or perhaps His greatest attribute, is creation, He sooner or later had to create a world. But the Cabala says how could He have created the world if He filled the world Himself. So according to the Cabala He had to create a vacuum in Himself. Then there could be space for creation. And He sent out a beam of His own light and this beam went through a process of evolution. But it was not the evolution of the Darwin evolutionists where things begin small and become big, but just the opposite. The nearer this beam of light was to God the greater it was. Then it became cooler and lower and the very last process of this creation is the material world, the stars, the earth, the sun, and man. Here in this world God has become matter. But even so since it is a part of God, it is also spirit. A part of something can not become something else. This is the process of creation. In the higher worlds, says the Cabala, there is no free will because they are so near to God. The difference between them and God is not great enough that there should be temptations or desire for sin. Everything is done according to heavenly will. Only here in this prison, in this dark den, where Satan and all the devils rule, only here does man have free will. He can choose between life and death, between evil and good, between wisdom and foolishness, and so on and so on. But this is a great gift. We know that a chain is as strong as its weakest link. Since we are the weakest link in God's chain, He depends on us. If we break, the whole Godly evolution breaks. In a way God depends on us.

F: We're responsible for the whole of creation?

S: For the whole of creation. For if we break down, everything breaks down. God would not break down, but creation would break down. Since creation is God's highest ambition, His most important deed, God in a way has given us power where He and His career depend on us.

F: How do you think we're doing?

S: I think we are doing very badly lately. However, this link, weak as it is, is still pretty strong and we cannot break it just like that.

F: Once we talked about the imps who are always tempting man, always putting him to the test.

S: It's all parables; we don't know what they are. It's man himself who is always . . . we are always tempted whether the imps do it or some other creatures. All these names are taken from folklore.

F: But don't deny your imps. Many people in interviews have almost forced you to.

S: I don't deny them. I believe in them.

F: I was wondering if in some ways God is also a tempter. God also puts man to the test.

S: The very fact that He has created matter, the material world, is already a big temptation. You mean that Providence itself works to send temptations to men. There is no question about it, because even though God has hidden himself, He is still there. And He sees everything. And His powers see everything and they all the time tempt man and they also see to it that man does his work no matter what the situation.

F: When I read your stories I'm always reminded of Job shaking his fist at God.

S: Sure, sure. These are the main questions. I'm sometimes astonished when I see writers who write things which have nothing to do with the crux of the matter. They'll just tell some little story which means nothing. To me every story must in some way, directly or indirectly, deal with the eternal questions.

F: You, like Job, ask the eternal questions, "What is man that thou makest much of him and turnest thy thoughts towards him, only to punish him morning by morning or to test him every hour of the day? My thoughts today are resentful, for God's hand is heavy on me in my trouble. If only I knew how to find him. Why should man be born to wander blindly, hedged in by God on every side?"

S: I will tell you. I say that even though men recognize that God had to create a world, just the same there is a great feeling of protest in men, and the higher the person the stronger the protest. I do not think this protest is anti-religious. I think it was meant that man should feel this protest. Let's say that you believe already everything is as it should be and there is no way out of this. So if someone drills your tooth and it aches you, you scream and this scream is the protest. And I will say that when higher peole protest it is even stronger. Although they may believe in God and although they know that His wisdom is great and his mercy may be great, just the same when they suffer or when they see their dear ones suffer, they protest. They say why couldn't God have created a different world? Why did You need all these temptations? You could have created a world of all bliss and justice. I say that protest is a part of religion. Even though according to the Christian belief Jesus was God's son, just the same when he was crucified, he protested, which is a human kind of attitude because he was a human just the same. And this is true about all of us, about animals, about men. The moment you are caught and you are hurt, you protest. And I don't think that God wants men not to protest. Because this protest is unavoidable. And this protest reminds God that He could have done perhaps differently. Like the Polish corporal who used to train the recruits. He said when you see a general salute him, but pierce him with your eyes. In other words don't be humble before him, don't cringe before him. He is a general, he deserves the honor, but look at him and make him realize that you suffer because of him. This is the way I feel about the Almighty. I admire Him. I'm sure He is infinitely cleverer than all of us, but just the same I feel . . . I am resentful towards Him at times.

F: Are you suggesting, as Herman Broder in *Enemies: A Love Story* puts it, that a Hitler reigns on high? That perhaps God is in league with the Devil?

S: No. A human being will say this only in moments of great despair. When he is in great, great strife, he may say so. But when I cool off I don't say this. I don't say He is a Hitler. I say He is great, He is wise, but since we are foolish and limited, we must protest. As a matter of fact I have built my whole morality on this protest. I say that because we are against God's so-called cruelty, we should behave in the opposite way so to say to spite Him. Hopeless as this is.

F: So man made in God's image and likeness must act inversely to what seems to be God's action.

S: He's made in God's image, but he has all the right to protest to God and to say, I don't like this kind of creation. It is true that I may be necessary for Your schemes, but how's about me? And if He tells me He will reward me later, then I can say, how's about now? Why should I suffer now? And this is the very essence of the Book of Job. At the end Job is rewarded. He has more beautiful daughters and more donkeys and so on and so on but we feel that this is not an answer to Job's suffering.

F: No, it isn't. Are we in some sense pawns in an eternally on-going struggle between God and Satan.

S: No question about it. Actually God does not have to fight Satan. If God would want, Satan would disappear in a second. The only thing is Satan must be here, because without Satan the material world could not exist. The material world is a combination of seeing and blindness. This blindness we call Satan. If we would become all seeing, we would not have free choice anymore. Because if we would see God, if we would see His greatness, there would be no temptation or sin. And since God wanted us to have free will this means that Satan, in other words the principle of evil, must exist. Because what does free choice mean? It means the freedom to choose between good and evil. If there is no evil there is no freedom.

F: So, although the characters in your books and all of us are like the Children of Israel of whom Isaiah spoke, "we wait for light, but behold obscurity, for brightness, but we walk in darkness," and although like Job we all cry out, "If only I knew where to find him," if He did show Himself in a sense . . .

S: If He showed Himself we would be lost, we would disappear.

F: So we are hedged in.

S: Our individuality would disappear because then we would become clearly united with the Godhead. There must be this blindness or this evil so that we should exist as free people.

F: Is this why so often when a character finally catches a glimpse of the splendor of God he then dies?

S: Or he almost dies or he becomes a saint or even if he does catch a glimpse of God there are powers which make him forget about it. Just like dreams. Sometimes you dream, you have a wonderful dream, you wake up with the feeling you have seen something. After five minutes the whole thing has evaporated. People who have gotten a glimpse of God forget it. The evil powers say it was nothing, it was an illusion or a delusion, and man goes back to his skepticism.

F: If they even remember it and if they don't forget.

S: They doubt it just the same; they doubt it.

F: And they can never communicate it to anybody.

S: They doubt it and even if they do communicate it there are people who say it's a lie or it's an illusion. It is made so. The creation of this world is made so that faith and denial should always be in balance more or less. In one person it's a little in one direction and in another it's in another direction, but there's always this balance where you never know where you are.

F: In "A Crown of Feathers" you say that truth is like a crown of feathers. What did you mean by that?

S: I mean you cannot always believe that it exists and if you see it, already it dissolves after a moment. But every time she saw this crown of feathers somehow when she tried to get it again it was lost. In other words it evaporates. And this must be so that the balance between good and evil should exist. If the crown of feathers would be here, this would create a whole revolution in everything. It is so made that all the experiences of man can never serve as scientific evidence. So this is the reason why the crown of feathers disappears, vanishes.

F: Could you say that in order to create God had to hide?

S: He had to hide. Yes, to hide His face.

F: So His absence you might say is a necessary condition for the continuation of creation.

S: Because if He would be fully present nothing could exist but Him. And even when He is absent it is also He, only that He gives kind of a lower grade of Himself. I compare it in my essay to a man of genius who has to teach a little child the alphabet. He cannot tell him all his theories and his ideas. He himself has to limit himself and for a while act like a child. And this is what God was doing in creating the universe.

F: Do you think that God might somehow resent man and resent creation?

S: Well I will tell you, this is in the Bible. Everytime man does evil God feels that He has made a mistake. The Bible says that God regretted creating man. But He hopes, He just the same hopes that man will sooner or later use his free will to strengthen this link instead of weakening it. If this link will ever break we will all go back to the Godhead.

F: And creation will be over.

S: And creation will be over. Or maybe there will be another kind of creation.

F: Here again is your optimism. In spite of evil, in spite of blindness, even when the weight of those eternal questions which you always ask seems almost too much to bear, always mixed with that pessimism of which we spoke is a kind of awe, akin to joy.

S: There is no question that there is joy in life, because if there would be no joy there wouldn't even be suffering. We wouldn't even know that we suffer because that would be the natural thing. There is joy in every life and hope in every life. And there is great joy in love and in sex and in food and in seeing nature and the greatest joy is free choice. God has bestowed upon men the greatest gift perhaps which He could have given us and this was free choice. The only thing is we don't make use of it. We use very little of it. In most cases we don't take into our hands our own lot, but instead we are pushed around. We are too lazy really to use free will. But once a man discovers the great quality of free will and begins to use it, he can always find some happiness in it. It's a great effort, but you are rewarded for your efforts.

F: If we have free will and can choose, then just how much responsibility does each of us have for the evil in the world? Your characters often seem helpless against it. If in a sense creation is a battle between good and evil, what part does man play?

S: I would say we are only responsible in the cases where we could have done something. Let's say if I see a poor man in the street hungry and naked and I could help him but I don't help him, then I am at fault. But I am not responsible for an earthquake or for tidal waves or for famines or for all kinds of things. It is the radical who thinks he could have made things better if he had gotten a better president or a better whatever. I know that this isn't so.

F: Does man somehow have a special responsibility for improving society in order to prepare it for the redeemer?

S: He has. But I would say you have to begin by improving yourself. You can never say I am just going to be one of the villains, but I will improve society. It's the same as if one would say, I will see to it that humanity will be clean but I myself will go around in dirty linen and befoul the world. If you want to preach cleanliness, you have to be clean yourself. Take a man like Stalin. He wanted a paradise but he himself was a devil so he turned this whole paradise into a devil's den. According to religion first of all you have to begin with yourself, where your free will is valid, where you have choices. When it comes to society your powers, or my powers, or anybody else's powers are very limited. This is what religion and real morality is: begin with yourself.

F: Many times the characters in your stories who are overcome by temptation or by evil are those who don't know themselves at all. I think of Zirel in "The Mirror" who looks in the mirror at her beautiful reflection but never sees herself.

S: To use free will we have to know ourselves. We have to know other people. But this idea of modern man that by choosing the right man for president or the right kind of system we will save the world is completely false. It is in your personal life where your free will is most valid.

F: Could you tell me something of Hasidism?

S: Well, the Hasids are actually Cabalists. Basically the Hasid believes what the Cabalist believes and this is pantheism, that every-thing is God. You sitting in this chair, this machine, this booklet, this carpet are all part of the Godhead. But while the Cabalists were an esoteric people who felt that the Cabala was only for the chosen ones, not for everybody, the Hasids popularized the Cabala. And they tried to live according to Cabala. Hasidism believed that religion is only possible through joy. If religion doesn't give you any joy, something is wrong with it. When Hasidism arose, religion had become kind of frigid or frozen. There was no more fire in it. They said to themselves, we must kindle a fire in Jewishness or it will disappear altogether. And Hasidism had this element which made people really hot about religion. They got their Rabbis and they used to go to them and they had all kinds of stories. Also it was kind of a brotherhood; one Hasid was like a brother to the other. The rich helped the poor; there was singing and dancing. So Hasidism is a belief in Jewishness, in the Cabala, and also a belief that religion without joy is not religion. As it happens with all movements with time it cooled off. Now it is already in a stage where Hasidism is almost cool but far from being completely so. There are still many groups of Hasidim in Israel and even here in this country who are very hot about their religion and this is what keeps them going.

F: In your stories sometimes religious ritual seems to box in people and makes them lose what religion is, while at other times ritual is the means by which they can have that joy of which you speak.

S: I will tell you this, if the ritual is done with the feeling of joy, if it is connected with joy, if it is connected with a gay way of life, it's good; if not, it becomes nothing but a burden or something for scholars or religious scholars to debate about.

F: So in a story like "Short Friday," which is one of my favorites, the ritual there is what gives the characters' life its joy.

S: Yes and there is joy in them although they die in the end, but this Thursday and Friday, the Sabbath, everything is connected with joy and love. By the way the Hasidists were not ascetics. I mean they were not sex maniacs, but just the same they believed in marriage and love and so on.

F: Even sexuality becomes a part of the ritual and joy, a part of God.

S: Absolutely. This is true not only for Hasidism but for the Cabalists. The Cabalist believes that not only bodies have sexual intercourse but souls too. They spoke about sexual copulation in heaven. The Cabala is full of it. I write about these things in my new essay which is called "A Little Boy in Search of God."

F: One of the philosophers whom you studied in your youth was Spinoza.

S: Well I was interested in Spinoza even before I studied him because I heard my father say that there was a heretic called Spinoza who believed that God is the world and the world is God. And even though what he believed was also what the Cabalist believes, still there was a great difference. The Cabalists believe that it is true that God has created the world and the world is a part of God, but for them God was an entity with will, with mercy, with great possibilities, with great goodness and beauty, while for Spinoza God and Nature were the same thing. In other words Spinoza thought that there was an indifferent kind of God, a God who did not care; let the poor die, let one animal devour the other, one person the other. Spinoza's morality was built on a kind of agreement of where I say I don't kill you and you don't kill me. We know that these kinds of agreements are never kept. The strong one doesn't want to make such an agreement. The wolf does not want to make an agreement with the sheep.

He wants to eat the sheep. So while both are pantheists, Spinoza and the Cabalist, Spinoza's kind of pantheism is a cruel pantheism and a hopeless pantheism. He says we should love God with an intellectual love. In other words don't ask any favors from Him, don't ask Him to be good, but we have to love Him just because we admire Him. The Cabalists believe that God is basically good and all our sufferings are nothing more than a small incident in eternal life. So there is a great difference. Just the same I was interested in Spinoza and when I read him I saw in Spinoza the Cabalist, not the materialist. And I still think that in spite of Spinoza's insistence that God is nothing but a kind of a machine, a Cosmic machine, there's more to it than he knew himself.

F: It has been suggested that your story "The Spinoza of Market Street" is your final rejection of Spinoza's thought.

S: It's not that I reject Spinoza. According to Spinoza the emotions were never good. Spinoza did not believe in emotions. As a matter of fact Spinoza believed people who loved to be insane. He considered all emotions, if they were a little exaggerated, a little too great, as insanity. I don't agree with him. I think that without emotions a human being would be less than a piece of wood. To me the emotions are of great importance. As a matter of fact I believe like Schopenhauer that the emotions are the very essence of a human being and the intellect is nothing but a servant of the emotions. So in this story I speak about a man who was a complete Spinozist, but then in his old age he acted according to his emotions and he found some happiness, while for many years he had nothing but the study of Spinoza.

F: The last time I was here I said that Herman Broder in *Enemies: A Love Story* seems to be a twentieth century Yasha in the *Magician of Lubin,* and you pointed out that there was a significant difference, that Yasha is a magician. Why is being a magician so important?

S: Yasha was an artist. What I call a magician is an artist. Yasha was a creative person himself so there was more joy in Yasha than in Herman.

F: Oftentimes you write of devils and imps as magicians, as jugglers, as tricksters.

S: Surely, the artist is beset by more temptations because he is not only morally tempted, but he is also tempted in his art. No matter how many good books you wrote, when you sit down to write a new book there is always the danger of writing something bad. The artist lives always between success or failure, between great success and dire failure. He can stumble more often than any other human being.

F: Right now in your life you are in the midst of great success.

S: I don't consider myself a success. Far from it. I think that a human being who really knows what great a gift free will is and how little he has used it, feels that he has failed. But for the little I have succeeded, for this I am grateful. But I know how much I have failed, how much more and better I could have done if I had made a greater effort. But I am still making that effort.

F: Sometimes I wonder how great a goal you have to set for yourself.

S: I think that a human being, a real artist, should set for himself the greatest goal. If you set for yourself a small goal you have already failed by the very fact that your goal is so small. Run as far as you can or at least try to. Never get tired. Never fall into despair. If you fail, begin again. This is what life is.

F: Oftentimes you write of God, too, as a great magician of the universe.

S: Well I will say that to me God is an artist. I say that His attribute is creativity. Creativity is also the attribute of the artist. So we can call Him the great artist, the almighty artist, or something like this. These are all parables. I mean we don't know really; it's all human, human ideas.

F: God is the artist of the world, and in creating the world He had to leave it. There's a silence there.

S: This is true about artists too. The artist cannot completely give himself in his art as some artists would like to. But they cannot. If the artist does not limit himself, does not dim his light, he cannot create. He becomes hysteric and he begins to outpour and becomes in a way boring. So I would say in every process of creation the writer has to repeat in a small way what God did in a big way, to give only part of himself, to create a vacuum. It's just the same, the same process, because what we say about God is actually what we know about ourselves. We don't know really what God is doing. The Cabalists, none of them were in heaven, you know. It's all man-made.

F: In a sense then, the artist fills the void left by the silence of God.

S: Yes, he fills it, and while he creates, he himself must create this kind of a void. And you know that many people complain to the artist the way we all complain to God. They say why did you make this character, why didn't you create a good ending instead of a bad ending, why didn't you elaborate, and so on. All these questions are asked because we don't realize that the artist has often to limit.

F: We ask the artist for answers that he cannot give without ruining his creation.

S: He really cannot give. They would like, for example, the artist to be psychologically sound, sociologically sound, very much interesting, and at the same time to be a scientist. They would like him to do more than he should do. If he did do all these things, he wouldn't be an artist. He would spoil his own creation.

F: Just as God cannot give us the answers even though, like Job, we ask the questions.

S: If He would give the answers, we say that creation would disappear, and the same thing would happen if the artist would go on and do all the things which the critics or the readers would like him to do. He would stop being an artist.

F: In the story "Pigeons" from *A Friend of Kafka* there is an old professor who has a revelation, and his revelation is that evil is the motivating principle of those who make history. He says, "their aim remains the same—to perpetrate evil, cause pain, shed blood."

S: Surely history was always evil. For whom are all these monuments? For killers, for murderers.

F: The modern devil and demon are men?

S: Sure. He always was man. About real demons, if they exist, we know very little.

F: You once told me that the demon is almost unemployed nowadays.

S: Because men do his work. The writers and the pornographers and the politicians do exactly what the demons used to do in the olden times.

F: But you do not feel that evil really has triumphed over everything. You do see goodness.

S: No, no. If evil would triumph over everything here again creation would cease, because if the link is broken God's experiment is gone. No, they have not triumphed. There are always good people. There are always those who destroy and those who build. It is only if humanity would give in completely to evil, which they did in Germany for a while, then they would . . . but then people fought Germany, they fought Hitler or Stalin.

F: The final story in this collection is "Something Is There." A rabbi who always withstood the Evil One begins to rebel against the Creator.

S: Yes, to rebel. This is what I mentioned about the protester. The great believer is also a great protester. As a matter of fact I am dreaming about writing a book which I want to call the True Protester, not the true protestant, but the true protester.

F: The rabbi, this protester, asks the coal-dealer, "Do you believe in God?" and the coal-dealer answers the way you did earlier. He says, "How do I know. I was never in heaven. Something is there. Who made the world?" And when the rabbi dies, he says, "Something is there."

S: He also says something is there. He repeats these words. Yes.

F: I guess the question is "What?"

S: What is there, which we don't know.

F: And we cannot answer that.

S: But something is there. He sees the moon!

F: And that somehow is enough. Except that there is that terrifying feeling sometimes in your stories that perhaps the something that is there is a Hitler.

S: I will tell you, evil maybe does not reach so far. Although according to the Cabala it reaches almost to the very top. There is an element of evil almost near to God. Except that in the last sense God is still stronger. In other words there is an opposition against God which is almost as strong as God Himself. God Himself must have an antithesis really to exist.

Isaac Bashevis Singer: "I Walk on Mysteries"
Kenneth Turan/1976

From *The Washington Post* (28 December 1976), C1, C3. Reprinted by permission © 1976 The Washington Post.

Let Isaac Bashevis Singer tell you a story.

"I have a Yiddish typewriter which is very capricious and highly critical," he says, partly whimsical, mostly serious. "If this typewriter doesn't like a story, it refuses to work. I don't go to a man to correct it since I know if I get a good idea the machine will make peace with me again. I don't believe my own words saying this, but I've had the experience so many times that I'm really astonished. But the typewriter is 42 years old. It should have some literary experience, it should have a mind of its own."

Isaac B. Singer is a pre-eminent teller of literary tales, a birdlike man with sparse, wispy white hair and nervous hands which fold and refold almost of themselves as he talks. His dark blue suit enhances the gravity of 72 years, but there is something in his manner, a bite, a sharpness, which says this man is hardly as innocent as he looks. But if you look closely at the arresting, demanding eyes, the sharp lines of his face, he doesn't look innocent any more, but impish, an aging Puck. He is not always what he seems.

Though the Yiddish language's only world-class author, called simply "the greatest writer of today" by Rebecca West, lauded by fellow writers as diverse as Kenneth Rexroth and Susan Sontag, and nominated for a Nobel Prize by Edmund Wilson, Singer's work runs strongly against the grain of both the Yiddish and modern novel. Associated with the small communities of Eastern Europe, he has lived in New York for more years than in his native Poland. Two-time winner of the National Book Award, he seems to strongly prefer children as an audience. And he never quite believes that he is indeed well-known.

"I don't even think that I am famous now, but if you say so, who am I to say no," he comments in his lilting, accented English, punctuated by an elegant shrug. "Today, to be famous, you have to be a Frank Sinatra."

In 50 years of writing, Singer has produced an enormous body of work, a body whose exact dimensions are unknown since healthy chunks of it remain untranslated. He has done everything from memoirs to journalism to children's books, but his world emerges most clearly in novels like *The Slave, Satan In Goray* and *The Magician of Lublin* as well as in short story collections like *Gimpel the Fool.*

Singer's works, set in an era of European Jewry that ended in the concentration camps, are paradoxical: at once concrete and fantastic, supernatural and down-to-earth. "I demand from a story to be both mystical and real at the same time," he says. "Even if I write miracles, these miracles are embedded in reality."

He writes with equal deftness and plausibility of demons and dybbuks, of surly peasants and agonized rabbis, of lust and impotence, of death, starvation and ecstasy. "In my stories," he has written, "it is just one step from the study house to sexuality and back again," and his full-bodied treatment of sex has in fact drawn cheers from the likes of Henry Miller. Critic Irving Buchen calls him "a conservative sensationalist" and writes that "his fictional world is so jammed with the dead that there does not appear to be any room for the living."

Yet the living in his books are so illuminated by the simple crystal purity of Singer's style that he can create character with but a single sentence, as in: "He was a short, broad-shouldered man; he looked as if he had been sawed in half and glued together again." He is a writer at ease with wonder, a writer who feels "literature without passion is like bread without flour."

The paradox continues on a personal level, for Singer describes himself as both "a skeptic and a mystic." Though a constant, inveterate questioner, he feels "the very fact that I exist is a mystery to me. I may not believe what is written in the holy books, but I feel the mysteries of creation are right near me. I walk on mysteries."

And though he considers himself religious, if not observant, he admits that "for the Orthodox Jews I am a nonbeliever. I like to write about sex and love, which is not kosher to the Orthodox people. I believe in God but I don't believe that God wants man to run away completely from pleasure. If he has created men and women with a great desire to love and be loved, there must be something in it, it cannot be all bad. Love and sex are the things which give life some value, some zest. Miserable as flesh and blood is, it is still the best you can get."

Despite this appeal for passion, Isaac Singer is a gentle man, a vegetarian for the past 14 years because "the truth is, all my life I felt terribly guilty about eating meat. I felt I can't speak of decency, mercy and all these nice things while treating animals that way. People always ask me, 'How do you get protein?' and I say, 'Who says one needs protein? That's only in the books.' "

For similar reasons, Singer has given up the uncaged parakeets he used to keep as pets. "They gave me a lot of joy, but they gave me also so much trouble," he says. "I suffered so much when they suffered, when they got sick, got lost or fell down, that in a way I am happy I don't have them anymore."

If Singer thus can be tolerant and gentle, he also can be waspish and uncompromising when he chooses, and when he turns to the subject of modern fiction, he so chooses with a vengeance.

"I don't see great writers in this century," he says, seemingly weary with the effort of looking. Stylists like Nabokov do not excite him, and neither do current Americans like Philip Roth and E. L. Doctorow. "The modern writer is so eager to be profound, to be symbolic, to show off his greatness, that the reader cannot enjoy him anymore. Never before in the history of literature have the readers been so fooled, so hypnotized against their will, to call mediocrity greatness. The net result is that we have many so-called celebrities, but there is nothing to celebrate."

So when Singer wants to read a good book, he goes back to the likes of Tolstoy and Dostoevsky, the people he calls "the masters," the people in whose footsteps he is still anxious to follow. "The masters were all great storytellers, and they wrote in a very clear way, they tried their best to be clear," he explains. "Language is made to communicate, it has to make itself understood, not become a mystery which has to be explained by other language.

"Look at the Bible. The Bible is not obscure, it is wonderfully clear. Yet I'm sure that when Moses came down from Mt. Sinai, the intellectuals of his time said, 'For this he had to go up to Heaven? Couldn't he have brought us something more profound?' But Heaven is not interested in phony statements," and neither, obviously, is Singer.

Convinced that whatever popularity he will admit to results from his firm adherence to the tradition of storytelling—"I don't hide behind puzzles, riddles, symbols which mean nothing. And readers who get tired of all these obscurities turn to me because at least they know what I am talking about"—Singer himself has turned a great deal to writing books for children because they at least appreciate what he has to give.

"Children are my best readers, I only wish adults should behave in the same way," he says, slyly. "A child loves a story, you cannot give to a child a book without a story. He is an independent reader, he is not influenced by reviews because children do not read reviews. He is not influenced by authorities, you can tell a child God Almighty himself wrote a book and if the child does not like it he will reject it. Where do you get among adults such readers nowadays?"

The closest Singer comes to such grown-up fans are the readers of the *Daily Forward,* New York's Yiddish-language newspaper, where all his novels except one have been serialized before publication. Though his sexual frankness and deviance from the language's sentimental tradition have put Singer well outside the mainstream of Yiddish literature—"They looked at me really as a strange kind of plant, until today they don't know what to do with me"—his *Forward* readers are tenaciously devoted.

"The Yiddish paper is so thin, there isn't much to read there, so I have many readers," he says, "and woe is to me if I make a mistake, like locating a Warsaw street in the wrong place. Once I had someone saying *Yizkor* (a prayer for the dead) on *Rosh Hashonah,* and the next day sacks of letters came. My readers are all old people, some of them have trouble with their eyes, but old people sometimes have sharp minds. Believe me, it is more difficult to fool a reader of the *Forward* than readers of *The* (New York) *Times.*"

Though he collaborates on translation to such an extent that translations turn into rewrites, leaving his English output three to four years behind the times, Singer still writes everything out in Yiddish, in longhand, generally on a piece of hard cardboard that "I put on my knee and scribble on." He uses college examination blue books, but since Yiddish is written from right to left he finds the red margins are always getting in the way.

There is, obviously, nothing of the cocktail party litterateur about Singer. In many ways, he is typical of many elderly Jewish residents of New York, fearful of walking the streets of his Upper West Side neighborhood at night and spending half the year in Miami Beach, were he lives in the no doubt archetypal Surfside Towers. Singer gets more work done in Miami than in New York, where "my main job is answering telephones." He is not kidding, as the constant ringing testifies.

"I write between one phone call and another," he says, adding in response to a surprised look, "This is not a joke. I don't feel for a moment the interruptions did me any damage. Sometimes it helps me; while I am on the telephone I may get an idea how to continue. Not all writers can do this."

In addition to all his other singularities, Singer is also half of one of the few novelist brother teams in literary history. His elder brother, I. J. Singer, was the author of *The Brothers Ashkenazie, Yoshe Kalb* and other novels, and was, in the younger brother's own words, Singer's "master and teacher." He introduced Singer to secular literature, giving him a Yiddish translation of *Crime and Punishment* when he was 10, and he was also the first to break with the family's Orthodox religious tradition.

Although he has been described as the descendant of generations of rabbis, Singer, born in a small settlement on the outskirts of Warsaw, shrugs that off by saying, "like every Englishman has a lord in his family, so has every Jew a rabbi."

As a child, he writes, "I suffered deep crises, was subject to hallucinations. My dreams were filled with demons, ghosts, devils, corpses. Sometimes before falling asleep I saw shapes. They danced around my bed, hovered in the air."

His father became a rabbi in a poor section of Warsaw, and the situations that were brought to him for resolution, the massive jumble of human experience which Singer witnessed and warmly recorded in his memoir, *In My Father's Court,* led to the spirit of acceptance of the bizarre and inexplicable which pervades his books. "Things happen in life," he writes, "so fantastic that no imagination could have invented them."

Singer started out as a proofreader—"the kitchen of literature," he calls it—and wrote his first stories in 1926. His first novel, *Satan In Goray*, was published in 1935, the same year Singer followed his older brother to New York. "I foresaw there will be nothing good in Poland," he remembers. "A lot of people said about Hitler, 'It's only talk,' but I know that the evil ones are not satisfied with talk. They are more energetic, they want to act. The good ones are the talkers."

His first years in the new land were distinctly unpromising, almost catastrophic: "Since I didn't know English I felt very bad. I had a feeling Yiddish is going to last here only a few years, I was afraid I'd be a writer who has written only one book." He felt, he has said elsewhere, like he was in a cemetery, and seven years went by before he was able to write again.

"I tried," he says of the lean years, "but somehow nothing came out. I wanted to write immediately a novel about America, about the life of an immigrant, his disappointments, but even this I couldn't do. When you are in a strange environment . . ." He shrugs. "Only dilettantes go to Spain for four weeks and come back with a novel about Spain. The net result is that to this day I only write about Yiddish-speaking people, either in Poland or the United States. I never venture out of these limits. If I would be the last man to speak Yiddish I would still write in this language. I know this language best."

Writing in Yiddish for a Yiddish-speaking audience, Singer did not really register on the American literary consciousness until Saul Bellow's translation of "Gimpel The Fool" appeared in the *Partisan Review* in 1953. Nearly 50 years old, he suddenly found himself discovered as a new figure on the fiction scene.

How has Singer taken to the kudos attached to his name in recent years? "I would say I take it like a man," he says, smiling. "I am not in despair, really, but neither am I rejoicing about it." In fact, in line with his traditionalistic view of literature, Singer leans toward feeling that time spent out of the sun is the way it ought to be.

"I had many years of complete privacy and they didn't do me any damage," he says wryly. "I never became bitter. I understood that when a young man begins to write the whole world is not going to embrace him immediately as they do in this country. Here when a young man writes two stories which make sense they celebrate him already as a genius. A young man sometimes loses his head, he really thinks he's God's gift to humanity."

All this strikes Isaac Bashevis Singer as sort of hopelessly droll, a game he is thankfully unable to play. "A writer who is famous in later years takes it with a grain of salt. A person who is famous at 26, he's forgotten at 36. One is not famous forever."

I. B. Singer, Storyteller

Laurie Colwin/1978

From *The New York Times Book Review* (23 July 1978), 1,
23–24. Copyright ©1978 by The New York Times Company.
Reprinted by permission of Laurie Colwin and The New York
Times Company.

Q: Readers of all ages, nations, backgrounds and creeds read and
love your books. Can you explain why you are so popular? What do
you think are the elements that make it possible for everyone to
appreciate what you write?

A: First of all, I don't think I'm so popular. All I would say is that, in
the languages into which I am translated, there are people who are
interested. A writer, like a woman, never knows why people like him
or why people dislike him. We never know.

Q: Why don't you take a guess?

A: The guess is that there is always a kinship between souls. Souls
are either close to one another or far from one another. There are
people who, when they read me, they like what I say. And there's
nothing else I can tell you. I wouldn't say Jewish people, because I'm
translated into Japanese. The Japanese translate everything I write,
immediately. They even publish me in English, with Japanese notes.
And how could I explain why some Japanese in Yokohama will like
to read what I write? Just as I would enjoy a Japanese writer, a
Japanese man may enjoy a Yiddish writer.

Q: What sort of things would draw you to a Japanese writer?

A: I will tell you. I know nothing about the Japanese—really
nothing. And, let's say, I read two Japanese books. I will say one is a
good book and one is a bad book. How do I know, since I haven't
lived in Japan? It seems that to enjoy a book you don't really have to
go there and to know the land and the people, because human
beings, although they are different, also have many things in common. And through this you get a notion which writer says the truth
and which writer is fabricating.

How does it come that we read the Bible, which was written, parts of it, 3,000 years ago, and we understand the story of Joseph and the other stories? It seems that we are very much today basically as we were 3,000 years ago, and we are able to understand what another human being does.

I even suspect that if books are written on another planet somewhere in the universe, and if someone would make a translation, a reader would understand what is good and what is bad. But this is already too far-fetched. Unless, one day, you would bring me a translation from the planet Mars, then we will see.

Q: You must have some notion of what you're doing that is this attractive. There must be some quality. You have been mentioned for a Nobel Prize.

A: Are you trying to convince me that I'm a big shot?

Q: You are a big shot. Now, tell me why you are.

A: I will tell you, Laurie: When I sit down to write a story. I'm not saying to myself I'm going to write a Jewish story. Just like when a Frenchman builds a house in France. He doesn't say he's going to build a French house. He's going to build a house for his wife and children, a convenient house. Since it's built in France, it comes out French.

When I sit down to write a story, I will write the kind of stories which I write. It's true that since I know the Jewish people best and since I know the Yiddish language best, so my heroes, the people of my stories, are always Jewish and speak Yiddish. I am at home with these people. But just the same, I'm not just writing about them because they speak Yiddish and are Jewish. I'm interested in the same things you are interested in and the Japanese are interested in: in love, and in treachery and in hopes and in disappointments.

Q: Do you very feel that, like a photographer, you're preserving the last part of a vanished culture?

A: People tell me this, and while they tell me this I have a moment of feeling, yes, it is so. But I never sit down to write with this idea. I wouldn't be a writer if I would sit down to preserve the Yiddish language, or life in Poland, or make a better world or bring peace. I don't have all these illusions.

I know that my story will not do anything else but entertain a reader for half an hour. And this is enough for me. The word entertainment has become, lately, a very bad word. I call it the 13 letter word which writers are afraid to use, because the word entertainer means for them a cheap grade of writing. But it isn't so.

The great writers of the 19th century—Tolstoy and Dostoyevsky and Gogol and Dickens—were great entertainers. And Balzac. They wrote a novel or a story so that there was some suspense in it. When you began to read it, you wanted to know what would happen next. And they also published, some of them, their stories in magazines and in newspapers, where it was written; "It continues next week." And the reader had to be interested to read the continuation.

Q: A serial.

A: A serial, yes.

Q: You still do that in *The Forward,* don't you?

A: I still do it in *The Forward,* and I know whatever I write is immediately read. I would say, at least by 15,000 or 20,000 people, because we still have about 40,000 readers. And, since *The Forward* is a small newspaper, those who read it read everything in it, even the advertisements.

So I'm still connected with the reader. And these readers also don't read my story because they are Jewish, because Jewishness is not something new for them. They have been Jews all their life. They judge a writer from the point of view: Is he interesting or not interesting? Also, although some of them are ignorant people and primitive people, they know that a writer's not going to redeem the world, as some of the young writers think.

So, in other words, I'm before everything else a writer, not just Jewish, and I'm not doing it with some illusion that I'm going to do great things. I just feel that I have to tell a story.

I have said this a few times before, and I can repeat it: I need three conditions to write a story. One condition is I have to have a plot. I don't believe that you can write a story without a plan—in other words, just sit down and write a slice of life hoping against hope that it will come out right. It happens once in a while, but most of the time if you don't have a plan there won't be a story.

The second condition is: I must have a desire to write the story—or a passion to write it. I must get up with an appetite to do this story.

And the third condition: I must have the illusion that I am the only one who can write such a story. Since I know the Yiddish writers, more or less, so I know what they could do and what I can do.

If I have these three conditions, I will sit down and do the work without worrying too much whether it is good for the Jews or bad for the Jews; whether it will redeem humanity immediately or whether it may take a few weeks until humanity is redeemed. I do the story, and I leave the rest to the reader, or to the critics—let them draw their own conclusions. Sometimes they find in it something.

Once I wrote a book called *The Magician of Lublin*. The hero repents at the end and hardens himself against the temptation of running after women. So once a psychoanalyst called me up, and he said: "I was delighted to see how you made your hero go back to his mother's womb." This had never occurred to me. But then I said to myself: He is just as good a reader as anybody else, and if he sees this, it's just as good.

In other words, once you have written a story, it's not your private property anymore. And if someone wants to find in it sociological truths or psychological truths, he's entitled to do it. In my case, all I want is to write a story.

Q: How do you go about making up a plot? Do you know the steps your mind takes?

A: No, I'm not making up a plot. The plot comes to me.

Q: How does it come to you? Are you walking around the street? Are you sitting looking out the window?

A: No. No. No.

Q: Does it just come like a flash?

A: I would say: if something happens to me. And things happen—I'm alive, I am with people, I also have memory. I've had affairs in my life and women and all kinds of things. And I think about these things. Suddenly, I say, here is a story. In other words, I don't wake up in the morning and go out into the street to make a plot. This never happens.

Q: So, in other words, your mind is like a soup kettle. And you keep stirring it. And suddenly the ladle comes up and there's carrots and cabbage.

A: Listen, we are doing the same thing. We think about things. You think about what happened to you, and I think about what happened to me. All kinds of things. And suddenly here is a plot for a story.

Q: What kind of things do you like to read?

A: I love to read a story with real suspense. I mean, not that there should be only suspense—I don't read detective stories—but if it has a literary value and it has suspense. I often go back to the writers of the 19th century. I'm ashamed to tell you.

Q: Why?

A: Why should I read old books?

Q: Everyone does that. What interests you? Love? Treachery? Sex?

A: Yes. Love and sex more than anything else.

Q: Treachery is second?

A: If there's love, there is treachery. And then, also, crime interests me. When I was a boy of 12 years old *Crime and Punishment* came out in Yiddish, and I began to read it. A large book—in Yiddish it's twice as large as in English—and I was fascinated. I couldn't put it away. And I must tell you, a boy of 12 years there in Warsaw, I knew nothing of the world except what I studied in school, but I suddenly felt: Here is a great work. I remember that in one case, when Raskolnikov speaks to the district attorney, there is a moment when Raskolnikov gets up to leave and then he sits down immediately. And I said to myself, this is wonderful. As if he would say, "I'm finished with the whole business," and then the sitting down—it pleased me so much.

So, if a boy of 12 years, in Warsaw, who had no experience in life could understand, more or less, *Crime and Punishment,* there is really no reason why the Japanese and the Turks should not understand what you write or what I write. So, actually, the writer should never be afraid that he is not going to be understood. Those writers who are afraid of that really underestimate the reader. The reader is—I assume so—an intelligent person; he knows about life and love and crime and everything, just as much as I and in some cases much more than I. So, I really don't worry that if I'm going to be translated one day into Chinese that no one will understand what a Hassid is and what a rabbi is. They will understand it very well. If they have learned in the last few years how to build machine guns and airplanes, they will also understand what I have to say. What I worry about is if what I do is good enough to be translated or to be read, and I work accordingly.

Q: Do you think that having that stable *Forward* audience—and you're probably the last writer who has that kind of audience—makes a difference to a writer?

A: I think it has good sides and bad sides. The bad sides are that the writer sometimes is bound to repeat himself. Because since I write, so to say, from week to week and from day to day, I don't see the manuscript before my eyes, and sometimes I begin a novel without really knowing how it will end. So, I'm bound to repeat myself and to make mistakes.

The good sides are that you don't speak to the wall, you speak to a reader. My readers—since I write mostly about Warsaw and Poland—also come from Warsaw and Poland. They have lived there. Woe is to me if I make a mistake. I once made a mistake and said that the prayer for the dead was recited in the synagogue on the second day of *Rosh ha-Shanah*. It was a mistake because there is no such thing. It's every holiday, yes, but not on *Rosh ha-Shanah*. So I got hundreds of letters. The letter carrier couldn't believe what's going on here. And every letter began with the same thing: How could a man like you make such a mistake?

Also, now, if I would make a mistake about a street, I would get these letters. So, in other words, I cannot be a solipsist like some of these writers who really feel that no one exists except themselves. I know that the world exists. It's not completely a dream. So this is a good thing.

Of course, whatever I write, there is always opposition if I write about sex. I remember that once I wrote a story—this is many years ago—and in the story there was a little bit of sex, and the sex was expressed in the words: " . . . and she did his will." That's all I said. So there came an angry letter from a man saying: "How do you dare to say such things? We have daughters and these daughters read this sometimes."

But it's a good thing to have an audience before yourself, just like an actor who is playing and the audience is there.

Q: You once said that an army of Kafkas was killing literature. What do you mean by that?

A: Yes, yes, I will tell you. Avant-garde writers like Kafka and Joyce say to themselves: I don't care for the reader or for the critic or for anybody. I am going to say what I want. I have to please myself and nobody else.

I assume this is what they say. I wasn't there to listen to them, but this is more or less how they think. To me, Kafka was made of the material of genius. But just the same, he did things which a writer who writes for people, who has the audience before his eyes, would not do.

Let's say, if a writer imitates Tolstoy—and I think that Solzhenitsyn tries to write like Tolstoy—there is no misfortune, because, if he has talent and if he tries to write like Tolstoy and even if it doesn't come out 100 percent, it's still good. But if you try to imitate Kafka, Joyce, and you don't have their talent, it will come out completely bad. Because only a great talent can afford to say: I'm speaking only to myself.

Q: If you were a Ph. D. candidate and you had to do your thesis on Isaac Singer, what would your topic be?

A: I would do what all the students do. I would read the author's books and I would try to find what they call the central idea.

Q: What would the central idea be in the work of I. B. Singer?

A: I would say that the idea behind everything is that one should not belittle any emotion. The philosophers all belittle the emotions— especially a man like Spinoza, who considered all emotions as evil. I have convinced myself that everything that goes through our minds, no matter how trivial, no matter how silly, and no matter how terrible sometimes, is of some value. In other words, take away the emotions from a human being, and no matter how much logic he will have, he will be a vegetable. The emotions and man are the same. And I'm interested, especially, in the emotions that become passions.

Spinoza says in his *Ethics* that everything can become passion, and I know that this is true. There is nothing that cannot become a passion. Especially if they are connected either with sex or with the supernatural—and I would say for me sex and the supernatural go very much together. I feel that the desire of one human being for another is not only a desire of the body but also of the soul. The two—a man and a woman, or two men, or two women—when they embrace and they say they cannot live one without the other, and they fall one upon the other with a madness, that this is not just an act of the flesh, it's more than the flesh.

Q: So, in other words, your topic would be emotion and excess in the works of Isaac Bashevis Singer?

A: Yes, and if I would be the dean I would give you the Ph. D. right this minute.

Isaac Bashevis Singer:
Nobel Prize-Winning Novelist

Donald R. Noble/1978

From *Horizon* (December 1978), 19–22. Reprinted by permission of Donald R. Noble.

The fame he never chased has at last caught up with Isaac Bashevis Singer. "I never wrote for prizes" he says. But on October 5, Singer was awarded the Nobel Prize for literature for, as the committee put it, "his impassioned narrative art which, with roots in Polish-Jewish cultural tradition, brings universal human conditions to life."

Singer has spent more than fifty years writing of a culture that no longer exists in a language that is dying. Had he been seeking fame all these years it is inconceivable that he would have continued to create his fictional world of the Polish *shtetl* in Yiddish when he has long been fluent in English. And it is inconceivable that he would wait until he was forty-six-years-old to have his first works translated into English and thus made available to a world that has come to love them.

So, when his wife told him, as they were about to walk to breakfast from their condominium north of Miami, that friends were calling to congratulate him, the seventy-four-year-old Singer replied: "It must be some kind of a mistake, or a joke," and, "in any case, let's eat breakfast. We have to eat. What do you think—you stop eating because of happiness?" At the coffeehouse they were greeted by a flock of reporters who had, of course, known about the prize before Singer himself.

It was a surprise to lots of people besides Singer; the Swedish Academy is notorious for passing over deserving writers—Joyce, James, Nabokov, Auden, and Malraux, to name a few—and awarding the prize to Scandinavian novelists and obscure third-world poets.

Besides all this, the academy had given the prize to Saul Bellow, another American Jewish writer, in 1976. The chances for Singer seemed slim. It may be that, as sometimes happens in the College of

Cardinals, the selection committee could have been deadlocked. If such was the case, their choice of Singer was an inspired one. Singer has produced twenty-nine volumes of work—eight novels, seven volumes of stories, three volumes of autobiography, and eleven children's books. He has achieved a global reputation, and is widely translated, even into Japanese. And, he is a writer with a devoted following, well deserved since he has been a devoted writer.

The wonder of it is that he became a writer at all. Born on July 14, 1904, in Radzymin, Poland, an area then governed by the czar of Russia, Singer was the son of a rabbi and the grandson of a rabbi. There was never any question in his father's mind about his vocation. Singer was raised for the rabbinate as he had been born to it and was educated in a seminary.

But just as Stephen Crane listened to the Civil War veterans of his hometown and the young Faulkner soaked up the stories of the hunters, farmers, and Negroes of Mississippi, Isaac Bashevis Singer lived in a world of stories in his father's house in Warsaw, stories of innocent girls from the ghetto abducted into slavery "and taken to Buenos Aires. There for a while they lived with unclean men, and then a dangerous worm would get into their blood and their flesh would begin to decay. . . . These tales were fascinating and horrible at the same time. Strange things were happening in the world. There were secrets, not only in heaven above, but also here on earth. I was consumed by the desire to grow up quickly and to learn all the secrets of heaven and earth from which young boys were barred."

Singer did grow up, to learn probably as many of the secrets of life as anyone is likely to and to write of them about as well as anyone has.

Singer's older brother, Israel Joshua Singer, set the example and led Isaac into the world of Warsaw journalism and belles lettres. Although I. J. Singer is now largely unread, his *The Brothers Ashkenazi* and *Yoshe Kalb* are distinguished novels that will one day be "rediscovered." They served, in any case, as an inspiration to I. B. Singer.

Rabbi Singer was himself a prolific writer. Singer writes in his warm memoir of his childhood, *In My Father's Court,* "No matter how little my father earned, he saved money to publish his books. He used to say 'a religious book is a permanent testament.'" But, to the rabbi, Jewish secular writing was at least suspect, probably heretical.

Some of Singer's Yiddish readers express similar feelings of discomfort. Although they admire the richness of the prose in the original Yiddish, they read, as Irving Howe puts it, "with pleasure and anxiety," for Singer can have a difficult moral outlook.

Singer is accused of pessimism, but he insists it is a qualified pessimism. Recently he said, "I am pessimistic but I am also full of joy. I was told that Schopenhauer was streaming with the joy of life. A pessimist is a pessimist because he would have liked life to be better than it is. In other words, he loves life. In an interview with Paul Rosenblatt and Gene Koppel, Singer elaborated: "I am a pessimist as far as our small world and our businesses are concerned, but I am not a pessimist as far as the universe is concerned. I am sure that the creator of the universe had a plan in it and that this plan was not a vicious plan. . . . I believe in a good God, not a malicious God. But a good God can also make a lot of trouble to little beings who don't understand his design. I have two parakeets. They fly around free. They are not locked up in a cage. But if I want to move from one apartment to another and it's winter, I have to put them into a cage and cover the cage in the middle of the day so that they don't catch a cold. But these parakeets don't know it. They see only cruelty. Suddenly I put them into a prison and I covered them. In the middle of the day I made darkness. From their point of view I am doing cruel things. . . ."

No, Singer is not a pessimist, but many of his stories do have an undeniable darkness about them, especially if they are told from the point of view of a dybbuk, imp, demon, or other of Satan's minions, and Singer, gentle, pacific little man that he is, is the master of the demonic point-of-view.

Once an imp, an agent of Satan, discovers the whereabouts of a vain, lustful, or otherwise vulnerable human, all hell breaks loose. The devil narrator of "The Mirror" makes a deal with a beautiful and bored young wife who dreams of being loved by a handsome stranger. The imp promises an assignation with Satan himself. She keeps her side of the bargain. As her reward she does meet Satan in hell, but not for pleasure; she is tortured for eternity. The imp tries to explain: "Is there a God? Is he all merciful? Will Zirel ever find salvation? Or is creation a snake? Is he all primeval crawling with evil? How can I tell? I'm still a minor devil. Imps seldom get promoted."

Singer is a strict moralist in his way. He believes in right and wrong. "It is a great tragedy that children are not taught in the school what is bad and what is good." Children should know what is forbidden and what is allowed. They would be safer from Singer's demons if they had some training in morals.

But it is not the fiction writer's job to moralize. He should just give the facts without accompanying commentary. To Singer, "a fiction writer is a reporter of a higher kind." Singer is a storyteller with no desire to be a spiritual leader.

Singer, who is so adamantly opposed to killing that he is a vegetarian, has strong feelings about human guilt and responsibility: "There is a saying in the Talmud, that a human being is always guilty if he does some damage. If an ox steps on an insect and destroys it, the ox is certainly innocent, but man having free choice and responsibility cannot just do damage because someone told him to do it."

Although he has never written about it directly, the holocaust, the consummate immorality, informs his work in subtle and mysterious ways. Singer writes of the people of the shtetl, the little rural Jewish villages in Poland and Russia, now made familiar to Americans through Singer's and Sholem Aleichem's stories and the play made from them, *Fiddler on the Roof,* and from the stories of Sholem Asch. It may well be that Singer's stories gain a certain power from what is not in them. The reader knows that Singer's world no longer exists because some madmen destroyed it. The reader knows, as the characters in the stories do not, how it will, in fact, turn out. We know not only that it is no more, but how it ended, grotesquely and abruptly ended.

But Singer is not a time-bound historian. In fact, one might call his fiction antihistorical. He has achieved what Edgar Allan Poe sought, escape from history. To the right-thinking Jew, time is of no importance. True, the characters move through the calendar, from Sabbath to Sabbath, from Passover to Rosh Hashanah, but it is of no consequence. What does matter is The Promise, the coming of the Messiah. There is no past, no future, only the present waiting. Although the stories are rich in historical context, this is not what matters.

Singer will brook no criticism of that context, however. When asked if his shtetl world is imagined he says, "I was deeply immersed in Jewish life when I was in Poland, so I am not just imagining things. I am remembering things. I convey millions of facts."

These facts are, as all the world now knows, conveyed in Yiddish, the vernacular of Central European Jews. "The only language," Singer says, "that has never been spoken by people in authority." Singer has been asked countless times why, after he became fluent, he never switched over to English as his countrymen Joseph Conrad and Jerzy Kosinski and his Russian neighbor Vladimir Nabokov did with such great success. "Yiddish contains vitamins that other languages don't have," says Singer, defending his choice. He has had a host of translators, including Saul Bellow, whose translation of "Gimpel the Fool" for *The Partisan Review* helped put Singer on the literary map.

Because he writes exclusively in Yiddish, Singer rejects comparison with other contemporary American Jewish writers: Malamud, Henry Roth, Philip Roth, and especially Saul Bellow. The Yiddish makes all the difference, he says, and if that were not enough, they write of different subjects. Singer never writes of people born in America. He is a Yiddish writer; the others are Americans who happen to be Jews. He doesn't denigrate their work; he just feels they know too little about being Jewish. They often have no knowledge of history, no Hebrew, no Aramaic, no Talmud, no real sense of the Jewish experience. Of Philip Roth especially he says, "one dimension." There may be a dybbuk in *Portnoy's Complaint,* but it is Mrs. Portnoy.

Also, Yiddish, a dying language, he says playfully, fits his material better. "I like to write ghost stories and nothing fits a ghost better than a dying language. The deader the language the more alive the ghosts. Ghosts love Yiddish, and as far as I know, they all speak it. . . . I am sure that millions of Yiddish-speaking ghosts will rise from their graves one day and their first question will be, 'Is there any new book in Yiddish to read?' "

Singer takes his ghosts seriously. He has often said that they inhabit his apartment and hide things from him—manuscripts, books, glasses, even his checkbook. "But they give everything back. Once I thought they stole my citizenship papers and I was mad at them. I thought about an exorcist. Then after a year and a half, I found them." The ghosts in his fiction might be tougher to get rid of, for the reader that is. One is made constantly aware of the terrible dangers in everyday life. One step off the path, and one is lost. One adultery, and decades of fidelity go down the drain. One act of greed, and the reputation for honesty is gone. One step out of one's place, and one's place may be lost forever. It is a dangerous world but, Singer says, an exciting one.

Although Singer would no more be purposely modern than he would purposely put a symbol into his fiction, he can be unexpectedly relevant. "Yentl the Yeshiva Boy" is the story of a bright girl who hungers for an education. To get it she dresses in men's clothes and goes to a Yeshiva in a distant town. There she falls in love with a fellow student, and even marries a woman in order to remain near the man she loves. "She had the soul of a man and the body of a woman." Singer may one day be discovered by the feminist critics as well.

The best of all his stories, however, is "Gimpel the Fool." Gimpel, the town baker, has an unfaithful wife; he has seen it with his own eyes. But he chooses not to believe and to live in, as it were, a fool's paradise. The fool becomes the philosopher. "The longer I lived the more I understood that there were really no lies. Whatever doesn't really happen is dreamed at night. It happens to one if it doesn't happen to another, tomorrow if not today, or a century hence if not next year. What difference can it make?" This can be called taking the long view, and it could lead to nihilism; but in this story it leads to heaven.

Lately Singer has taken to writing more and more for children. They are, he feels, a better audience. Children are the best audience because they read for the story; they don't "identify." "Does a child identify himself with intrigues about some kings who lived in the fourteenth century and who had twenty concubines and seven elephants? It is the opposite. The child is delighted to read something which he doesn't know, which has nothing to do with him."

In his acceptance speech for the National Book Award, won for a children's book, he lists ten reasons why he prefers children as readers. Some are: they read books, not reviews; they ignore critics; they are not searching for identity; they don't read for psychotherapy; they hate psychology and sociology; they don't read Kafka or *Finnegan's Wake*; they still believe in God, the family, angels, devils, witches, goblins, logic, clarity, punctuation, and other such obsolete stuff; they love interesting stories, not commentary, guides, or footnotes; they yawn when bored; they don't expect their beloved writer to redeem humanity.

For the first time, Singer's work is providing the basis for a major motion picture. An international cast recently completed filming of *The Magician of Lublin* with Alan Arkin in the title role.

Now that Singer has won the Nobel Prize and the $160,000 that goes with it, more may be demanded of him, but he has no plans to change. "Everything will remain the same—same typewriter, same wife, same apartment, same telephone number, same language. I am thankful, of course, for the prize and thankful to God for each story, each idea, each word, each day."

Has the Nobel Prize Changed Singer's Life?
Tony Schwartz/1979

From *The New York Times,* 129 (17 October 1979), C21. Copyright © 1979 by The New York Times Company. Reprinted by permission.

"Oh, you want the Nobel prizewinner," the handyman at the apartment house in the West 80s, said. "Take the elevator at the next entrance."

Isaac Bashevis Singer met his visitor at the door and ushered him into the living room, where the late-afternoon sun streamed in through two large windows. The winner of the 1978 Nobel Prize in Literature seated himself in an overstuffed chair, his back to the windows, and put a pair of dark glasses over his blue, Rip Van Winkle eyes. "Too bright out," he explained.

In the mornings, when it is not so bright out and the sounds along Broadway are not so distracting, Mr. Singer carries his tiny, pie-crust table over to the window, sits down shortly after 9 o'clock with a small composition notebook and writes in longhand for the next two and a half hours—"three at the most"—right to left across the pages, in his native Yiddish. By then, he has already taken a brisk hourlong walk in the courtyard of his apartment building and shared a light breakfast with his wife, Alma, at the coffee shop across the street.

Winning the Nobel has not altered the essential rhythm of Mr. Singer's life, but inevitably, he says, there have been some changes. Before the prize, it had been his practice to speak with whomever phoned him, offering advice when it was solicited, and even making luncheon appointments with young writers and admirers eager to meet him. After the prize was announced, his phone rang so unceasingly that for a month he took a room in a hotel, where he wrote his acceptance speech, returning to the apartment only in the late evening to sleep.

And for the first time, Mr. Singer had his number removed from the phone book. His current number is unlisted. "I resented having to

do it," he said. "I don't think it is right for writers to isolate themselves from readers. But finally there was no choice."

Indeed, the biggest difference Mr. Singer has discovered is how
others view him. "Some people treat me now as if I'm God's gift to
humanity," he said. "It's silly. Many great writers didn't win the prize,
and they are still great writers. No prize changes a man's character.
I'm still one of the millions of miserable people who eat, think, hope,
worry, sleep, pray and die."

As for the $165,000 cash prize, Mr. Singer can now afford to pay
for a full-time secretary, and he intends to spend some money
publishing full-length Yiddish versions of some of his work that had
previously only been serialized in *The Jewish Daily Forward.* But
most of the money he has placed in six-month savings certificates. "I
don't go to the theater, or to fancy restaurants, and I don't dress
well," he said. "This is not my fashion. I live the same life that I did
when I was a poor man."

And at the age of 75, Mr. Singer is scarcely resting on his laurels.
On Nov. 1, Farrar, Straus & Giroux will publish *Old Love,* a new
collection of his short stories, to add to the 30 books he has published since his immigration from Warsaw in 1935, among them 8
novels, 11 children's books, 3 volumes of autobiography and 7
volumes of stories. "Complacency does not go well with perfec-
tionism," he said. "I don't feel I have done my job now. I pray to
God that I can do something better."

Only that day, Mr. Singer completed a short story intended for *The
New Yorker* and sent it to his agent. "I wrote it and rewrote it, and I
don't know if they will take the story," he said. "Now I've begun to
brood about it, and I have some corrections I want to make."

Even with an unlisted telephone number, the calls have not ceased,
and a visitor was not in the apartment long when the phone began
to ring. Mr. Singer sprang from his chair and scurried into the next
room with the eagerness of a substitute quarterback summoned suddenly from the bench. "He's very possessive about the phone," said
Mrs. Singer, who had been sitting across the room, quietly doing
needlepoint, and interjecting an occasional comment. "Usually it's for
him. My girlfriends have stopped calling because they're afraid to
disturb him."

The call, Mr. Singer explained when he returned, was from his

editor at *The Forward,* which continues to publish nearly all of his
work before it has been translated into English. In the past, his work
was translated by others, most often his nephew Joseph Singer, and
Mr. Singer did the editing. Increasingly now, he does the translations
himself, not just because his nephew recently decided to pursue his
own career as a painter, but also because Mr. Singer has grown more
comfortable with the English language. Nonetheless, he still writes
everything first in longhand in Yiddish, and types his manuscripts
on the durable Yiddish typewriter he purchased in 1935 for $35.

With the arrival of a photographer, Mr. Singer insisted on putting
on his suit jacket and pulling his tie tight at the neck. "I'm from the
old world," he said. "I feel naked without it." The phone rang again.
This time, the caller was a television producer—"for '60 Minutes' I
think"—whom Mr. Singer had recently met. The man wanted to
drop off a present: composition notebooks with no red lines down the
left margin. "I don't like the red lines. I write from right to left, and
for me the red is a disturbance. We will see what he has. He will soon
be here."

"I love to speak on the phone," Mr. Singer said. "I don't know
why. Why do you like one girl and not another? But for me, letter-
writing is a nuisance. My letters are written with great speed, always
with apologies for not writing sooner."

The talk of letters suddenly triggered the memory of one that Mr.
Singer had intended to mail that morning. He began emptying his
pockets of bills, notes, pencils and pens. For several minutes he flitted
about the apartment riffling through stacks of papers. And then,
again quite suddenly, he remembered posting the letter after all.

"I have such crises every day," he explained matter-of-factly. "I
need suspense, not only in my novels, but in life itself. If there is not
positive suspense, then there is negative suspense." Mr. Singer will
brook no psychological interpretations of his perpetual crises. "A
psychologist would say that this means I am in love with my grandmother, or some such. I did love her, but that's not the explanation.
We need suspense in life almost as much as we need bread."

The absence of such suspense, Mr. Singer added, warming to his
subject, was the central failing of most modern fiction. "It is so much
into psychologizing and sociologizing that the suspense is lost. Once
you lose all the complexes, and all the crises are gone, you have

nothing. It is too smooth. I create suspense in my work, and fate creates it in my life."

The doorbell rang, and the man with the notebooks walked in. He had 100 of them in a package, all without the red margin line, and he also had a packet of old reviews of Mr. Singer's books. The author, obviously delighted at his windfall, perused a review from *The Jewish Current*. It was a pan. "They always give me a bad review," he said. "It is a Marxist paper, and they complain that what I write is pornographic. Well, let me tell you, I like to write about sex. They say what I write is antisocial. So it is. Or they say it's not in the spirit of Jewishness, and so what if it's not? I don't consider this criticism. These reviews I ignore."

Two hours had passed by the time Mrs. Singer gently mentioned to her husband, whose energy showed no signs of flagging, that they ought to be thinking about dinner. The next day they were scheduled to leave for an eight-day stay in Florida, where they have a condominium.

"I hear it's been very hot down there," Mrs. Singer said.

"Maybe we shouldn't go," her husband replied. "Let's just forget the whole thing." A wry smile suggested he was gently teasing her, but she looked at him aghast.

"I'm all packed," she said.

"So unpack," he replied.

"But we've told everyone we're going," she said.

"Didn't I have enough heat already this summer already?" he said, obviously enjoying the byplay.

"We've made the reservations," Mrs. Singer said.

"Then cancel them," he said.

"But we can't cancel them. We have the Super Saver fare."

Isaac Bashevis Singer smiled benignly at his wife. "So then," he concluded, "we will go."

Isaac Bashevis Singer in Texas

Stephen H. Garrin/1980

From *Texas Studies in Literature and Language,* 22, no. 1 (Spring 1980), 91–98. Reprinted by permission of the University of Texas Press.

Isaac Bashevis Singer, the 1978 Nobel Laureate for literature, and the first Yiddish writer to be so honored by the Swedish Academy, was born in Radzymin, Poland, in 1904. The son and grandson of rabbis, he attended the Rabbinical Seminary in Warsaw, but chose instead to follow in the footsteps of his older brother, the novelist I.J. Singer. Isaac Bashevis began his literary career as a journalist for the Yiddish press in Warsaw. He also entered the "kitchen of literature," as he called it, by translating into Yiddish Thomas Mann's *Der Zauberberg,* Stefan Zweig's *Romain Rolland,* Erich Maria Remarque's *Im Westen nichts Neues* and *Der Weg zurück.* From Norwegian letters Singer translated Knut Hamsun's *Pan* and *Victoria.* Hamsun is a significant influence on Singer's own work.

In 1935, realizing what was to be the tragic fate of European Jewry, Singer left Europe and settled in New York where he began to write for the *Jewish Daily Forward,* a Yiddish language daily. Most of his narratives, even today, are first serialized in the *Forward* before they appear in translation. In 1953, Saul Bellow, later to receive the Nobel Prize himself, rendered Singer's "Gimpel Tam" ("Gimpel the Fool") into English, after which his fame quickly spread. Today Singer is as widely read in Japan as he is in this country, South America, Europe, and Israel.

In bestowing the Nobel Prize, the Swedish Academy cited Mr. Singer for "his impassioned narrative art, which, with roots in a Polish-Jewish cultural tradition, brings the human condition to life."

On May 11, 1979, Isaac Bashevis Singer visited the University of Texas at Austin. His appearance included an informal meeting with faculty from various departments in the College of Liberal Arts, a public lecture entitled, "My Philosophy as a Jewish Writer," after which there was a brief opportunity for members of the audience to pose questions. Some of the more significant inquiries and answers are printed here with a transcript of a private interview with this writer.

I

Query: [An inquiry about the influence of William Blake on his work.]

Answer: All I can say is that William Blake was very near to the Cabbalah. I love him very much and I admire him highly. I don't think he has gotten enough recognition. He was a Cabbalist without studying the Cabbalah.

Q: [In response to the indication in Mr. Singer's talk that an important change in his personal philosophy was his skepticism regarding rationalism, a question on his belief that rationalism, per se, was evil.]

A: No. I wouldn't think in this way. I admire science highly. We could not have gone to the moon, let's say, with our emotions or poetry, or even the power of religion. We use computers, mathematics, physics, and so on. I think logic is a great gift of God, just like mysticism. What I am against is when people think that we can grasp everything with the power of logic. What is outside of logic and so to say exact science, is superstition and silly and damaging. This I am against. In other words, I think only a person who recognizes both science and intuition, science and religion, science and good emotions, can bring us nearer to knowledge. This is my way of thinking. This I think is good. When I call a man a rationalist, it is only if he considers rationalism the only power which man really possesses and he should really use.

Q: [A query about the influence of Immanuel Kant.]

A: When I was a boy I studied Kant's *Prolegomena*. In a way I would say that Kant was, in a way, a highly religious person. And even I would call him a mystic. It is a fact that Kant has written a book about the famous Swedish mystic Svenborg and he tells there stories which I could not believe that a philosopher like Kant should believe in them. The great rationalists of the olden times knew that logic is logic and other powers are other powers. It is only the petty rationalist who really thinks that he knows all the secrets of the universe and he has reached the summit; like those, let's say, who believed that all Marx has said is holy, and the rest is junk. It is this kind of rationalism which I dislike.

Q: [A question about the author's earliest impressions in New York.]

A: All I can tell you is that all immigrants feel lost. I felt doubly lost. I came here with the intention to be a Yiddish writer. The impression I had when I came here was that Yiddish was not going to last more than five or ten years. When I went to my editor at the *Jewish Daily Forward* and asked him for a permanent job, he said that a permanent job in Yiddish is like building a house in the crater of an active volcano. That was his feeling and that was mine also. My only comfort was that I had written one book already in Poland called *Satan in Goray,* and I said to myself there are writers who only write one book and I am going to be one of them. But in the years I realized that a writer should never worry about who is going to read him, or if his language is going to last, or even if he himself is going to last. We are all not perfectly immortal. He should do his work. And I got out of this melancholy and began to write. Today I am more sure than ever that Yiddish is not going to be forgotten. I told the professors today, we Jews suffer from many sicknesses, but amnesia is not one of them. I also told some audiences, I am ready to admit that Yiddish is a sick language, but in our history between being sick and dying is a long, long way.

Q: [A remark about the English renditions of his narratives.]

A: As a rule all writers lose in translation, and I would say humorists and poets are the greatest losers in translation. And a writer who is connected with folklore is a very bad loser too. And I would be a very bad loser because I have a little humor and am sometimes connected with folklore, and maybe I have a spark of poetry in me. With all these things I would be very vulnerable. I knew it from the very beginning but I decided to work on the translation. In the 1950's, when my works were being translated, I had been in this country almost fifteen years and had learned a little English. And I am working on the translation all the time. If I wouldn't work on the translation, it would never come out. I have had very good translators; somehow it never comes out right. In my case it was especially necessary since all my works are being translated into English. So I take care of the English translation as much as possible. What they do to me in Japanese, I will never know.

II

Garrin: Who were the main influences on your work? Are there any specific writers who have affected your own writing?

Singer: I would say that I was influenced when I read Edgar Allan Poe in Polish, not in English, and was delighted with his writing. Later on I read him in English, of course, and although there are many people who think Edgar Allan Poe was not a great poet, I think that he was great. There is divine music in his poems. Also, he was a wonderful critic. I was partially influenced by Edgar Allan Poe, but not where I could point out and say, "This is the man." Even my brother who influenced me much . . . still I wouldn't say that he is my only influence. I hope that I really found my way sooner or later. When you are young you try to imitate everybody, and then when you get older, if a writer is really a writer, he finds himself, his style; and I hope this happened to me so that I cannot really point out very special influences except my brother, Aaron Zeitlin, and such writers.

SG: What about E.T.A. Hoffmann?

IBS: Yes, Hoffmann also to a degree. I didn't read enough of him, but of course Hoffmann was a writer of my kind. I especially loved Gogol's stories. There was a time when I loved Knut Hamsun, the Norwegian writer. I cannot point, like some writers can say, I was influenced by Sholem Aleichem, or by Peretz; I could not say this.

SG: To what extent did you follow in the footsteps of your brother I. J. Singer, a superb author many people are not aware of?

IBS: Very much so, very much so. I loved his short stories. I loved very much *The Brothers Ashkenazi*. He's a superb writer, but he didn't live long enough to get the recognition he deserved, which is a great shame.

SG: Are there any classics of literature which have influenced your life and work?

IBS: I think highly of *Crime and Punishment,* and of *Anna Karenina,* and of *War and Peace.* Since I loved short stories, Chekhov and de Maupassant have created love in me for the short story. Again I would say I have my own way. I just try to find my own way, and I think that in a small way I found it.

SG: You have written a number of children's books, and some of them are quite exceptional. Do you have a special theory of children's literature?

IBS: I consider children the best readers because children read books, not reviews. They are not influenced by advertisements. They do not give a hoot about authorities. If a child doesn't like a book, it will reject it. They are the most independent readers. To write for independent readers is a great pleasure because most of the adults just go where the vogue goes. If the vogue is abstract, they become abstract; if the vogue is concrete, they are for concrete. But a child doesn't know what vogue is. He has his own opinion. He has his own mind. The less we have such good readers among the adults, the more I love to write for children.

SG: How would you characterize the state of modern literature?

IBS: My brother always told me something which I repeat to myself even today. A writer should tell a story, not explain a story. In other words you bring together a girl and a boy and say that they have fallen in love. I don't try to explain to the reader why a man and a woman fall in love. First of all, it cannot be explained; and second, if it could be explained, the reader is as intelligent as the writer. He knows life, he has fallen in love himself and is not in need of explanations. Interpretation has become a great malady of modern literature which has done great damage. In the nineteenth century the writer did not explain. Balzac knew that the French reader knew just as well as he. They were all storytellers in the nineteenth century. That is why literature did so well in the nineteenth century and is doing so badly in the second half of the twentieth. Writers try to explain their heroes either from a psychological point of view or a sociological point of view. I call them the "psychologizers" and the "sociologizers." And it is not good for literature. Its essence is storytelling.

SG: How has the Nobel Prize affected your work?

IBS: Well, I would say I am of course the same man. I never wrote for prizes and I never dreamed of getting these prizes. It didn't affect me, but it affected other people. People are more after me than they ever were, although I have no reason to complain. I got a lot of recognition, but of course this prize has a kind of charm. When you say the Nobel Prize, it means the highest, which is far from true, because there were many great writers who lived in the time of the

Nobel Prize and didn't get it, like Tolstoy himself who was a candidate, and a French writer got the Nobel Prize. There are such
writers like—whom shall I name—Joyce and Proust and many of
them. But since it came, I'm grateful. It helped, I would say it helped
in a big way the cause of Yiddish. The Yiddishists feel that they have
finally been recognized by the highest authority, and it gives them a
lot of courage; and it's good for me too because it is my language.

SG: There is a rumor that since you have been discovered by the
Swedish Academy, Hollywood is also interested in your narratives for
adaptation to the screen. How do you feel about this prospect?

IBS: I will tell you, there are options; but what will happen I don't
really know. First of all, the movies I think they make from literary
works are almost always bad. But even if a miracle would happen, it
would be good, I wouldn't feel it's my work. I only feel about a work
that it's mine if I write it; then I'm responsible for every line. In a
movie, there may be a good actor, a good director, a good photographer; many people take part in it. Because of this, it's a collective
creation, and I love the creativity which belongs to one man.

SG: In an ironic development, do you think Israel, where Yiddish
was until recently despised, is going to be the center for Yiddish
studies?

IBS: I think so. They have there a good chance since some people
in Israel are interested in Jewishness and since they are learning that
Yiddish is not such a stepchild—a stumbling block, as they used to
think—they may return to Yiddish in a big way. It's never going to
be the first language in Israel, and no one wants it to be the first
language: but they will study it and find other treasures which are
hidden in this language.

SG: What about the Jews in the Soviet Union and those who are
now at last leaving, why are they abandoning Yiddish in favor of
Hebrew?

IBS: I will tell you, the Russian Jews, many of them are assimilationists. Their ideal used to be for many years the revolution. Now
their ideal is the antirevolution. Now they have to assimilate themselves with Hebrew. Again, it's the language of the authorities. Later,
they may rebel against this. I will tell you, there are many Jews who
are by nature or conviction assimilationists. They just have to do what
the others do. In Russia they learned Russian and wanted to be

Russians. The only thing is the Russians don't treat them like real Russians. In Israel they will become a real part of the society. There are a number of Russian Jews who are interested in Yiddish; I wouldn't say all of them.

SG: What do you think is the future of Yiddish?

IBS: It will never be forgotten.

SG: Are there any prospects for new Yiddish writers?

IBS: I don't know. I don't foresee any great writing in the near future in Yiddish because there are no young people now. Even if there would be, it would take a long time until they grew up. There is a movement called "Yugentruf" ["Youth for Yiddish," a New York-based organization of Yiddish students]. I don't expect from them any great writing, but you never know. If a talent is born he will make his way in any language, be it Esperanto, Yiddish, or the language spoken on Mars. Talent has this kind of power that it ignores all formulas and all rules. It does always something unexpected. So I just don't undertake to be a prophet, either a good one or a bad one.

SG: I would like to return to your philosophy and work. Could you summarize your personal religious belief?

IBS: My own religious belief is that there is a God. There is a plan to this universe. There is a high intelligence, maybe even a purpose, but it's given to us on the installment plan. Every generation gets a little. We still don't know if the universe has a message or if we have a message. We still don't know it clearly. I would say that man is not born to know God but to search for God. The search in itself is a way of serving God. If we search for God and we are good to human beings, we are doing more or less our job. I could never believe in this business that evolution did it all. It's sheer nonsense. Evolution is nothing more than a word which has almost no meaning. I am ready to admit that there was an evolution . . . that the horse did have more than one toe, or whatever you call it, but evolution itself . . . there is a plan behind it. It's not blind; this is the main thing. Modern man is inclined to feel that there is no purpose to the universe, no sense even. There were atoms and they combined and combined, and this is how the universe came out. This to me is sheer nonsense. It is as if one would say there is a printing shop in heaven and letters were dropped down to earth and the result is Homer, de Maupassant, and the Bible. I just don't believe in this kind of nonsense.

SG: Almost all of your narrative episodes are populated with hobgoblins, spirits, and ghosts. Are these to be understood meta-phorically?

IBS: They are both metaphorical; I use them as symbols for humanity. But I also believe that although there's no evidence to it, that there may be entities of which we don't know, and they still exist. Three hundred years ago, if someone would have told that in the mud in the street there lived thousands of millions of creatures, they would have considered that the worst superstition; they would have laughed. If you would have told this to Spinoza, he might have said this was sheer nonsense. Now we know that in a little mud in the street, in a little garbage, live millions of creatures. Why can't there be other creatures of which we don't know, that exist and take part in our life? So I assume that although there is no evidence, or scientific evidence, I assume that there may be such creatures. By the way, I believe in telepathy, clairvoyance, and premonitions. I know that these things do exist. I did research myself in my small way. I'm inclined to believe that we are far from having reached the summit of knowledge. There are millions of things to learn, and I hope some-times that in the twenty-first century they will pay more attention to what we call psychical research than we do now.

SG: Do you ever get "writer's block"?

IBS: I got one big block when I came to this country, to the United States in 1935, and my impression was that Yiddish was not going to last more than five years—ten years maximum. I went to my editor, Abraham Cahan from the *Forward,* and he promised to publish my sketches. I said I would like to have a permanent job. He said, "A permanent job in Yiddish is like someone building a permanent house in the crater of a volcano. Yiddish is not going to last more than a few years, so why do you need a permanent job?" So I thought there's no sense in my writing in Yiddish if I am going to be translated into some other language. So I stopped writing altogether, except that I wrote some little sketches for the *Forward,* just to be able to make a living. To make a living meant for me . . . my idea was to make $15 a week because if I could make $15 a week, I could pay my rent, which was $4 a week, and eat in cafeterias and enjoy myself. Several years passed and I saw Yiddish was still there. At least it was not an active volcano! But every story is a crisis.

Demons by Choice:
An Interview with Isaac Bashevis Singer
Parabola/1981

From *Parabola,* The Magazine of Myth and Tradition, 6, no. 4 (Winter 1981), 68–74. Reprinted by permission.

When we first began discussing an issue on demons, one of the people we felt we would most like to talk with was Isaac Bashevis Singer. Certainly no writer in our time has described a world so filled with devils in fancy dress, demonic beings who fly through the air, dybbuks taking up residence with the innocent, imps who play dastardly tricks, ugly old witches, or human beings, like the Magician of Lublin, so possessed. And certainly no one else has done so with such intelligence, grace, and compassion.

Singer, who has just had the second volume of his autobiography, *Lost in America,* published to great critical acclaim, came to the United Stated from his native Poland in 1935. From that time to this, virtually everything he writes first appears in story or serialized form in Yiddish in the *Jewish Daily Forward.* He has written some eight novels from *The Manor* and *The Family Moskat* to *Shosha* and *Old Love;* endless short stories from *A Friend of Kafka* to *A Crown of Feathers;* books for children—*The Fools of Chelm, Why Noah Chose the Dove, Naftali the Storyteller and His Horse, Sus;* and autobiographical works: *In My Father's Court* and the first volume of his autobiography, *A Young Man in Search of Love.* In 1978 he was finally (and many of us fell belatedly) awarded the Nobel Prize for Literature. He has been unstintingly generous with his time and energy—talking to everyone about everything— sharing the stories. Until the prize, which brought with it recognition and unbelievable demands, Singer was one of the very few resident authors who was listed in the New York phone book or who answered his own phone. He continues to be a visible part of New York's West Side— strolling the streets, or eating in one or another of his favorite neighborhood restaurants.

We spoke to Singer in New York in the midst of a 95°

heat wave. He had just finished an exhausting lecture tour and a series of book-signings, and was beleaguered by a bad toothache. But he gave of himself once more—because, he said, the subject of demons "interests me."

Does Singer believe in the devil? Do Demons exist as a separate reality? After reading the novels, the stories, the memoirs, after talking with the man himself, one is left with what may be the greatest gift of the very great storyteller: a richly-etched, deeply-felt portrait of our condition; no easy answers; and a million more questions that will enrich us and actively engage us in a search that Singer himself pursues with such benefit for us all.

> Only on rare occasions did Rabbi Benish cross the threshold of his house. He would glance about him, and inquire of a passing porter or school boy:
> "How will it end?"
> "What does God want?"
>
> *Satan in Goray*

Parabola: Do you think we need demons?

Isaac Bashevis Singer: Do you mean do we need them in life?

P: Yes.

IS: It's a good question. I think it would be necessary. Because if people would never see anything of the supernatural, if we would never have any contact with other entities, we would live out our life with the feeling that this is it: our so-called reality is the only thing which exists. And that would make the human spirit much smaller than it is.

P: Do you feel that the demons we deal with are as you say in "Gimpel the Fool" like "shoulders and burdens" from God?

IS: If they exist, they certainly are from God. There is nothing in the universe which is not from God. If a person believes in nature, everything is from nature, which is again everything. There is a unity in the creation. We cannot believe in anything else.

P: But does everything have a dark side, an "other" side?

IS: I think that everything might have God knows how many sides! We don't know ourselves how many. Because if you take a pebble, you can look at this pebble from a chemical point of view, from a gravitational point of view—from many other points of view. According to Spinoza, the number of attributes of God are endless. And even if you believe in nature, you can say the same thing: that this pebble still can be seen from very many points of view.

P: One of the things that seems very strong in your work is an idea that the "demons" are put here to test us . . .

IS: I would say that behind all my ideas, the strongest idea of mine which is conveyed in my thinking, even more than in my writing, is the freedom of choice. I feel that the freedom of choice is the very essence of life. Although the gifts which God has given us are small in comparison to the gifts which He has given maybe to the angels or to the stars, we have one great gift—and this is to choose. And we always indulge in choosing. If we pay attention to one thing, we have chosen to pay attention to it. If we love somebody, we have chosen this person for love. This is in every act of humanity. To me, God is freedom. And nature, to me, is necessity. Everything in nature is necessity. In God—who I think can overrule nature, is above nature—everything is free.

P: But what about a situation like the one situation you describe in *Satan in Goray*? Would it make a difference if we acted differently? Or is it inevitable that we must encounter demons?

IS: No, no . . . it makes all the difference. When people leave free choice, the demons appear. The demons are in a way the dark side of nature which we choose. If we stop completely believing in our power, then other powers can come upon us. In other words, the demon to me is a negative side of free choice. But we have free choice in every time of our life, in every minute of our day, so we can always choose. Even if we have a bad choice to make, there is always something which is better than the other.

P: Can we be *easily* possessed by demons?

IS: I don't think they can take us over so quickly. They only come when people resign almost from everything. When people say to themselves, "I'm not going to make any choices anymore. I will just let the powers work for themselves." It is then that the demon is bound to appear.

P: Do you think we are in a time similar to the one you painted in *Satan in Goray* where the Evil One is triumphing again?

IS: I would say we are always in such a time. If not the whole of humanity . . . you look what's going on, let's say, in this country with crime: how really wherever you go—if you go to a court where there should be justice, there is the very opposite—people who you can buy for money . . . I would say human life is one big crisis. The moment you have conquered one crisis, there is already another one lurking.

P: But is that a part of what "moves" us?

IS: I think it is a part of being alive, of choosing. In other words, the danger is always there: the danger of turning love into hatred, of turning justice into injustice, of turning talent into non-talent, and so on and so on . . .

P: Do you think that your God would fight for us? Is God at war?

IS: I will tell you: He doesn't fight for us. Since He gave us free choice, He gave us a great gift, and we have to use it or misuse it. In other words, when it comes to choosing, we must rely mostly on ourselves. In this respect Judaism is a little different from Christianity. Where the Christians believe that once you belong to the Christian religion, the powers are resolved: when Jesus died, all the others should be redeemed forever. We believe the opposite: that the crisis is always there, the danger is always there—like a medical doctor who will tell you that the microbes are always there in your mouth and in your stomach, and if you become weak, they begin to multiply and become very strong.

P: And if we lose our control, the microbes, or the demons, can take over.

IS: Of course. Nothing which one man did, no matter how great he was, can really redeem you or guarantee you redemption forever.

P: And in your story, "The Mirror," it seems that you are suggesting that everyone has a demon in the mirror.

IS: Of course. Just as we are medically surrounded by dangerous microbes, so our spirit has always to fight melancholy and disbelief and viciousness and cruelty and all kinds of things.

P: But in some of your stories, even in "Cunegunde," your demons have a kind of melancholy . . .

IS: Oh, but the very essence of demons is melancholy. Because it's the very opposite of hope.

P: So you have some sympathy . . .

IS: Of course, I have sympathy for everyone who suffers and lives. Because we are all living in a great, great struggle, whether we realize it or not. Sometimes we realize it. This is a very difficult thing—we very often say how difficult life is.

P: Do you think we learn from our encounters with the demons, from facing those demons?

IS: We learn all the time, even if we don't use all the time what we have learned—because just as you learn all the time, we also forget all the time. There is a permanent amnesia planted in us, which just as we keep on forgetting our dreams, we sometimes keep on forgetting our reality. You see a certain thing; you think you have learned. And then you make the same mistake again, which shows that you didn't learn.

P: So, is there any hope for us?

IS: I will tell you: we have to go through this kind of struggle. In a way, the hope is that life does not last forever, the crisis does not last forever, and behind all this crisis, behind all this darkness, there is a great light. We have to struggle, but we are not lost, because the powers which have created us are actually great and benign powers.

P: And you think we have the equipment to fight back?

IS: We have the equipment. The only thing is we should not let it rust, we should not forget about it, we should not put it away, and say, where is it? We must be very much aware all the time—on the watch. This is true in science, it's true in literature . . . If you don't all the time watch what you are doing, you're bound to make mistakes. In my own life, I feel it all the time. it's true in love, it's true in everything.

P: You don't really feel that "evil" is a separate force?

IS: It's a part of what we call life. I don't think that the rocks have free choice, or the meteors. They live in the world of necessity— which is again a different kind of war. What can you call it? A higher war? But we are, so to say, soldiers. We have to fight.

Our life doesn't last forever. The moment we leave this world, the great struggle is over—at least for a time. In a way, death is not such a curse, but it's a time of resting. People are afraid of death because they were created so, to be afraid, because, if not, they would mishandle the body. Actually death is in a way a great resting after the struggle.

All the powers work so that you should come to a bad ending, but our soul works for the opposite—that the ending should be good. Actually, the ending is always good.

A Shmues with Isaac Bashevis Singer

Mark S. Golub/1981

From *Studies in American Jewish Literature*, 1 (1981), 169–175.
Reprinted by permission of Kent State University Press.

Golub: I guess the first question I want to ask you is: When did it begin? When was the first time that Isaac Bashevis Singer took pencil to paper?

Singer: Well I took pencil to paper when I was a boy of twelve years old. I read in Yiddish a translation from Conan Doyle's *Sherlock Holmes*. And immediately I tried to imitate Conan Doyle. But after half an hour or so I got tired of it, and I saw I didn't like it. Then I waited another few years, and I began, about sixteen, to write in Hebrew. And I wrote in Hebrew a number of years. I even published a few things. But in this time, when I began to write, Hebrew was not yet what it is today. It was a language of The Book. You had to look up in the dictionary words which didn't really exist. I remember I wanted to look up how you say "salt shaker" in Hebrew. They didn't have salt shakers in those times.

Golub: There's no salt shaker in the *Torah*.

Singer: Not even in the *Mishnah*. So I began to write in Yiddish, where we did have salt shakers—very many, of all kinds. And also, the people whom I describe were speaking Yiddish. Yiddish was the natural language for me. I, myself, spoke it with my parents—with my friends. And since then I'm writing Yiddish.

Golub: When did you publish your first book?

Singer: The first story I published when I was, I think, about 23 years old. And the first book, which was called *Satan in Goray,* I published when I was about 29 years old.

Golub: And when was your first translation into English?

Singer: Oh, the first translation in English came out in 1950—*The Family Moskat.*

Golub: I believe you have said that a book loses something like 40% in translation.

Singer: It depends on the translator. If he's very bad, it can lose 80%!

Golub: Are you comfortable with the translations into English?

Singer: I am not comfortable, but I'm prepared to lose. The only thing is I do the editing in English lately, so whenever I feel I lose, I work on it in order not to lose. So I am not really a bad loser in English. The only thing is what happens to me in Japanese, this is the question.

Golub: How many languages have your books been translated into?

Singer: I always say the truth—16. And the printers make it 60. I don't know why—it's wishful thinking, wishful mistaking.

Golub: Do you find it difficult to write? You are obviously a creative person when it comes to writing. Is it difficult?

Singer: It may be difficult. But since I love to do it it's not difficult. You will not call a work which you love really, which gives you pleasure, difficult. If a writer says that I hate writing—and there are such writers—I have some doubts about their talent.

Golub: Really. I have heard writers say that the typewriter drinks blood. It has not drunk your blood.

Singer: I hope not. Maybe it does it stealthily—without my knowledge.

Golub: Why *always* in Yiddish? Why have you not written lately in other languages, like English?

Singer: I will tell you. It is my mother language. It is the language which I think I know best. Also I feel best in this language. I am not self-conscious. In English, I always think I'm going to make a mistake—like all foreigners. So I have to think about the language all the time, which is not good for a writer—to put too much stress on the grammar and the syntax. Where in Yiddish, I feel like a man at home—you take off your tie, you take off your jacket—although I don't take off my tie and my jacket at home, but this is my own business.

Golub: Am I correct that your father was *chasidic* and your mother came from a family that was *misnagid* (opposed to the *chasidim*)?

Singer: Not completely *misnagid*. My maternal grandfather also went to a "rabbi" from time to time, but he wasn't so hot about him.

Golub: Were you frightened of your father?

Singer: Never. But I loved him, which is even better than being frightened.

Golub: What was he like?

Singer: A most good-natured human being. He had blue eyes, and a red beard, very white skin. And his life was his religion. There was nothing but religion, in his life. He ate religion, he slept religion, he studied religion, he breathed religion. And he wanted his children to be like him. He also wrote books—

Golub: He was a scholar.

Singer: A scholar, sure.

Golub: He was also a *dayan* (a judge).

Singer: Yes.

Golub: So obviously, one of your books refers to . . .

Singer: *My Father's Court* was our house—this is a memoir. My mother was also a very sweet person. But already there was a sharpness about her.

Golub: She sounds, by the way, from the little I have read about her, like a very unusual person.

Singer: Very unusual—very clever—and logical. Let's say, my father would come back from his "rabbi" and he would say, "Ach! The 'rabbi'—he's such a saint." So my mother said, "How do you know that he's a saint?" He said, "He was praying—" So my mother said, "This is his business!" This is the kind of person she was, sceptical, clever—and highly religious, of course.

Golub: She had a sense of humor, too, obviously.

Singer: A sense of humor. He also had a sense of humor, my father. They were both excellent storytellers. I all the time milked them for stories, though my father didn't have as much time. But my mother she always had stories to tell.

Golub: Have these stories worked their way into your books at all?

Singer: Into my books for children, mostly like *Mazel and Shlimazel, Zlateh the Goat*—a number of stories, and they all have roots in my mother's stories.

Golub: Were they proud of you?

Singer: No. They were ashamed both of my brother and of me, because we shaved our beards. My father was especially ashamed that we wrote books because he considered all secular books blasphemy—pornography. So my father used to tell people when they asked him, "What are your sons doing?" he would say, "They sell newspapers." He considered this a very dignified way to make a living. But a writer?! So after a while he began to believe in it. Once when he came to Warsaw and he asked me, "Are you selling enough newspapers to make a living?" I said, "Not too many, but somehow I manage."

Golub: They at no point in their lives ever came to accept the fact that you and your brother were writers?

Singer: I don't think so, no. They wouldn't have. My mother might have accepted but the only trouble is that my first book, *Satan in Goray,* is full of diabolic business and *sex*—and *this* they certainly would not accept! They would have rather accepted *The Family Moskat,* let's say, or *The Slave,* than *Satan in Goray*—which was really away from the Yiddish tradition as much as possible.

Golub: Where did it come from in you? You certainly were steeped in the *chasidic* tradition, you were a part of traditional observant Judaism.

Singer: Yes. But I was also a sceptic. In other words, my father believed that every little law—every Jewish custom—was given to Moses on Mt. Sinai, of course. But I saw, already as a young boy, that most of these things are man-made. It is true that man, himself, was made by God—so what is man-made is also, in a way made by God. Just the same, my belief in all these customs was not as strong as it was in my father. I am until today an ardent believer in God. I never doubted the existence of God for a moment. But I don't keep all these dogmas and all these things. According to my father, I am a complete *goy.*

Golub: Is there any wistfulness in you for those days when you were observant?

Singer: Yes. I still have great respect for these Orthodox Jews, for these pious Jews, because they had a compass—they knew exactly where to go, what is right and what is wrong. And even if they were overdoing it, it was also no tragedy. Of course, they were overdoing it mostly when it comes to what man does to God—*shehbayn adam l'Makom,* not *shehbayn adam l'chavayro* (what man does to his fellow man). When it came to *shehbayn adam l'chavayro,* they were like all other people. I mean, they were not worse than other people; but neither were they much better. There was competition, and envy, and greed—like among other people. Of course, this was a contradiction to what, really, a religious person should be. But of course, according to my father, a man had to believe, and not to ask any questions—not to have any doubts. He had no doubts; he didn't ask any questions.

Golub: Why do you think it is that the *mitzvot* (commandments) do not lead to a certain kind of higher ethical life?

Singer: I will tell you why. Because the *mitzvos* between man and God are very easy to keep. Let's say you eat *matzah; sh'murah matzah* (the specially prepared *matzah*), you make a benediction. But to tell a man, "Don't compete with another man; don't swindle; don't desire another man's wife," these are very difficult commandments. They go against the very essence of the nature of the body. The body *is* greedy, and is angry, and is lecherous by nature—and so on and so on. So in other words, the people do always the things which are easy—they keep—they even overdo them; and what is really difficult they neglect. This is true among Jews, Christians—among all religions.

Golub: Have you ever known a *tzaddikf*?

Singer: Yes. I will tell you that my parents were *tzaddikim*.

Golub: They were?

Singer: Absolutely! And since I'm a critical person, I wouldn't just sit there and give compliments to my parents.

My father was ready to give away his last penny. And sometimes he did things which were foolish. Once he had 60 rubles, which then was a fortune. You could give a dowry to a girl with 60 rubles. So a poor man came to him and complained that he's in a bad situation. He gave him away the 60 rubles—which was his whole capital. Everything he had!

My mother was also very charitable, but not as much as my father because she knew that she had every day to give her children to eat, you know. I have seen my mother give away bread and potatoes in a time of famine when we, ourselves, went around hungry all day long. This was in the time of the First World War. And there I saw she took out these potatoes and these pieces of bread—which were for us a question of life and death—and gave it to a man who needed it even more.

And not only this. My father never said a bad word about anybody. He was a real saint. When a woman came in to ask a ritual question, he immediately turned away, because it's written in The Book that if you look at a woman, you may desire her. And if you desire her she may be somebody else's wife. So the best thing is, don't look. And he kept it. My mother also kept every *mitzvah*.

But they were not the only *tzaddikim* I knew. I knew quite a number of people who were saints. And I always measure saint-ness about human relations, not the relations of God because there it's easy to be a saint.

Golub: You have a healthy respect for the *yetzer ha-ra* (the evil urge).

Singer: I don't applaud him.

Golub: No, no I don't mean it that way. I mean that you understand the power—

Singer: Of course. The *yetzer ha-ra* is actually the human body— the human nerve system—the human character which tells you, "Grab as much as you can. Today you are alive, tomorrow you may not be alive." The usual way the *yetzer ha-ra* persuades people. And if it doesn't go easy, people are ready to swindle a little bit—to bend the law—all kinds of things. And this is the measurement where you see, really, who is a pure man and who only just follows the routine.

Golub: As we know, there is a great deal of mysticism in your writing—there's a great deal of demonology in your writing. Is this a literary tool, or are you—

Singer: It's both. It's a tool and it's also a belief. I believe in higher powers and in lower powers. I feel that we are surrounded with powers of which we have no inkling, but they are here just the same. Just as the people didn't know before the microbe was discovered that we take a little mud from the soil, there are millions of creatures in it. So if you would have told it to somebody they would say that you are fanatic—that you invent. So we don't know what powers might still be discovered. So, we're not at the summit of knowledge. I'm sure that there are powers of which we don't know, or sometimes we feel their presence, but we cannot define them. And this I call a

mystic. Not a man who says, "I have seen angels and demons."
Because these things you don't see them so often; you may get a
glimpse of them once in a lifetime, and there are greater realities—
more profound. This is the way of my kind of mysticism.

Golub: You say you have never doubted the existence of God.

Singer: No!

Golub: What about the existence of Satan?

Singer: Well I will tell you. Satan I call "human nature." We are
born satans. And God wants to make us the opposite of satan. But
sometimes I mention demons just instead of saying "a bad man"
I would rather say that he played around with the demons, or something. Also, there may be powers—there may be demons. How do
we know that they don't exist?

Golub: It is different asking the question than knowing the answer.

Singer: Of course.

Golub: What is your favorite story in the *Torah*?

Singer: Favorite story in the *Torah*? Is there a single story in the
Torah which is not beautiful? They all are. Absolutely all. The story of
Sodom, or the story of Joseph and his brothers, and the story of Lot,
and Jacob and Rachel, Isaac and Rebecca—it's all beauty.

Golub: What about the *Akkedah* (the binding of Isaac). Is that a
disturbing story to you?

Singer: No, it's not a disturbing story. I mean, I would be very
much disturbed if I would see a man with a knife going to slaughter
his son waiting for an angel to say, "Don't do it." But as you read it,
it's beautiful. Beautiful. And also the idea that God had to tempt
Abraham to see if he really—you know, as if the Almighty wouldn't
know the truth, He needed proof, which is in a way a primitive way
of thinking. But it's beautiful anyhow. From a literary point of view, it
is sheer beauty, most of it because it is so short.

Golub: You know, there is a line in *Enemies,* one of your later
books, in which Tamara says to Herman, "A woman who demands
such sacrifices doesn't deserve them." Of course she's talking about
when Masha wants Herman to leave Yadwiga just before Yadwiga is
about to give birth.

Singer: Yes, yes.

Golub: There are some people who feel that a God who would
demand the sacrifice at Mount Moriah does not deserve them.

Singer: But He didn't demand the sacrifice. At the last moment He sent an angel to tell him not to do it.

Golub: That's not fair. Did Abraham know beforehand?

Singer: He didn't.

Golub: So He made the demand.

Singer: Well, listen. If this would be the only question about the Almighty—We can ask a million questions about Him. Since He's a silent God—He doesn't talk to all of us every morning and every evening—so we have to live with it, that He is silent. And we, ourselves have to answer ourselves, or to say that we don't know the answer.

But I will tell you. The best thing: since He's a silent God, we should be silent people. We shouldn't keep on criticizing Him. If you are given a book, and this book has twenty billion pages, and you read only one sentence, you cannot sit down and write a review about this book. And this is the way we see God. We get such a little part of His creation that *any* criticism is silly.

Golub: You know there is a big argument about whether Isaac Bashevis Singer is a pessimist or not.

Singer: Yes, I will tell you what I am. When it comes to the bigger things, about the universe, I'm kind of an optimist. I say most probably the Almighty knows what He's doing, and He has created such a large universe and so many galaxies. Creation was not done by a fool, or by a person who doesn't know what he's doing. Neither did Creation come from an accident, as they say, " 'evolution,' 'a physical accident,' 'a chemical accident' "—it's a lot of nonsense! There is a plan behind the whole thing, and consciousness, and greatness— great wisdom.

But when it comes to humanity, I'm kind of a pessimist. I don't feel that human beings will ever really reach these ideals which they have been preaching for thousands of years. Again and again, you know, it seems that the *yetzer ha-ra,* somehow, the body, dominates the soul—not the soul the body. This in itself may have some purpose.

Conversations with the Singers

Grace Farrell/1981

From the *Sacred Heart University Review*, 1, no. 2 (Spring 1981), 3–18. Reprinted by permission.

I

Isaac Bashevis Singer is used to questions. They fill his head; they fill the pages of his books; they take up all his time. Each of his stories hones a series of questions to a brittle edge, and then quickly, ever so fleetingly, opens up as if to reveal an answer, but never quite reveals it, only forms another question in its stead.

"You don't get answers," Singer tells me. "Questions are all you get." The last line of "Yentl the Yeshiva Boy" reads, "Truth itself is often concealed in such a way that the harder you look for it, the harder it is to find." Now that I have come to know the man, I torture him, as he laughingly puts it, with my questions, until he asks with wonder, "Grace, do I know?"

Isaac Bashevis Singer: We talk about philosophers, but I'm more interested now in psychic research. Philosophy is able to reveal that we are unable really to know the thing in itself, but psychic research still gives us hope.

Grace Farrell: Are you involved in the center for psychical research at Duke University?

IBS: No, I'm not involved in it, but I read Professor Rhine and his wife and the proceedings of the Psychic Society. Lately so many books about it are being published that you could spend a lifetime reading them. But I have been interested in this business all my life.

GF: In Hasidic thought time and space don't really exist . . .

IBS: Not only in Hasidic thought, but for Kantian philosophy. They are only categories of our thinking.

GF: Does this tie in at all with psychical research?

IBS: In a way it does; in a way it does, sure, because if time and space are only categories of human thinking, and we don't know what thinking itself is, then this gives way to many phenomena. It is a fact that Kant believed in the supernatural. He was interested in Swedenborg, who was a Swedish mystic. There are many things which seem to us to be contradictory, but we discover in nature that they are not. There can, for example, be a God and there can also be evolution. These two ideas, which some people think are contradictory, are not really contradictory in nature. This is true about other things. There is a place for logic and there is a place for the supernatural, for philosophy and for mysticism. All these things go together.

GF: You told me that we are always making folklore. Even the patient on the psychoanalyst's couch is making folklore.

IBS: To me psychoanalysis is folklore. Folklore is a grain of truth veiled or mixed with a lot of fantasy; but fantasy itself is a kind of truth. It is eternal truth, although it may not be external truth.

GF: And folktales are very often one of the only ways in which we can get that grain of truth.

IBS: I think so. I mean, we also get grains of truth from science and mathematics, but this is a different method altogether. With folklore we get it by instinct and feeling. It's a different way of getting at truth.

GF: How do you connect folklore and ritual?

IBS: They are very closely related to one another. I don't believe that all the rituals were really given to people by God who revealed himself and told us to do these things. They are also a product of human feelings about the godhead. As far as this goes, they are actually a form of hope.

GF: Is there a power, if not a magic, or some kind of energy involved in just performing a ritual?

IBS: There is psychic energy.

GF: And just in telling a story there is some kind of energy involved.

IBS: Yes. It's the same kind of energy. Except in ritual, it may be even stronger because it's repeated by many people, and it becomes more real the more it is practiced. Let's say, if you are a very believing Catholic, then for you the holy communion is very, very real. Even if others may doubt it, for Catholics, who were brought up in the ritual for years and years, it is real. The ritual has a kind of subjective reality, and since we don't really know the difference between what is subjective and what is objective, it has reality. I would say that everything we feel is, in some way, real. I also believe that everything which we imagine exists, really does exist. We cannot outdo the creativity of nature. All our fantasies are truths somewhere—if not here, somewhere else; if not on this planet, then on some other planet. If you imagine that you are walking with your head down and your feet up, I am sure that there must be some planet where there are such animals who walk this way.

GF: That reminds me of a passage in one of your books, where a rabbi gives four proofs of God. One is that if we can imagine a perfect, almighty being, then one must exist.

IBS: Exactly. That's a good idea; it's in my book, or did you read it somewhere else?

GF: I think it's in one of your books.

IBS: I will tell you, if it's in my book, it's right; if it's in another book, it is absolutely ridiculous.

GF: Do you really believe in demons?

IBS: I believe in them. I am even afraid of them. When my wife goes out of town to visit a relative and I am alone in the apartment, I leave the light burning because I am afraid of the demons. If you are afraid of something, then you must believe in it. Furthermore, it is my deepest conviction that all demons speak Yiddish and all imps speak Hebrew.

GF: Who speaks Aramaic?

IBS: Aha! The angels. It is written so in the . . . in the Talmud.

GF: Were the demons in "The Black Wedding" real?

IBS: In "The Black Wedding" I really describe a case of insanity. She was completely insane. As a matter of fact, part of that story was published in a psychiatric anthology.

GF: So the demons were not real?

IBS: No. The whole thing was a delusion.

GF: How can we tell?

IBS: The woman saw only evil. Everything was devilish; the whole wedding and every person there was demonic. In such a case, when everything is so one-sided, it must be insanity. However, you can also interpret it differently. I always make these stories ambiguous, so you can explain them either from the point of view of psychology or from the point of view of psychic phenomenon. I don't compel the reader to believe what I believe. I leave a way out for him.

GF: Do you remember the advice given in the story "A Piece of Advice?"

IBS: If you are angry, play the part of one who is not angry, and if you play it long enough, you will lose your anger. If you are compelled for a certain time to play the one who is good-natured and if you play this part long enough, you will become good-natured. It is known in the lore of Hasidism that if you have a bad habit and you make believe that you don't have this habit, you cure it by making believe. In other words, as we were saying before, to make believe is a real power.

GF: At first I thought that the advice was a bit hypocritical.

IBS: You thought it meant to flatter everybody for eight to ten days? No, it's not hypocrisy. Actually even life itself is a play. Behind our clothes we're all naked, but we put on clothes and we make believe almost that this is what we are. We forget our nakedness and we see ourselves as always dressed. When you wear a mask long enough, it becomes a part of your face.

GF: In *The Manor* the Rabbi of Marshinov gives similar advice about the Ten Commandments.

IBS: You don't have to believe; just keep them and you will begin to believe. How do you feel about the Ten Commandments? Do you think they are good advice?

GF: Yes, I do. They seem basic to human dignity. If they were all kept, then the dignity of each human being would be maintained.

IBS: If people would live by these Ten Commandments, if they really would live by them, this world would be a paradise, or at least half a paradise. And if people break them, the world becomes a hell. It is not easy. Not to kill and not to steal for people like you and me is very easy. We would not steal; we would not kill. But there are other commandments which are sometimes difficult to keep. Like not to commit adultery or not to covet other's riches. People are tempted very much. It's not easy. Just the same if people kept all ten of them, life would be almost wonderful. The whole of the Talmud and all of the commentaries are actually about how to keep the Ten Commandments. They look simple, but they are really very profound. It is within human possibility to keep the Ten Commandments, but the Sermon on the Mount is something which we cannot keep. It's almost impossible, the demands are so great. They ask a maximum of ethics: to turn the other cheek and to love your enemies!

GF: My students always want to know where Herman is [the polygamous hero of *Enemies, A Love Story*] and now they also wonder where Yentl is [the woman who had to disguise herself as a man in order to study the Torah].

IBS: Yentl is supposed to be in a yeshiva, if she is still alive. And Herman supposedly either committed suicide or is hiding somewhere in another hayloft. The question is what would happen if Herman should meet Yentl. This never occurred to me. How's about this?

GF: I don't think they would get along.

IBS: No?

GF: Yentl wouldn't put up with Herman.

IBS: Do you think you could put up with Herman?

GF: No.

IBS: Also not, huh? You wouldn't take him?

GF: I don't think so.

IBS: Well, there's no danger that Herman is in Connecticut. Too small a state.

GF: How do you feel about Yentl. Do you think that she should not have gone to such lengths to do what was forbidden a woman?

IBS: I think that every human being must do what they must do. I mean, this is just how she felt. She was a woman with what was then thought to be a man's desires or ideas. She loved the Torah more than the kitchen. Since she could not study the Torah as a woman, she had to dress up as a man, and, having lived among men and having worn this mask for so many years, it became a part of her life.

GF: Do you think that she could be happy in her next yeshiva?

IBS: I will tell you, no human being is really happy. I don't believe in happy people. People have happy moments, but the course of happiness is not in human nature. At least this is how I feel about it. A person like Yentl could not be happy because, although she is living according to the way she wanted to live, she is also a woman and she also has the desires of a woman. I would say the conflict between being a woman and being a man stayed with her for the rest of her life. This is the way I see it.

GF: You have a story called "The Psychic Journey."

IBS: Yes. This story is half ironic. I feed pigeons, and while I feed them, I find another pigeon feeder and we get acquainted. I carry my magazine about the supernatural and she also carries such a magazine. She makes her living teaching awareness and such things. She persuades me to go to Israel with her, and I go. This is more or less the story. There are all kinds of other things in it as well. In it I make fun of the supernatural and at the same time I show that I believe in it. In this story I am both the scoffer and the believer.

GF: In your story "The Seance" you also make fun of the mystics.

IBS: Here I also make fun of them. I do so because many of these people are swindlers or they fool themselves. It is only once in a while that they touch on a spark of truth. But in most cases the spiritualists fool themselves. So when I write about this subject, I always try to give both sides of the case, both their belief and their cheating, whether others or themselves.

GF: In "the Shadow of a Crib" Dr. Yaretzky has a debate with himself about whether the world is seeing will or blind will.

IBS: He was a complete pessimist and a disciple of Schopenhauer. According to Schopenhauer the essence of the world was blind will, nothing but blind will. He's actually a materialist. From Schopenhauer's point of view there is no redemption whatsoever. No hope and no redemption.

GF: In this story Dr. Yaretzky somehow did not follow his fated path. He comes back after he dies, looks in the new rabbi's window, sees the woman whom he didn't marry and a cradle of an unborn child. Is it as if he had a path which he should have taken, one which the seeing will had set out for him, but which he did not take?

IBS: I would say, yes. According to this story he feels that he didn't accomplish what he had to accomplish. He made mistakes. He believes in blind will when actually there is sense to the universe. He avoided women because he believed that all women are treacherous, but because of this he avoided a woman fated for him. He had to come back to atone for his mistakes or to correct them. In a certain sense he had to apologize.

GF: But do people have one fate which they must live out?

IBS: I don't know. I only write the story. I know just as much as you, and maybe less. Who knows, maybe you know something which you do not want to reveal. As I've said to you before, if you could tell me why we are born and why we must die, I could answer all the other questions.

II

"He lectures too much," Alma Singer tells me with much concern. "He says yes to everything and tires himself out."

"She lectures me not to lecture," the Nobel Laureate chuckles from the bed on which he is resting. Her concern for him inspires my concern for her, and as she brushes a bug off the bathroom door, I swoop down upon it, to the rescue, slamming my foot where it lands.

"Murderers!" booms an accusing voice. And while I stand horrified and without excuse, Alma Singer tells a story.

"Once it happened that my Uncle Karl, who was also a great lover of animals, was rowing on a lake near Munich. The 'beautiful people' went there; it was a very popular resort. He wore a bathing suit and a raincoat. He put a couch in the rowboat and he took a book and he sat in the couch and he rowed himself out. Suddenly he saw a bee drowning. He was trying to save her with the oar when his whole boat tipped over and he fell into the lake. All he could see was his raincoat which was spread like a lotus flower around him. So he swam to save his life. I don't know what happened to the bee."

Grace Farrell: And did you really have pet birds which flew around the apartment?

Alma Singer: We had oodles and oodles of them. One day I came home from work on a winter evening and Isaac said, come into my study and I will show you something. I went in and there was a little bird sitting on a table. It seems that Isaac had gone to the window, and although it was already darkish, he could see that there was snow on the windowsill. Then he saw a little yellow bird sitting there, so he opened the window, and with his hand he pushed the little bird in. Right away it was very much a personality and very much at home. But we didn't know what to do with it. We had never had a bird. We had no cage; we had nothing. So we asked the handyman for help, and he brought an old cage up from the cellar. Isaac gave the bird oatmeal and a little water on the bridge table and the little bird picked at it and ate. The cage the handyman brought up was dirty and had no bottom, so the next day we went out and bought a proper cage for him. And he began to sing and to talk. He was a very intelligent parakeet, that one. And then later, before we went on vacation, we bought him a wife. Isaac said, how can we leave him alone; he has to have somebody to be with. But I will tell you, it went from bad to worse. As long as we had a relative to send the birds to when we were away, it was okay. Then sometimes we found a decent person to take care of them. But most of the time it ended with tragedy. We had to put them into a pet shop or there were people who were not reliable or the bird went under the bed and wouldn't come out or we couldn't find the bird or the bird died . . . there were so many things that when the last one died, I said, for God's sake, no more: I can't take it. You know, you get attached to animals. So the last one lived a long time alone. When he went I said, I don't want any bird anymore. We took out the cage. By then we had a beautiful, big cage. But I do not want a bird anymore. We travel too much.

GF: You came to the United States in 1936 and you met Isaac in 1937. In the Poconos?

AS: No. In the lowly Catskill mountains. The Poconos would have been one notch higher! It was on a farm.

GF: What was your first impression?

AS: Oh, it was very strange. He was lost! He had on a blue shirt with short sleeves. His white arms had a lot of freckles and he had very red hair—he had a little hair left then. He had friends in a summer colony nearby and he went to visit them, but he got lost. A farmer told him how to go, but somehow he missed the way. He didn't get there. So he came back to where I was and asked instructions. And I thought to myself, that's funny that a young man can't find something nearby. And that was my first impression. We had an occasional meal together, but then he would disappear and go to New York. One day we got into a conversation about literature and right away we agreed on many things, and then we had regular sessions on the porch about literature. That's how we got acquainted.

GF: And he used to bring you Emeraude perfume.

AS: Oh, that was later. Not in the Catskills! . . . We were married in a terrible snowstorm, a real blizzard. I had gotten a new hat and a new dress and I had my fur coat, and still the wind went right through me. We had to battle our way to city hall through snow, oh so high! We were the only couple there.

GF: At what point did you know that he was writing really great literature?

AS: When I read *The Family Moskat* and later *The Slave* I knew that this was the real stuff. How do you know? I can't put it in mathematical formulas; you know through the emotions. It has to do with reading a lot. You know what's good and what is not. I was very enthusiastic about *The Family Moskat,* but for some reason Isaac always picked on that book. He always said, yes, it's a good book, but it has flaws. I thought it was a superb work. And *The Slave* is wonderful, and recently I reread parts of *The Manor.* My favorites are *The Manor, The Slave, The Magician of Lublin, The Family Moskat,* "Alone," which is a fabulous story about Miami, "The Admirer," about the woman who comes to the apartment in New York, "The Joke" is very good, and of course, "Yentl."

GF: I loved "Yentl" on Broadway. When will it be a film?

AS: I think the job Cheryl Crawford did with "Yentl" on Broadway was superb. She had a good cast; she had a nice theatre; she had nice stage designs and props. Everything was very, very fine. With this we were lucky. We were definitely unlucky in the beginning with "Yentl." This story was originally bought by a man who was a jeweler who had a wife who was a casting director. She foresaw that this would make a wonderful play or a wonderful movie, and she visualized Barbra Streisand in the title role. But for some reason Barbra Streisand postponed it and postponed it. The jeweler and his wife were not rich people and she felt that unless they had an actress of Streisand's status, with all her theater publicity, that they could not undertake the project. They did not want to risk it with another actress. Finally this jeweler found himself in financial straits, so he sold the story to Barbra Streisand's company. All of this went on for many, many years until one day Isaac gets a telephone call from a young man saying that he wants to do "Yentl" as a play. Isaac says, I don't own it anymore; it's out of my hands; it belongs to Barbra Streisand. But the younger man, Robert Kalfin, was determined to contact Barbra Streisand in hopes that arrangements could be made to let him do it on the stage. And so it was. The only thing was that she did not want to give him the right to do it with music. With music it would have been an even greater success. We were only allowed to put a few notes in. She wanted to have that for when she was ready to do the movie. Anyway now she has begun to do it. She must have bought it a dozen years ago.

GF: In his writing your husband always maintains a reverent silence on the Holocaust. *Shosha* comes as close as any of his novels in treating it, and there he does so by omitting it. We see his characters just before and just after what is the central fact of their lives. Can you talk to me about your experiences?

AS: It's very hard to explain to an American. In Germany where I was born, the Jews felt part of the nation; they were born there, they were raised there. They thought some miracle would happen and nothing would happen to them. But the miracle never came. But still, it was very hard to decide in the middle of one's life to suddenly pick up and go.

GF: Did all of your family get out?

AS: No. My grandmother had a niece in Geneva who was willing to take her. My uncle, Uncle Karl, got out at the last minute. He left penniless because he waited so long. But he was lucky. My father waited too long and my mother didn't make any move to leave. We wrote to them and urged them to leave. We couldn't get them straight to America, so we tried to get them to Cuba. We collected funds from the family and rented a room in Cuba. But my mother never made up her mind, so nothing came of it and they perished. My father was put under such enormous pressure. They said that he should bring foreign funds to the government. He didn't have such funds, but they didn't believe him or made believe that they didn't believe him. They told him that if he didn't raise it by a certain time, he would be deported and my father knew exactly what this meant. Luckily he had a heart attack and he died in his business, surrounded by his employees. Then my mother didn't want to leave. She lingered on. She thought that nothing would happen to her. But the truth was that one morning she was summoned and put on a train and the train left for an unknown destination. I have somewhere a letter. All that is known about it is that this train never arrived. They were in the middle of Poland or somewhere. They pushed them into cattle wagons and then in the middle of a field they were herded out and they were machine-gunned. This is the report we got. So.

GF: Yesterday you were talking to me about Oscar Wilde's thoughts on bitterness.

AS: He said you are lost not if you lose standing or money or anything that you consider important. You are lost only if your soul becomes bitter.

GF: It would be a most difficult thing, in this context, in the context of the Holocaust, not to feel bitterness.

AS: In two weeks a woman comes here who, with her husband, was rounded up in the night and shot. They fell when the shots rang out and pretended to be dead. When the Nazis left, they waited a while and then they crept out. She's alive. She is here to tell the tale. I would say it's harder for these people to be alive, to have gone through this, to have lifted themselves up from this, than it is for those of us who lost others.

GF: A friend of mine, who was in two of the concentration camps as a very young child, firmly believes in God. But I have talked with other people who reacted to the Holocaust by saying that never again will they believe that there is a God.

AS: No. I stopped believing right then and there. Perhaps I wasn't a very strong believer right from the start, but it all seems so senseless, because what did these people actually do to anybody. Nothing, except that they were born in a religion like you are born in your religion. That's all. This persecution was senseless and was cruel and it just doesn't make any sense. How can you believe in a higher power that lets this happen? After that I said, no more for me. No. No.

GF: Herman Broder in *Enemies, A Love Story* thinks at one point that perhaps a Hitler reigns on high, that maybe there is an evil God.

AS: Well, then again many things in creation are so perfect, so beautiful, that they could not be the product of an evil mind. When we consider the wings of a butterfly or a snail or a stone . . . there is such untold beauty in the universe. There must be something behind creation. I would not call it God. There must have been a power in the beginning, a first cause, and then creation evolved and refined itself. Who did it, or what did it, who knows? Let's substitute Power or Original Motor for God. God connotes a divine person.

GF: In your husband's fiction, he asks these questions and he has characters who are filled with doubt and disbelief not unlike your own, but ultimately he believes.

AS: Yes. He believes.

GF: Do you debate it with him?

AS: No. I don't like to let him know that I have a contrary view, because those people who believe in God are happier than the ones who doubt. Why disturb him? I think that it's better to leave him his belief that there is a God, that there is a hereafter. Good for him if he feels that way. I just say I don't know what there is.

But I want to tell you something that is very significant to me about destiny in life. Perhaps it is the only really mysterious thing in my life which ever happened. Actually as this thing with Hitler started to get worse and worse, my husband, who was not Isaac, of course, was more alert than I was to the problem. The trouble with me was that I really hated to give up the business. It was a fantastic business which we had in Munich and there already were two children. I thought, only in extreme need will I give this up. Maybe we can live through it. One day I wheeled my baby carriage with the children around a big square near our house. It was a nasty day; there were not many people on the square. Suddenly I saw an elderly man who also pushed a baby carriage. He pushed; I pushed. It was unavoidable—we got into a conversation. While I talked to this man it became very clear to me that we had to leave. Why he talked to me, I do not know. People were already very careful to whom they talked and what they said. He told me terrible things were going on in the east. They were building concentration camps, extermination camps. He said that he had a relative who came from the east and saw all these things. When I heard this I asked him questions, and he said, they are going to wipe out all the Jews. They will be shipped there and killed. When I came home that day, I said to my husband, I think we'd better make it final. I want to go. But why on a rainy day an old man wheels a baby carriage and comes over to me and tells me this! It does seem like providence. This is the one thing in my life that seems inexplicable, almost supernatural.

Later, when I ask Mrs. Singer if her husband really believes in demons, she says, "I don't know. He says sometimes that they are a means of expressing something. Why don't we go and ask him."

AS: Isaac, Grace wants to ask you something.

IBS: So what is the situation now? Did you get all the information about us? All the intimate details?

GF: I know I'm not going to get a straight answer on this one. Actually I wanted Alma to tell me if you really believe in demons.

IBS: I absolutely believe in demons and I will give you proof of it right now. I will tell you, it happens once in a blue moon, very seldom, that Alma goes away and I stay home alone . . .

GF: I've already published that one.

AS: This is the one about leaving the lights on?

IBS: Yes. Actually there have been times in my life when I was so afraid of the demons and the supernatural powers that I was half mad with fear.

AS: You were?

IBS: Yes.

AS: Not me.

IBS: I will tell you more. Even until today whenever I have the slightest problem I pray God, and I always suspect that the higher powers and the lower powers are after me. Whenever I was in love I always felt there was a telepathic *esprit* between the person and me. I always feel that if I'm angry with a person, this person knows about it, or if I like a person very much, I feel that an *esprit* of sympathy flows between me and him.

AS: This is true about everybody.

IBS: Yes, but what is true about everybody doesn't make it less true. It's true about all of us. I don't believe in the history of love that any real love affair between a man and a woman can develop without telepathy.

GF: Did you have this with Alma?

IBS: Yes. As a matter of fact we have a case where I went somewhere and waited for her and in the most unexpected way she just promptly came there. To the library. Remember?

AS: This was just an accident.

IBS: You see, she is a rationalist. You call it an accident, but I do not. I feel that streams of knowledge and of love and of hatred and of all kinds of emotion exist.

AS: I will tell you the way it was. I asked him once, what do you do in New York; where do you do your writing? He told me that he goes to the periodical room on the first floor of the library. So one day, several months later, I decided I would go to that library and maybe by chance I would see him. I found the room and walked in and the first person I saw sitting there was Isaac.

IBS: Yes! But I went there that day with the idea of meeting her! I wouldn't say that this is really evidence of telepathy or of clairvoyance, but I believe that there is no evidence that even love exists or that talent exists. There is no evidence for these things, but these things do exist just the same. I believe.

Isaac Bashevis Singer

Miriam Berkley/1983

From *Publishers Weekly,* 223 (18 February 1983), 65–6. Reprinted by permission of the publishers, R.R. Bowker Company, a Xerox company. Copyright 1983 by Xerox Corporation.

A soft Yiddish-accented "Coming!," a slight movement at the peep-hole and Isaac Bashevis Singer opens the door to his spacious upper West Side apartment in New York. We walk down the Persian-carpeted hallway, with its walls lined with books and magazines on Judaism, mysticism, the Cabbalah, the occult, into a white-walled living room.

It's eight o'clock on the eve of Singer's annual winter departure for Florida, which has suddenly been pushed forward a fortnight, meaning a last-minute rush of preparations. Alma, his wife, greets us then leaves, reappearing briefly with glasses of freshly squeezed orange juice. Singer, born in Poland, and Alma, German-born, who understands but doesn't speak Yiddish, communicate in English "in our own way."

We are here to speak with Isaac Singer as a writer for children. The 77-year-old Nobel laureate is cordial but seems tired. Still, as the hour wears on, he grows more animated and answers our questions eloquently. The 1978 Nobel citation to Singer referred to his "impassioned narrative art," the ability to tell a story unlike anyone else, and this spills over into his conversation.

Zlateh the Goat (1966), a kind of love story between boy and beast, was Isaac Bashevis Singer's first story for children. He was past 60 at the time, and the book was written in response to a request for a story about Chanukah from his friend Elizabeth Shub, then editing children's books at Harper & Row. It won Singer his first Newbery Honor.

Since then he has continued writing for children, mostly short story collections or picture books that have been illustrated by such people as Maurice Sendak (spying the typescript for *Zlateh the Goat* on Ursula Nordstrom's desk, Sendak reportedly said to her, "What! You have a manuscript here by Isaac Basheveis Singer, and you haven't offered it to me?"), Uri Shulevitz (who did Singer's latest, *The Golem* from Farrar, Straus & Giroux), Margot Zemach, Nonny Hogrogian and Eric Carle. All are written originally in Yiddish, translated into English and eventually into other languages; Hebrew, French, Spanish, Italian, Swedish, Japanese, etc. Among these books are a National Book Award-winner, *A Day of Pleasure* (1969), two additional Newbery Honor books, *The Fearsome Inn* (1967) and *When Schlemiel Went to Warsaw,* (1968), and a number of books named ALA Notables: *Mazel and Shlimazel* (1967), *When Shlemiel Went to Warsaw* (1968), *The Wicked City* (1972), *Naftali the Story-teller and His Horse, Sus* (1976) are four examples of these.

Did Singer's immediate success in children's books surprise him? Not so much. "I read the story myself, and I liked it, and my editor liked it, so if I got a prize, I thought, so maybe the committee also liked it. And this was the end of the surprise."

What *does* surprise him is the range of languages his books appear in. Many are translated into Japanese, for instance. "What do Japanese children know about Poland? But then, it's not really such a surprise. When I read Andersen's stories or the Grimm stories as a little boy, it was also an environment far from me. And I loved them. Everything which is good is international—a good picture, a good story, good philosophy, good science. What I'm surprised at is that people don't understand each other to such a high degree—or maybe I should say to such a low degree."

The fact that children like his stories is a source of great satisfaction to Singer, who finds children wonderful readers, more independent than adults. In the statement, "Why I Write for Children"—a list of 10 reasons prepared for his National Book Award acceptance speech, read in Stockholm and published with his Nobel lecture—he wrote, "Children read books, not reviews."

He repeats that now, adding, "A child will accept or reject a book only because of his real taste, what he likes and what he doesn't like. If you tell him that Freud or Moses praised this story, he will be unimpressed."

What makes a good children's story? The same qualities that make a good adult story: "It must be a real story with a beginning, a middle and an end. There must be suspense in it—the child must not know when beginning the book what the end will be."

Although Singer's stories for young and older readers come "from the same source, the same mind," he says that when writing for the young, "I will not write a love story with sex. I have lately seen people who really have sex in children's stories, but I don't believe in this. I don't think children would appreciate it." Love is a different matter. "Oh, yes, love, love. Absolutely!"

The picture book titled *Why Noah Chose the Dove* ends with the words, "the Truth is that there are in the world more doves than there are tigers, leopards, wolves, vultures and other ferocious beasts. The dove lives happily without fighting. It is the bird of peace."

Does he, then, believe in morals or happy endings? Not on principle. "If my publisher would tell me, 'Write a moralizing story,' I couldn't do it. But if I sit down to write a story by myself, and if I feel there is some moral in it, it will be there. The main thing is that a writer should not be pushed by anybody."

"This is the reason, I think, why in Soviet Russia and in other such countries the writers are terribly confused. They get orders; you have to write so that the Bolshevik Revolution should come out beautiful and useful and necessary and so on. Once a writer gets these orders he is in a bad way. I would say writing is like sex. If a man is told, 'You have to satisfy me; you have to give me six orgasms,' he is *kaput.* If people are relaxed, and they love one another, there will be success."

What about children? Must a children's writer know children? Singer was separated from his own son at five, an emigré with his mother from Poland to the Soviet Union, until the young man was in his 20s.

Singer's four grandchildren live in Israel, and he doesn't see them often. Also, they speak Hebrew and, although Singer reads Hebrew, he has trouble pronouncing it. So communication with them is less frequent or full than he likes, and they probably know him best through the Hebrew-language editions of his books.

Singer does have contacts with other children—at readings. "I look at these children when I read the story to them, and I have the feeling they don't care. They don't listen. It's just a burden to them. And suddenly they begin to ask questions, and I realize they heard every word, they understood every sentence. These little children are something remarkable."

Singer's own childhood, and the child within him, remain vividly alive to him. One early memory, about which he has written much, is of the *cheder* (school) to which "they carried me the first time" at the age of three. There he learned the Hebrew letters used both in Hebrew and Yiddish.

Isaac Singer had only a few toys but he played with books before he could read, pretending to be a scholar like his father or a writer like his brother Joshua, 10 years his senior.

He listened to folk tales told by his father and mother, many of which form the basis of his own stories today, or he listened to stories from the Bible. "My children's books were the Bible. The Book of Genesis is full of beautiful stories—the Joseph story is a sublime story, the Book of Samuel, the Book of Kings."

At age eight or nine, Singer discovered Sherlock Holmes, who inspired his first literary effort—an imitation that lasted for a page or two. The Holmes stories, read in Yiddish, had "all the qualities for which I looked—adventure, suspense."

Understanding "one sentence in six or so," he read *Crime and Punishment* in Yiddish while barely in his teens. "But I understood that he was a great writer." The novel "kind of lifted up my spirit. I felt terribly sad, yet very happy that I could read something like this."

Not long after, he was also reading German; the language in which he read was a matter of what books he could borrow from friends. "Who could buy a book in those days?" In Hebrew, he read *The Picture of Dorian Gray,* which he found very beautiful, and *The Pickwick Papers,* and in Polish the stories of Edgar Allan Poe ("he was as marvellous as he is in English"). Today it is Poe, along with such other 19th century writers he first read during that period— Tolstoy, Dostoyevsky, Gogol, Pushkin, Flaubert—whom Singer admires the most.

Eventually, after a spell in a seminary, he moved to Warsaw and there, under his brother Joshua's tutelage, he became part of the Jewish literary scene, working one or two days a week as a proofreader for a journal Joshua co-edited.

Singer attended a club called the *Literatenferein,* the Union of Writers, with a guest card from Joshua, a member. When Isaac had published some dozen stories, he was presented with a card of his own: "A great day in my life."

In those early, pre-America days, when he was struggling as a young writer, one of the things Isaac Singer sought most was his brother's approval. Now, however, no one tells him how to write.

"Sometimes when an editor tells me that there's some mistake, in grammar or something, of course I tell him, 'correct it by all means.' But they never really try to teach me how to write. It's too late for teaching."

Nor does he worry overly much about critics, although he does look at reviews. "If the reviewer would try very hard, he could manage to hurt me," he says. But, "I'm not easily hurt. All I say to myself, there are different tastes, different readers, different opinions. You have to make peace with it that you cannot please everybody. But, as a rule, I've no complaints."

The Passions of a Nobel Laureate:
Isaac Bashevis Singer

Tom Teicholz/1983

From *Interview*, 13 (August 1983), 36–38. Reprinted by permission of Tom Teicholz.

Tom Teicholz: Your works are known for their lush sensuality, and the perversion in which your characters indulge. Why does this interest you so much?

Isaac Bashevis Singer: Why shouldn't it be interesting to me? Isn't it the thing about which people think and act on all their lives? Isn't sex the way—don't we all come from sex? You might as well ask why people are interested in food.

TT: But it's not always the subject matter of literature.

IS: I wouldn't say it always is, but then I don't do things that are always done.

TT: One imagines, though, the world of the Hassidim and Polish Orthodox Jewry to be a world of many restrictions.

IS: It's true. My father was a Hassid, but I am not exactly a Hassid at this stage in my life. I am a religious man. I believe in God, but I am not a Hassid. I do not believe that man's love and passion is something against God. He created it.

TT: But do you think that a life in which there are restrictions imposed leads to greater or more unbridled passion?

IS: I think that if you restrict one energy, it will come out in another energy. If you restrain yourself from sexual achievements, you will get other things. Your desire for literature or photography or any other work will be greater. This energy is in us. Of course, it can also become religion—it can become anything. The truth is that, if people didn't restrict themselves, they wouldn't be able to exist together. Our whole civilization and culture is based on restriction.

TT: Do you think in modern life today there are the same restrictions or are—

IS: There are not the same restrictions, but we restrict ourselves just the same.

TT: Do you think life today is more passionate?

IS: I think that in people who restrict themselves, there is more passion because the passion doesn't want the restriction. It tries to get out of the restrictions, so there is more of a battle. But in the end, there is some bookkeeping in life, so that if energy is spent in one way, it will not be spent in another way and so on.

TT: In one of your books, you talk about how, as a young man, you wrote many rules for yourself, one of which was that one should only be married for fifteen years. Do you still believe that?

IS: I would say I believe that: if marriage is a contract, it should not be a contract for life. It should be a contract for a number of years until the people bring up a family. Then, if they still love one another, it should be prolonged.

TT: But is fidelity possible?

IS: I think it is possible. If it weren't possible, people wouldn't talk about it. As a matter of fact, every human being restrains himself one way or another.

TT: But your stories are all about people who don't, or can't, restrain themselves.

IS: Well, they do, but sometimes their passion is so great that they burst their restrictions. I would say that the whole civilization is built on restrictions. You would not be able to do anything if you would only let go.

TT: In terms of literature, do you think there are some writers who are memorable for their writings about these passions, about sex?

IS: Many, like Henry Miller and also Chinese writers and other Asiatic writers and writers in African languages.

TT: Which, for you, are the most memorable writers about sex?

IS: Well, we still think that Boccaccio knew his profession quite well.

TT: Do you think the elements you write about between men and women are so basic—do you think that's why your works are read all over the world?

IS: I have the illusion that I am read because people like what they are reading. Why they like and what they like, I don't know.

TT: Or what they understand?

IS: I don't write so that my writing is obscure, so that I need commentaries. I try to make it clear.

TT: Do you think that fiction should be moral; that writers have a moral responsibility?

IS: I don't think that a writer should sit down and try to write a moral story or a novel. But, if he is a moral man, and a man who thinks about ethics and culture—real culture—there will be some message and insight. But if a man sits down to write and says, "This novel is going to make people better, and bring the glorious future they are hoping for," he will never succeed.

TT: So you feel that your ethical training . . .

IS: Was not lost. Except for a real outcast, no writer features crime or something like this. There are such writers too, I am sorry to say, but I don't belong to them.

TT: What does God think of all the passions?

IS: I know that after this interview, you are going to interview the Almighty so that He will tell you all about it. I don't know what He thinks.

TT: Well, what do you think about Him?

IS: All I can say is that I can see very well His great and divine wisdom. I cannot see His mercy all the time, but He has to hide something. He's not going to tell me all the secrets.

TT: When you create your stories, do you feel more in touch with your Creator?

IS: I think I feel in touch with Him every minute of my life. I feel that He is there, and His providence is there, and His computer is so great that it can take care of all the billions of people and all the planets that have people.

TT: But you believe in free will?

IS: Yes.

TT: So He doesn't predetermine?

IS: According to Maimonides, both are true: determinism and free will.

TT: How so?

IS: Maybe you don't understand how so—it looks like a contradiction, but it's only a contradiction to our way of thinking. Not to God's way of thinking. In a way, it's possible, even in this world.

You can say that under such and such a circumstance a man is going to feel this way, and he really does. That doesn't mean that he did not have free choice. He had free choice; only he decided not to use it.

TT: What about suicide? You once said, "For me, a person who does not think about suicide is almost not a person."

IS: I think a person who does not think about suicide does not see the tragedy of humanity. So he is not a highly sensitive person. I think a highly sensitive person would, sooner or later, play with the idea that a man can put an end to it if he really wants to.

TT: Do you still think about suicide?

IS: Why not? We all do.

TT: You've been quoted as saying that you believe we've all been here more than once.

IS: I believe in it, but I have no evidence that it is so.

TT: No one has called you from the Beyond and said it's so.

IS: No one has called me, but when I walk in the spring and I see the leaves and the roses, I recognize them from last year. They are the same. In a way, they have been here last year. The same is true about us. We have been here the last century or so. It's not a question of evidence, only a question of feeling.

TT: Are you as curious today about the world as you were as a young man?

IS: Yes. I almost wanted to say more so, but if I am as curious as I was, I am very curious.

TT: Have you found any answers to your questions?

IS: No answers at all. We find parts of answers, answers in certain circumstances, some personal answers. But the great answer to why we were born, why we are here, why we have to die, why we have to witness, and why we suffer, can never be answered in a really satisfying way. I would say that man is going to ask these questions to the very end of his existence.

TT: Are there still some questions that you think you will find answers to?

IS: Small ones I find all the time. I write a story, and I ask myself should I finish it so or differently, and I find an answer. But when it comes to the so-called "Eternal Questions," I don't think that any answer is waiting for us.

TT: But, do you still believe, as Gimpel does, that anything is possible?

IS: I wouldn't say *anything*. If you would tell me that we could walk on the ceiling I would have my doubts. But knowing what causality is, and what human will and human freedom are and what the human passions are, many things have happened—many things which limited people think cannot happen. But these things can happen and do happen and have already happened.

TT: You've been writing since the 1930s and have only been published in English since the 1950s. There is a lot of material that continues to appear in English without any regard to its chronological order. How do you choose what to release?

IS: What I think is worth being translated, I translate. Where I think I did not succeed 100 percent, I would leave them [untranslated].

TT: Do you re-work them?

IS: If I find time, I do.

TT: So some of the old material is as good as the new material?

IS: I don't think we have time to search and search and find them. I think there is a lot of my material which should be translated. There is a lot of material that I would like to re-work.

TT: Work that has been published in Yiddish?

IS: Yes, published in Yiddish. There are unpublished things also, but mostly things that have been published in *The Jewish Daily Forward*.

TT: Stories or whole novels?

IS: Stories, even novels and novellas—all kinds of things. Essays— scores of essays that I wrote just because I had to deliver stuff every week to the editor.

TT: Do you feel that being a serial writer was good training?

IS: I think it was good for me. It was good in the Nineteenth century. Many writers wrote like this. It has its shortcomings too. One of the shortcomings is that the writer is bound to repeat himself. But this repetition does no damage if the writer later edits his stuff and takes out the repetition. It is a very wonderful discipline for a writer. It is a whip that drives you to write, and in writing he tries not to be obscure because what he writes today, 20,000 or 40,000 people will read tomorrow or next week. You know that you are really talking to people and not to yourself. You don't try to be an obscure writer who needs commentators to explain his work all the time.

Isaac Bashevis Singer: Conversations

TT: What is lost in translation in your work?

IS: I would say a lot would be lost if I didn't work on them, but I work on the translations. I have learned enough English to work on them, and I am a reader myself. If I see that something is not right and I don't like it and would not publish it, I will rewrite it. I would say that I do a lot not to lose anything. Sometimes I even gain through the forces of translation because while I read it I get new ideas. I would say that people who read me in Yiddish and people who read me in English, if they know both languages, will see how many changes I've made in the process of translation.

TT: With your present knowledge of English, are there any works that were translated 20 years ago that you think deserve to be re-translated?

IS: No, I have no complaints about the translations because my nephew, the son of my brother, I. J. Singer, was quite a good translator. I think I would find mostly faults in my writing, not in the translation.

TT: How did Saul Bellow come to translate "Gimpel"? Was that just a coincidence?

IS: He undertook to publish a kind of anthology of Yiddish stories, and his assistant, a Mr. Greenberg, knew that I wrote "Gimpel the Fool," and he read it to him. Bellow knows Yiddish, but not too much. He knew enough for an American man. He liked it and he translated it. This was the only time that he translated a story.

TT: In many ways, it launched your career in English.

IS: In a way, yes. It was published in *The Partisan Review.* That was read by most of the writers, and I got some attention.

TT: Does wearing the cloak of being one of the last Yiddish writers carry a burden with it?

IS: If I wear that cloak I am not conscious of it. When I sit down to write, I don't think about whether I am the last or the first or whether I will help Yiddish or do damage to Yiddish. I think about the story—is it going to be a good story or a bad story? So, because of this, other things I leave to the critics. If they want me to be the last Yiddish writer—actually, no one knows. No man knows if he will be the last one. There will always be someone else.

TT: Do you see yourself primarily as a writer of short stories?

IS: No, I have written novels. Of course, I love the short story. The short story is a great challenge to a writer because you have to say, in a few pages, a lot of things. I think that the short story should really be short. I think that the short stories in *The New Yorker* are almost all longer than my stories. Mine are really short. But if you manage to really say a lot and to bring out character and personality in a story, or bring out suspense, you have achieved almost the impossible.

TT: And what about your career as a writer of film treatments and as a playwright?

IS: I would not say that I am a playwright, at this point, certainly not with film—I wrote one little treatment once. I think of myself seriously as a writer of novels and short stories. If I succeed in making a play, I consider it a miracle.

TT: Now *Yentl* is being made into a film.

IS: It is being made into a film. That's true. What kind of a film, I don't know.

TT: Have you seen any of it?

IS: I wrote a script, but they didn't take it. Barbra Streisand wanted a musical with songs. There are no songs in my script. So they made a different script and there will be songs. It is not really my child.

TT: But more and more you're writing children's books?

IS: I have written ten or eleven books—small books. Each one contains a story or maybe two, but never 20 or something like that.

TT: Does this come from being a grandfather?

IS: I think I began writing for children before I became a grandfather.

TT: But you like writing for children?

IS: I love it. They are a great audience. Children are really independent readers. You cannot hypnotize them with reviews or advertisements or by authorities. The child has to like it. If he doesn't like it, it's rejected. So they are real independent readers.

TT: You've been called a curator of a lost world. Do you feel more able to write about this lost world because you did not witness its destruction?

IS: First of all, the lost world is the world of my childhood, of my younger days. This is the world between the time of my being born and the time of my leaving—I'd say I was about 30 years old when I left Poland. So a large part of my life, though not the largest part,

I lived in Poland. We are bound to write about the things of our younger days and to remember them better than the things that happened yesterday or the day before. Of course, I write also about people here in America, but mostly I write about people from Poland—Yiddish-speaking Poles, Jews—I do this to be sure that I write about people that I know best. I know their language best and their way of thinking. I would almost never write about people born in this country. Once in a while I will bring in someone, but just for a while.

TT: What about assimilation and the loss of culture? Your work seems to emphasize being true to one's . . . .

IS: I don't believe in assimilation. I think assimilation is when a man, who is a member of a minority, tries to adjust himself to the culture of the majority. I think this is not right. You should stay what you are and stay with your roots and not adjust yourself to people because they are more in number or stronger and so on. For instance, I don't mind if you know all about Shakespeare. But if you know all about Shakespeare, and you don't want to know anything about the Jews or the Jewish writers, I would say that you are trying to adjust yourself to a strong majority. I consider that wrong from an ethical point of view, and from the point of view of human dignity.

TT: Why from the point of view of human dignity?

IS: Because it's not dignified for a man to deny his home and to try to imitate and own what belongs to somebody else. In other words, if you have parents and a home and a language and you say, "My parents and home and language are nothing. But my neighbor—his parents are important. His home is important. His language is important"—you have no dignity.

TT: You can't imagine that the two together can become more than the individual?

IS: Yes, I can imagine it, and it is so. But it is not so when one party is completely weak or nonexistent. That really means that you have decided that you are nothing and the other one is great because he has more power, or more numbers, which is not as the thing should be.

TT: You studied to be a rabbi, and your works are full of scholarly religious references. Do you keep up with this? Do you still read the Talmud and the commentaries?

IS: If I open it, I read it. Sometimes I am curious and I read it, but

I have no discipline where I have to study every day so much of the Talmud or so much of the Bible. Sometimes I take out the Bible and I will read it for two or three hours wondering, since I have read it scores of times, why do I read it? But I always find something new in it. This would be true about the Talmud or all of these old books.

TT: You've called vegetarianism the greatest achievement of your life.

IS: I don't mean a financial achievement. I mean an achievement in the sense that I had the courage to do what I wanted to do for many many years and I didn't.

TT: When did you decide this?

IS: I would say I made my last decision about 20 years ago.

TT(teasingly): But when one writes a great deal, one is killing many trees.

IS: Well, I don't worry about the trees. I have not yet heard any tree crying. Let the Almighty worry about the trees. We will worry about creatures of flesh and blood, like ourselves.

TT: When did you feel comfortable as a writer and a journalist?

IS: I never felt comfortable. I always felt like I haven't done enough and haven't polished enough. I should polish more and improve more. So going around feeling comfortable is not in my nature.

TT: And today?

IS: Today I don't feel comfortable at all because I am thinking about my next story and what I should do about it. Who wants comfort?

TT: Is there any recognition that you haven't . . . I mean, you've received practically every prize there is to get.

IS: I would say that I'm getting recognition, but I did not really work for recognition. This was not my sole condition [for becoming a writer]: either recognition or nothing. I would have done the same thing if I had not gotten any recognition. I would still do my work. Of course, I was glad that some of it I got, but recognition and money are not everything.

TT: Although your father wrote commentaries, he didn't believe in secular writing.

IS: No. He was very much against it. He considered secular writing, as a matter of fact, sinful writing. He had no respect for secular writing and always warned me not to go in this direction because my brother I. J. Singer did it. He believed that a Jew, especially his son, should have one thing in his life and that was religion.

TT: Was it difficult to make the choice to go against him?

IS: It wasn't difficult for me because he was against it—I didn't want to bring him grief or spite him. I loved him too much to enjoy opposing him. But I had no choice. I didn't have his belief that every restriction and all the laws, which rabbis have handed down generation after generation, were really given by Moses on Mt. Sinai. Without this belief, I couldn't have become a rabbi. I couldn't have become a man who studied the Talmud all the time and does nothing else. It was a conflict between my beliefs and my love for him and my mother, which never diminished for a moment because I knew they wanted the best for me. But what they considered the best, I did not consider the best. Their intention was certainly very good.

TT: Did they ever read anything you wrote?

IS: Very little of it. My father, almost nothing. They read once in a while and what they read, they criticized. They never went around boasting about their son the writer.

TT: Do you think they would have been shocked by some of the material you now write about?

IS: I'm sure that if my father were alive now, he would still not read anything of my writing. He would say I had made the mistake of my life. My mother would be a little more tolerant, but not too much so.

TT: Is there a point at which you limit yourself, at which you censor yourself?

IS: Yes, I would say that if I hadn't censored myself, my stories would have been even more sexy. I would have written more about sex than I do today. But I don't believe in four-letter words—this I really dislike. I think it adds nothing to literature—it diminishes literature. I would have been more outspoken, but I think literature can do very well without it because my readers know as well about sex as I do; they know what it is all about. I don't have to explain it to them.

TT: What's the difference between erotic literature and pornography?

IS: Pornography to me is a man who sits down to write just to excite people and has no other goal. It's very boring. I tried to write, once in a while, a pornographic book. It's boring, it's repetitious, it adds nothing to literature. If you read Boccaccio you can enjoy both the story and what he writes about.

TT: I'm sure you're asked the same questions over and over.

IS: I don't mind.

TT: Is there any question that you would ask of I. B. Singer that hasn't been asked?

IS: No. I would leave him in peace.

I. B. Singer Talks to I. B. Singer about the Movie *Yentl*

Isaac Bashevis Singer/1984

From *The New York Times,* 133 (29 January 1984), sec. 2, col. 1.
Reprinted by permission of The New York Times.

In the 1950s, Isaac Bashevis Singer wrote a story titled "Yentl the Yeshiva Boy," about a rabbi's daughter with "the soul of a man and the body of a woman." The young woman, Yentl, is so hungry for learning that she defies Talmudic law by disguising herself as a man in order to attend a yeshiva, or religious school. The story, set in 19th-century Poland, was adapted for the stage in 1974 and recently became the basis of a big-budget Hollywood musical produced and directed by Barbra Streisand, who also plays the title role. Herewith, Mr. Singer asks himself a few questions about Miss Streisand's "Yentl."

Q: Have you finally seen the Yentl movie?

A: Yes, I have seen it.

Q: Did you like it?

A: I am sorry to say I did not. I did not find artistic merit neither in the adaptation, nor in the directing. I did not think that Miss Streisand was at her best in the part of Yentl. I must say that Miss Tovah Feldshuh, who played Yentl on Broadway, was much better. She understood her part perfectly; she was charming and showed instinctive knowledge of how to portray the scholarly Yentl I described in my story. Miss Streisand lacked guidance. She got much, perhaps too much advice and information from various rabbis, but rabbis cannot replace a director. The Talmudic quotations and allusions did not help.

Q: Did you enjoy the singing?

A: Music and singing are not my fields. I did not find anything in her singing which reminded me of the songs in the studyhouses and Hasidic *shtibls,* which were a part of my youth and environment. As a matter of fact, I never imagined Yentl singing songs. The passion for learning and the passion for singing are not much related in my mind. There is almost no singing in my works. One thing is sure: there was too much singing in this movie, much too much. It came from all sides. As far as I can see the singing did nothing to bring out Yentl's individuality and to enlighten her conduct. The very opposite, I had a feeling that her songs drowned the action. My story, "Yentl the Yeshiva Boy," was in no way material for a musical, certainly not the kind Miss Streisand has given us. Let me say: one cannot cover up with songs the shortcomings of the direction and acting.

Q: Is it true that you wrote a script of the play which Miss Streisand rejected?

A: It is true, and when I read her script and saw the movie I understood that she could not have accepted my version. In my script Yentl does not stay on stage from beginning to end. The leading actress must make room for others to have their say and exhibit their talents. No matter how good you are, you don't take everything for yourself. I don't mean to say that my script was perfect, or even good. But at least I understood that in this case the leading actress cannot monopolize the stage. We all know that actors fight for bigger parts, but a director worth his name will not allow one actor to usurp the entire play. When an actor is also the producer and the director and the writer he would have to be exceedingly wise to curb his appetites. I must say that Miss Streisand was exceedingly kind to herself. The result is that Miss Streisand is always present, while poor Yentl is absent.

Q: How do you feel about the writing?

A: It is not easy to make a film from a story. In most cases it is impossible. The great plays such as Shakespeare's, Moliere's, Ibsen's, Strindberg's were written as plays. My Aunt Yentl used to say to my Uncle Joseph, "In a pinch I can make from a chicken soup a borscht, but to make from a borscht a chicken soup, this is beyond any cook." Those who adapt novels or stories for the stage or for the screen must be masters of their profession and also have the decency to do the adaptation in the spirit of the writer. You cannot do the adaptation against the essence of the story or the novel, against the character of the protagonist.

Let's imagine a scriptwriter who decides that Mme. Bovary should end up taking a cruise along the Riviera or that Anna Karenina should marry an American millionaire instead of committing suicide, and Dostoyevski's Raskolnikov should become a Wall Street broker instead of going to Siberia. This is what Miss Streisand did by making Yentl, whose greatest passion was the Torah, go on a ship to America, singing at the top of her lungs. Why would she decide to go to America? Weren't there enough yeshivas in Poland or in Lithuania where she could continue to study? Was going to America Miss Streisand's idea of a happy ending for Yentl? What would Yentl have done in America? Worked in a sweatshop 12 hours a day where there is no time for learning? Would she try to marry a salesman in New York, move to the Bronx or to Brooklyn and rent an apartment with an ice box and a dumbwaiter? This kitsch ending summarizes all the faults of the adaptation. It was done without any kinship to Yentl's character, her ideals, her sacrifice, her great passion for spiritual achievement. As it is, the whole splashy production has nothing but a commercial value.

A Singer of Stories in His Ninth Decade

Linda Matchan/1985

From *The Boston Globe* (25 August 1985) ed. 3, sec. Sunday
Magazine, 15 ff. Reprinted courtesy of The Boston Globe.

Yiddish writer and Nobel laureate Isaac Bashevis Singer, 81, is taking
a mid-morning walk. Head bent forward, eyes down, he is striding a
dozen brisk steps ahead of his slightly breathless wife, Alma, to whom
he has been married for 45 years.

As he usually does at this time of the morning, Singer is returning
home to his beachfront Collins Avenue highrise in the Surfside area
of Miami Beach; it is not far from Isaac Singer Boulevard, a street
named for the author after he won the 1978 Nobel Prize in Literature. The walk is just a short one for Singer, who usually walks five
miles—80 New York City blocks, he says—every day. But it is an un-
varying part of the routine. He and Alma have just had their breakfast where they begin most days when not at their other homes in
New York or Wengen, Switzerland.

He passes a corset shop, a store with orthopedic shoes, a bakery
that specializes in low-salt baked goods. This is an old people's neighborhood. Pedestrians move slowly. Drivers move slowly. Everywhere
are signs of retirement and advanced age, of spare time to kill: large
bellies, Bermuda shorts, bronzed, wrinkled skin, varicose veins.
Yiddish—Singer's native tongue and the language now spoken in
this country mostly by a shrinking community of aging Jewish immigrants and by Hasidic Jews—is heard on Surfside's streets as often as
English is. Restaurant menus offer prune juice, stewed prunes, Jell-O.

Yet here in this aging world of his Yiddish-speaking contemporaries, the Polish-born Singer looks conspicuously out of place. He
walks quickly, and he hasn't a hint of a suntan even though the
temperature has been in the 70s and 80s for weeks. He is a thin
man, and unlike virtually everyone else in Surfside, he is wearing
a tie, a white shirt, heavy black shoes, and a lightweight, blue suit
jacket; there is a dressy straw hat on his head. The suit and tie, the

227

hat: It is an Old World appearance that he almost never sheds. He will say later this day that he doesn't know what Bermuda shorts are.

He is in a hurry, he says as he walks. It is 11 a.m., and he has only an hour to spare, because "they" will not leave him alone. "They," Singer explains, is "the telephone." All morning he has been bothered by phone calls—requests for interviews, requests from his readers to review their manuscripts, questions about his work, greetings from admirers, invitations to social gatherings. "They always call, and they say, 'I'm a great fan of yours' and that 'I read you even before the Nobel Prize,'" Singer says, a little sardonically, in his Polish-accented English. He looks beleaguered as he rides silently in the elevator of his apartment building and then unlocks the door of his sunny, one-bedroom condominium.

Although it is Sunday, it is a busy day for Singer. He must prepare for the creative writing class that he teaches every Monday with his friend Lester Goran, a professor of English, at the University of Miami. He has agreed to be interviewed, an obligation that seems more of a burden to him than anything else but one he puts up with because he says he doesn't like to disappoint people. He has a dinner party to go to this evening that he doesn't want to attend. And, of course, he must make time for his writing. He is working on a novel, *Der Veg Aheim (The Way Home)*, which has been running in weekly installments in the New York-based Yiddish newspaper *The Jewish Forward*. His editor, Simon Weber, is waiting for the next installment, and so are all his readers.

But before long the telephone rings. It is the woman who has invited him for dinner.

"I want to tell you that I don't really feel too well," he objects. "If you can free me . . ."

It doesn't work. "Who is going to be there, tell me?" he asks. "It's a restaurant, isn't it, or in a house? What time will the car come? . . . I will tell you, I don't really feel too well, so if I don't feel well, I will leave earlier."

The woman persists. There is a long silence while Singer listens. Finally, he relents.

"Okay, my friend, I will tell you, even though I don't feel well, maybe I will begin to feel well when I see people around me. Okay, okay, we will make it. . . ."

There is a pause. "And give my best to your husband. Thank you."

In the ninth decade of his life, Singer is at the height of his popularity, appeal, and productivity. In the past year he has launched two new plays off Broadway; published four books, *Love and Exile, Stories for Children, Gifts,* and *The Image and Other Stories;* written articles for *The New York Times;* and published several short stories, including three in *The New Yorker,* two in *Partisan Review,* and two in *Moment,* a Jewish Magazine. His serialized Yiddish novels and stories still appear every week in *The Jewish Forward,* which he has written for regularly since 1935 and which has published most of his major translated works, including *The Magician of Lublin, The Slave, The Manor, The Estate,* and *The Penitent.*

He is said to be the only living Yiddish writer whose translated work has caught the imagination of American readers. Read in 16 languages, Singer has produced a voluminous body of writing, some of it rooted in America, but much of it in the now-vanished world of the shtetls and ghettos of pre-World War II Poland.

In simple, uncluttered prose, he describes a world of horse-drawn droshkies, of pushcarts, fools, wise men, whores, penitents, fanatics, psychics; a world where pious young men wear long gabardines and sidelocks; where intellectuals meet in Warsaw cafeterias to discuss social revolution, Zionism, Kafka, Spinoza. It is a world where the spirits, demons, and dybbuks of Jewish folklore hold court in daily life.

Above all, it is a world that reflects the perpetual human struggle between morality and passion, good and evil, tradition and modernism. His stories trace the direction of human destiny: A married Jewish magician with hidden powers and several gentile lovers eventually isolates himself in penitential solitude to escape the licentious life he loves and fears. A woman is so fiery, vindictive, and filled with rage that fires run after her and ultimately consume her. A vain married woman from Krashnik is consumed by erotic fantasies, finally entering the mirror in her boudoir after a demon seduces her.

Singer's is not exclusively a world of darkness and conflict, however, and it is in part his diversity that has earned him the respect of readers. There are also hilariously funny Singer stories, and children's stories that are gentle and reassuring. And there are tender tales of love and devotion, such as "The Little Shoemakers," a moving story about a hard-working family of shoemakers who hold onto their beloved cobbler heritage despite their move to America; or the celebrated "Gimpel the Fool," about the victim of a thousand practical jokes who narrates his own story with an insight and humor that belie his pathetic gullibility.

Nearly seven years after being awarded the Nobel Prize, Singer still draws huge audiences when he lectures and reads his work. He is constantly sought as a speaker, and he manages to lecture or attend book signings at libraries, Jewish community centers, and colleges an average of four times a month, mostly in New York but sometimes in other parts of the country as well.

He is also sought by interviewers, who are almost always charmed by what they find. They inevitably describe Singer as a captivating and grandfatherly storyteller whose blue eyes literally twinkle when he reads, who is a master of memorable one-liners ("I am a vegetarian for the sake of health—the health of the chicken!"; "God has given me so many fantasies that my problem is not how to get them, but how to get rid of them"), who is witty and energetic and warm. Last April, *The New York Times Magazine* named Singer one of the "101 Reasons Why New York is Terrific," along with Carnegie Hall, the Brooklyn Bridge and the Rockettes.

Part of the reason he is so admired and adored is because he is thought to be a sort of walking museum of Jewish life in Eastern Europe. At his talks, people line up—young, old, students, professors, readers—to tell him how grateful they are to have access to the shtetl world in Poland. "So many of their comments sound the same," says Dvorah Menashe, Singer's secretary and personal assistant. " 'You've brought back my heritage. You've brought my grandparents' world alive.' "

Rosaline Schwartz, curator of the current exhibit about Singer at the YIVO Institute for Jewish Research in New York, says some people are so moved by Singer's work that they have returned to the exhibit two and three times. "I've heard people say they have cried here," she says.

"No matter where you go, interest in him never flags," says New York writer Dorothea Straus, the wife of Singer's publisher, Roger Straus; her book *Under the Canopy* is the story of her 20-year friendship with Singer. "I don't know another writer like him," she says.

Singer continues to draw critical praise as well. Critic-historian Irving Howe has written that Singer is a "genius" whose Yiddish prose has "a verbal and rhythmic brilliance that can hardly be matched." Author Leslie Fiedler, a professor of literature at the State University of New York at Buffalo, has described him as a "truly mythic writer." Tufts University provost Sol Gittleman, who teaches a course in Yiddish culture, calls Singer "one of the great fantasizers of Yiddish literature, the Chagall of Yiddish literature."

To be sure, Singer also has his detractors, and they are not in short supply. His writing has been called "bad for Jews," his depiction of women termed "hostile" and "derogatory," his books "too dirty." Some who know him personally say he can be churlish and rude and narrow-minded. They point to the way in which he disparaged Barbra Streisand in newspaper interviews, lambasting *Yentl,* her film version of one of his stories, as "artistic suicide," that "was absolutely not in the spirit of the story." They say that last spring Singer refused to be interviewed by a film crew from Finland, after he had first agreed to the interview and after the whole crew had flown to Miami.

What is clear, though, to almost everyone associated with him is that there is something truly remarkable about this writer, this small, frail-looking man with a fine, white feather of hair and the ears that rise impishly to a point, whose only formal higher education consisted of 18 months at a rabbinical seminary.

He is extraordinarily prolific, even now, in his 80s. Singer himself isn't sure exactly how many books he has written, but according to Farrar, Straus & Giroux, which issues most of his translated writings, the works that have been published in English include 10 books of short stories, 13 children's books, three collections, and four books of memoirs. Many other stories that have appeared in the *Forward* have yet to be translated. "I am working now in my old age, together with Dvorah, to rescue some of them from oblivion and publish them in Yiddish and English," Singer says.

Although he has received the most prestigious award that a writer can hope for, and though his stories have appeared in the finest American magazines, he first submits almost everything he writes to the humble *Jewish Forward.* The 88-year-old weekly, once a daily paper read in virtually every Jewish home across the country, is now a shadow of what it used to be. Its Yiddish-speaking readers are dying out, and its circulation has plunged from 220,000 in 1924 to 25,000 today.

Yet Singer says proudly that he never missed a day of work for the paper, with the exception of the high holy day Yom Kippur, even though editor Simon Weber says the paper pays Singer "a pittance, compared to *The New Yorker.*" Why does he do it? Simply because, Singer says, he has been connected to it and its readers for so many years. It is part of his routine and keeps him disciplined. It is simply what he does.

His fidelity to the paper is all the more remarkable in view of the fact that some of its readers—people who are in a position to have known the world that he evokes, or at least to know Yiddish well— are among the first to criticize him. Some have viewed Singer with suspicion, accusing him of being sensational, grotesque, profane, and obscene, and arguing that the evil characters, demons, and imps of his fiction are humiliating and inconsistent with Jewish life. "I had been an admirer of Isaac Bashevis Singer until his gremlins and demonology plus his near pornography chilled me," says Lewis Weinstein, a Boston attorney. It has been said that there are religious men in the *Forward*'s linotype room who refuse to touch his copy, so traif (tainted) is it to their Orthodox sensibilities.

In a way, Singer is a sort of prophet without honor in his own land. Aaron Lansky, who heads the National Yiddish Book Center, an Amherst-based organization devoted to the preservation of Yiddish literature, recalls being in a Jewish library in Montreal the day the *Forward* arrived announcing that Singer had been awarded the Nobel Prize. The library was filled with Yiddish-speaking men, and he said the news caused an uproar in the reading room. They began to yell and to argue, pulling the paper out of one another's hands to scrutinize it as though they couldn't believe what they had read.

"They were all furious," says Lansky. "A whole debate started over why Singer shouldn't have gotten it."

Why he shouldn't have gotten it, according to some who know Yiddish literature, is that other Yiddish writers deserved it more. The name of poet-novelist Chaim Grade, who died in 1982 and wrote about Jewish life in Eastern Europe between the two World Wars, is one that is frequently mentioned; he is perhaps best known for *Rabbis and Wives,* his posthumous collection of three translated novellas.

Some Yiddish readers complain that Singer places Jews in a bad light. Some say he should write more like the real Yiddish writers, the 19th- and 20th-century classicists such as Sholem Aleichem, I. L. Peretz, and Mendele Moykher Sforim. In their books, critics say, there is still a place for Jewish life in the modern world; in Singer's work, it's either "obedience to law or utter licentiousness," as Aaron Lansky puts it.

Others say they simply find Singer's writing—his contemporary work, at least—unimpressive. "*Der Veg Aheim* is boring," says one New York reader who has followed Singer's writing in the *Forward* for decades. "After I read half a column I'm tired of it. He will start out with whatever hits him—I wouldn't start in with the trees and the sunshine always. Sometimes he goes right to the story, but sometimes he keeps writing a lot of description when description is not appropriate to the subject matter."

Yet Singer is apparently unfazed by such reactions. "It is the nature of readers, especially our readers, the Jewish readers, always to complain," he says. "There is no sense in worrying about them. When I sit down to write, I don't write to please the readers. I'm the first reader, and I have to please myself."

Isaac Bashevis Singer has been writing to please himself since he was 16 years old. He was born in 1904 in Leoncin, Poland, the third of four children. His talented older brother, Israel Joshua, whom Singer often calls his "father and mentor," was the first in the family to make his mark as a writer, publishing such distinguished novels as *The Brothers Ashkenazi* and *Yoshe Kalb;* even today some readers call Israel the "real writer" in the family. Their elder sister, Hinde Esther, who lived and died in obscurity and was a depressed, troubled woman, was also a writer of some talent who published under the name of Esther Singer Kreitman. Her autobiographical novel, *Deborah,* has recently been reissued.

Both of Singer's parents were descended from rabbis, and his father, Pinchos Menachem, was a rabbi as well. Materially poor but spiritually rich, Singer's father was entirely immersed in Hasidic piety, and his one desire in life was "to have the strength to serve God and to study the Torah," as Singer recalls in his autobiographical work, *Love and Exile.* He believed in miracles and was convinced that mysterious forces were at work in the world. He spoke often in the Singer home about spirits of the dead that possess the bodies of the living, and about houses inhabited by hobgoblins and demons. The secular world was of little interest to Pinchos Menachem, who considered secular writing heretical; when people asked him what his sons did, he would reply, "They sell newspapers."

Like his father, Singer's mother, Bathsheba, was devout, but, as the son writes, "what a difference between the two of them." She was by nature a skeptic, inclined toward more rationalistic views of religion and human behavior. The contrast in their natures and their world views is characterized in a delightful tale by Singer in one of the memoirs of *In My Father's Court.* He writes of the time that a dis-traught woman visited Pinchos Menachem with what she called "a very unusual problem": the slaughtered geese that she had bought to cook would shriek when she banged one against the other, even though their heads had been removed. Pinchos Menachem main-tained triumphantly that this proved once and for all that omens were sent from heaven. Bathsheba ignored him, insisting that slaughtered geese don't shriek.

The tension in the family mounted. The mighty drama made everybody tremble; the young Isaac, torn between his parents, began to cry. In the end his mother prevailed: It suddenly occurred to her that the woman must have forgotten to remove the windpipes from the birds.

Yet this conflict—the simultaneous attraction to and away from or-thodoxy and faith, and the erosive effect of modern beliefs on tradi-tional ways of life—remained part of the son's psychology, and it shows up in much of his writing, even today.

But there were other influences, too. There was Krochmalna Street in Warsaw, the ghetto tenement area where Singer's family moved in 1908 and where his father established a *Beth Din,* or rabbinical court. It was "a kind of blend of a court of law, synagogue, house of study, and, if you will, psychoanalyst's office where people of troubled spirit could come to unburden themselves," Singer explains in *In My Father's Court.* There, as a small boy, he silently gathered much of the material that years later Singer the storyteller would recall and embellish in his work: The tales told by *Hasidim,* the settling of business arguments, the conflicts between couples who seek divorce.

"My father's courtroom was like a school to me, where I could study the human soul, its caprices, its yearnings, its barriers," Singer writes in *Love and Exile,* a collection of three of his books of memoirs that he characterizes as "spiritual autobiography, fiction set against a background of truth." A boy who loved to read, to fantasize, and to question, he absorbed all of the activity in the courtroom with a curiosity and appetite for detail that astonished and even frightened his mother. "What a memory!" she used to say. "Let no evil eye befall you."

In 1917 Singer went with his mother to visit her father, the rabbi of Bilgoray. He stayed for four years in the Orthodox, old-fashioned shtetl that had remained unchanged for generations. It, too, proved a strong inspiration for his writing, possibly serving as a model for Goray in his novel about 17th-century false messianism called *Satan in Goray,* and for many of his short stories.

But it may have been his brother who proved the most decisive influence in Isaac Singer's life. I. J. Singer introduced his brother to Yiddish journalism and theater, and brought home Yiddish translations of Tolstoy, Dostoevsky, even Mark Twain. He was a nonbeliever, challenging the father's Orthodoxy and leading the young Isaac toward a new set of secular, worldly, modernistic possibilities.

He also led the way back to Warsaw, where Isaac followed in 1923. There, in the lively city that was Eastern Europe's center of Jewish social and cultural life, Isaac eked out a meager living as a proofreader. He spent hours in libraries where he voraciously read scientific journals and books on philosophy, psychology, astronomy, physics, biology. He developed a fascination with the occult and with psychic research.

And he became acquainted with the diverse community of Yiddish writers and intellectuals who frequented the Writers' Club that appears in many of Singer's stories, although he stayed on the periphery of it himself. He abhorred ideologies and was not won over by the arguments he heard from the Hasidim, anti-Hasidim, atheists, Zionists, Bundists, or socialists. He regarded himself as a skeptic and a loner, though he still felt connected to his Orthodox roots, and ultimately developed his own brand of religion and philosophy. In *Love and Exile* he called it a "private mysticism: Since God was completely unknown and eternally silent, He could be endowed with whatever traits one elected to hang upon Him."

In Warsaw, Singer also worked on his writing. But even as a writer he forged his own path. "The themes employed by Yiddish writers and the writing itself struck me as sentimental, primitive, pretty," Singer writes in *Love and Exile*. It was marked by "cliches about social justice and Jewish nationalism, and had remained provincial and backward."

In any case, Jewish literature surely didn't deal with the kinds of concerns Singer was preoccupied with, such as the intense and varied sexual relationships he was beginning to experiment with in Warsaw, one of which produced a son named Israel. Nor did it speak to the resulting sense of conflict and shame that Singer felt about his gnawing and consuming passions. He was, afterall, the son of a pious man and one who admitted he still "retained an idea of a wife as my parents conceived it—a decent Jewish daughter, a virgin."

"I liked women," he writes candidly in *Love and Exile*. "From the very first I wrote about sex in such a way as to shock the Yiddish critics and often the readers, too."

In Warsaw, Singer contributed stories to Yiddish anthologies and periodicals; the novella *Satan in Goray* was serialized in the magazine *Globus,* a Warsaw periodical. But this was not overall a period of great productivity for him. By the time he was almost 30, he writes, "all I had accomplished in Yiddish literature was one novella and several short stories that I had published in magazines and anthologies no one read." In 1935, at the urging of his brother, who had emigrated to America, and because "I was afraid any day Hitler was going to invade Poland," Singer came to New York. He had already parted from his young son (now a journalist living in Israel whom he sees occasionally) and the boy's mother, Runya, who also lives in Israel.

In America he met and married German-born Alma, who helped support him by working as a salesclerk at Lord & Taylor. Here he wrote articles and stories for the *Forward,* though little more of note until after the premature death of his successful brother in 1944. Many who know him say that until then, he had been intimidated and constrained by his brother's awesome talent. Singer has never returned to Poland.

But in many ways, Singer has never really left it. Most of his characters, even in stories set in America, have ties of some sort to Poland, and his portrayals of Polish life in his European stories are so vivid and fresh and captivating, it is hard to believe he is not still immersed in it. He still writes about the issues that preoccupied him in Warsaw—about the destiny of the modern faithless Jew, about the powers that watch over human beings, about the conflict between passion and morality. In his stories, there is still "just one step from the study house to sexuality and back again," as he writes in *In My Father's Court*. It is difficult to fully comprehend his fidelity to the Old World after half a century in America. Singer's explanation, like most of his explanations, and like his writing, is spare and simply put.

"Writers always go back to their young days, to their young loves," he says. "If a writer writes about his life, and he is serious, he will go back there, just like a criminal goes back to the place of his crime. An artist goes back to the place where his work began. He goes back to his roots by instinct."

But there seems to be more at work than instinct in Singer's writing. It is as though he is conscientiously tending the Old World so that it won't disappear. "I have a feeling he doesn't see anything he can't use in his books," says his friend Dorothea Straus. "Consciously or unconsciously he is interested in preserving the culture he left. He notices only what's useful to his writing. I don't think he has ever been on the beach. He never spends money on anything, as far as I can tell. He'll turn wherever he is into the streets of Poland."

He seems practically oblivious to the world beyond his own internal one. He rarely goes to movies or watches television, and he says he doesn't read much fiction, "because I have no time." He has never learned to drive a car or ride a bicycle. He isn't sure what number his apartment is and has to check with Alma when he is asked. He has no conception of how to find his class at the University of Miami. The English department has hired a limousine to pick him up each week, and all he can tell the driver is that he has to go "near a fountain." There he waits quietly until someone in the class comes to find him.

He depends on two women to run interference with the outside

world for him. There is his devoted and fiercely protective Alma, who
tries, usually futilely, to discourage Singer from working so hard; who
packs his lunch in a paper bag every week before he goes off to
teach, even though he brings it back untouched because he forgets
to eat it; who fondly calls him "Duelly" and refers proudly to the time
"we won the Nobel Prize."

And there is Dvorah Menashe, his 31-year-old, vivacious personal
assistant who 10 years ago attended a class Singer taught at Bard
College, two hours north of New York City, and spontaneously
offered to be his chauffeur. He accepted. She now arranges his
appointments, helps him with research, and translates some of his
stories. With her dark, thick hair, her penetrating blue eyes, the
jeweled drop earrings and lacy black sweater she wears, she looks
uncannily Eastern European, like a character from one of his books.
She has even begun to talk like Singer. "God forbid something
should happen to him," Menashe will say, "he should live until 120."

After all these years, writing remains at the center of his world,
which is in many ways routinized and unglamorous. He eats simple
meals, frequently in cafeterias—eggs, hot cereal, boiled potatoes,
kasha. He seldom attends synagogue, though he says he believes in
God and prays all the time. "But at my age, why should I go to *shul*
(synagogue) to say to the Almighty what I want to say? I can say it at
home, or in the street."

His routine begins "in the morning, about 8, 9, and if they let me
do my work, I sit down to do my work," Singer says. He writes
longhand in a small Yiddish scrawl on 6-by-8-inch pieces of lined
paper, drawing on remarkable powers of discipline and concentration. Interruptions are barely noticed; he will answer the telephone in
the middle of a story and pick up its thread as though the conversation had never happened. Watching him compose "is like watching
a movie unfold," says the University of Miami's Lester Goran, a
novelist who has worked with Singer on translations and says Singer
has an extraordinary rapport with his characters. "He experiences all
the attitudes of the characters. He even changes his voice with different characters" while working on the translations.

Afternoons are also spent working, answering letters and the
telephone, reading proofs, working with a translator to refine his
stories in English. He prefers to write in Yiddish because he says it

is the only language he really knows well. He maintains that "their English is more real than mine. Mine is like taking out from a book."

"He is so much a perfectionist," says Dvorah Menashe. "Every story, he says, 'I will polish until it will shine.'" Sometimes he meets with work associates or friends, among them the *Forward's* editor Simon Weber, Roger and Dorothea Straus, and Lester Goran; his friends, Menashe says, tend to be people connected with publishing. "His work is so much his life, his breath. That's his social life." Often he takes time to talk with readers. And despite his protests that he "could do with less" attention, it is clear that part of him thrives on it. He will obligingly stay for an hour after his readings to sign books and chat: "I don't want suddenly to push away people just because I got the Nobel Prize," says Singer. His telephone number is listed in the Miami phone book. Despite a warning to an interviewer that he has little time to spare, he can hardly restrain himself from interviewing her, and the hour stretches on. "Have you read my book *The Penitent*?" "Have I signed your book?" "Do you get at home *The New Yorker*?"

Still, he is a challenge to understand. It is difficult, for instance, to reconcile the Singer who is an avowed conservative about marriage (Alma, he says proudly, is "a good wife") with the one who says openly, "If I have sinned I have only sinned in this respect—love," and who last year told an interviewer from a Jewish women's magazine: "It is true that after having a home, I still behaved for years, and I still do, like a man who lives in furnished rooms. I mean I try to steal some of my bachelorhood pleasures."

Many who are close to Singer describe him as "hard to peg" and "a loner." "There are many things I don't understand about him," says the *Forward's* Simon Weber, who considers himself one of Singer's closest friends. "I just take him as he is."

Publicly, though, Singer is a virtuoso. He is animated, courtly, warm, and genuinely curious about the people he meets with, striking up conversations about almost anything; with women he can be flirtatious and irresistibly engaging. Stories roll off his tongue— how the imps have hidden his mail, how he buys shoes that don't fit "because I didn't want to disappoint the clerk."

"He's really nice to talk to," says Maxine, the waitress who serves him every day at Sheldon's Drugs in Miami. "He told me about when he got the award from Sweden. He tells me stories of his hometown. He always makes you feel good."

And so he continues to be pursued by fans and to write, apparently caring little that some of his recent works have met with mixed, even harsh, reviews, and that some critics have said he has passed his prime as a writer. In 1983 *The New York Times Book Review* called *The Penitent* "his worst book," and his newest work, *The Image and Other Stories,* which he describes as "one of my very best," has received both praise for its stunning prose and criticism for its formulaic sameness.

Writing, he has said, is the only thing he can do, and it is inconceivable that he would stop. Sometimes he gets nervous before he starts to write, but that doesn't matter much at this stage of the game: "And if I get nervous, so what? So I'm nervous."

Yes, he will acknowledge, it is still a struggle to write. "But I like to struggle," he says. "You can only be victorious if you fight, so if I struggle and I think that I have managed to do what I wanted, to me this is a little victory."

Conversations with Isaac Bashevis Singer
Richard Burgin/1985

From *Conversations with Isaac Bashevis Singer* (New York: Doubleday, 1985), chapter 10. Reprinted by permission of Richard
Burgin, author of *Conversations with Borges, Man Without
Memory,* and *Private Fame.* Burgin's conversations with Singer
were held from 1976 through 1983.

A little island . . . The limits of philosophy . . . Experiments in free
choice . . . A true protester

Burgin: When we were talking about Nabokov you mentioned that
although you have mixed feelings about him, you were relieved to
discover that he believed in the supernatural. I wonder what you
mean by that term, "supernatural."

Singer: I don't really believe that there are two things—the natural
and the supernatural. I would not say that gravity is natural and
telepathy is supernatural. If telepathy exists, it has as much right to
call itself natural as gravitation does. We call the things which we
don't know or for which we have no evidence supernatural. For example, there is no real evidence that there is a soul or that there is
free will. The same applies to ghosts or spirits or other entities whose
existence we cannot prove.

Can we prove that there is such a thing as love? There are a number of people who will tell you that love is nothing but carnal desire.
Some extreme behaviorists don't believe that there is such a thing as
inborn character or personality. They say everything is conditioned,
except for a few instincts like the fear of loud noise or falling. Now,
for thousands and thousands of years men married women and had
children, and the fathers called themselves fathers even though there
was no scientific evidence that they were the fathers, since there
were cases where they were not. Still, most of the people who have a
wife and children believe that they are the fathers of the children.
Although Strindberg wrote a play, *The Father,* in which he tried to
show that no man can really maintain that he is the father of his

241

children, we know that in most cases, especially in former times, women were faithful. What I want to emphasize by this is that the supernatural is only a word for things whose existence we can't yet prove.

Burgin: That reminds me of a saying of Conrad's that the real world is so fantastic that in a sense there's no difference between the so-called supernatural world and the real one.

Singer: Yes, we still don't know what magnetism is and why a magnet will attract a nail and not cottage cheese. The atom is more of a riddle today than it was three thousand years ago. We don't know really what light is. We don't know what life is. We speak of electrons and we know how they work, more or less, but not what they are and how they came to be. Actually, our knowledge is a little island in an infinite ocean of non-knowledge. And even this little island remains a riddle.

Burgin: When you affirm the so-called supernatural, are you saying, "I'm trying in my writing to call attention to the fact of how little we really know"?

Singer: You have expressed exactly my way of thinking. I try to call attention to the things which we cannot prove but in whose existence some of us still believe.

Burgin: Socrates said, "I know nothing except the fact of my ignorance."

Singer: When it comes to these things, no one can be original because of our common ignorance. Originality is not the only important quality of a writer. Sometimes we have to repeat emotions and ideas because we cannot function without them. If a man is in love with a woman and says, "I love you," he knows very well that millions of people have said it before. But this word "love" is, for the time being, adequate and it expresses more or less what he feels. There are people who are original by nature. They use phrases which have been used many times but the sum total of what they say or write creates a feeling of originality. There are also writers who try to make every sentence original; they don't allow themselves to write a single sentence unless it has some queerness—and the net result is banality. Now, Tolstoy was an original man, even though he begins *Anna Karenina* with a saying which is quite banal. When you finish *Anna Karenina* or *War and Peace* or his other works, you feel here is an original person. There are other writers about whom you feel that there is nothing original in them. All you can see is the frustrated ambition to be original all the time.

Burgin: Can you think of any such writers?

Singer: I can think of such writers but I'm not going to mention names.

Burgin: How did your interest in the supernatural develop? Can you trace it to its source?

Singer: I was interested in the supernatural all my life. I knew even as a child that the world which we see is not the whole world. Whether you call them demons or angels or some other name, I knew then, and I know today, that there are entities of whom we have no idea and they do exist. You can call them spirits, ghosts, or imps. Of course, I also use them as symbols in my writing. I can express with them many things which would be difficult for me to express if I only wrote about people. But it is not only a literary method, it is connected with a belief that the world is full of powers that we don't know. After all, let's not fool ourselves, a few hundred years ago we didn't know about microbes, we didn't know about electrons and all those powers connected with radiation. So who says that we have already come to the summit of knowledge?

Burgin: On the other hand, we're learning or we think we're learning more about microbes and electrons, but where can it be proved that we've learned or discovered anything at all about the spirit world? Our knowledge of it doesn't progress.

Singer: It's not something with which you can progress. When it comes to human character or to ethics we don't progress.

Burgin: But if these entities exist, why have we learned nothing definite about them?

Singer: Because they are not made to be discovered. And the reason is that if we did discover them, free choice would disappear, and I think that free choice is such a great gift of God that if it disappeared it would be a profound misfortune. It would finish human history. If we could prove that there is a God and there is a Satan and that there is connected with them a world of punishment and reward, free choice would completely disappear. All people would be afraid of these powers, they would act accordingly, and it would do away with man's struggle. Because of this, I don't think you can ever take

these powers into a laboratory and demonstrate them. Although I like
to do in my own way a little research to prove certain things to myself, I know that no final proof can ever come as long as humanity
is going in the direction in which it is going. The moment people
began to investigate the physical world one discovery came after the
other, and they will continue to come for maybe a million years from
now. But when it comes to these things—the existence of God,
Providence, free will, and so on—no discovery could ever come
which would convince us once and forever.

Burgin: When I spoke with you a couple of days ago you were
emphasizing that the primary purpose of literature is entertainment—
its level of entertainment depending, of course, on the audience one
is writing for. But I was a little confused about your view of the purpose of philosophy.

Singer: Philosophy is a kind of learning in which you really have
to believe. There are no proofs, as in exact science. Spinoza has not
proven that there is a Substance with an infinite number of attributes.
But you can still say, "I believe in Spinoza. I love his way of thinking."
When Schopenhauer said that the thing-in-itself is will, he believed he
had found some truth. All philosophers are in a sense dealing with
the truth of their belief.

Burgin: Do you feel that philosophy may have nowhere to go, in
fact may have no real future and may simple dissolve?

Singer: At the beginning, the philosophers believed in the power
of logic. Then came critical philosophy and it told us that logic is all
definition and nothing else. It can never cross those limits.

Burgin: The limits as Kant defined them.

Singer: Not only Kant, also Locke and Hume. Kant came after
them. Then there was a revival of metaphysics—as in Hegel, who
tried again with the power of definition and logic to create something.
Lately such philosophers as Wittgenstein and others tried to turn
philosophy into a discipline of language. Sometimes philosophy looks
as if it would be at the very end of its efforts.

Burgin: Perhaps that kind of man is dying out?

Singer: But to say that philosophy is finished would be too much
guesswork, because we never know what will come. There may
suddenly come a man who may be another Spinoza or another
Descartes or another Leibnitz. I feel that since the desire of human

beings is to know, and since this hunger is still with us, we cannot say that philosophy has been finished.

Burgin: So you've moved away from the position of at least partially aligning philosophy with science?

Singer: While it pretends to be a science, it's actually a part of human character, of the way human beings think and feel. It has to be repetitious, just as the human spirit is.

Burgin: I'm curious *how* you read philosophy, assuming you still do.

Singer: I seldom do.

Burgin: Well, when you've most recently read philosophy how do you read it? As a curious branch of literature?

Singer: I know now that nothing the philosophers have said and are now saying and perhaps nothing they are going to say in the future ever can have the kind of evidence which one can have in physics or in chemistry. We have to make peace with this. People have tried to find absolute truth and failed.

Burgin: But they're still interesting failures to read . . .

Singer: Yes, and they will continue to try and they will continue to fail. It's the fault of the discipline.

Burgin: Do you feel that perhaps Kant came as close as a philosopher can come towards making an empirical case for his categories of understanding when he says our minds are constructed to perceive time and space the way they are? That seems almost irrefutable.

Singer: It has been shown by Salomon Maimon and the neo-Kantians that even existence is nothing but a category of thinking. We cannot say that there *is* a thing-in-itself, because perhaps existence itself is only a way of thinking, not being. It's good that all these philosophers have finally made us realize that "reality" is only reality from our point of view, from the point of view of our senses, of our consciousness. They have destroyed many illusions, but they have never created anything positive. Spinoza, who tried to give us something positive, ended up with something that became nothing but an arbitrary definition. His Substance with its infinite attributes is only a game of words. We just don't know what a piece of wood is if we take away man's perceptions of it. Since we are imprisoned by our senses and by our way of thinking and this prison will last as long as we live, we have to make peace with it and deal with things in this "prison," as Plotinus and Philo called the body and the senses.

Burgin: How do you reconcile this with your belief in free will?

Singer: Of course, I cannot prove that it exists, but I prefer to believe that there is free choice. And in my own way, I make experiments with free choice. I sometimes want to convince myself how free I am. Can I make a decision and keep it or can't I? Because all my life I made, God knows, myriads of decisions and I broke so many of them.

Burgin: What do you mean?

Singer: For example, I made a decision to get up at eight o'clock in the morning and I got up at ten o'clock instead. In Warsaw, almost every day I made a decision not to waste my time in the writers' club, take part in the gossip and immediately I went there and wasted my time in talking nonsense. Even now, in my old age, I try again and again to make decisions and keep them, hoping against hope that it is not too late and that I may succeed one day. Hope and the idea of free will are entities which one cannot give up completely.

The truth is, I have been wasting time since I grew up, but somehow I succeeded in doing a little work. I would say that wasting time is my passion Number Two, and the feeling of guilt for wasting time is my sickness Number Three. To me, this feeling of guilt proves that I really believe in free choice.

Burgin: Aren't there some areas of life where you are reacting according to nature, not really consciously making a decision?

Singer: I don't need to make a decision to eat breakfast. When I say making a decision, I mean making a decision *against* my desires. The Ten Commandments are commandments against human nature. Many people would like to steal if they knew that they could do it without being punished. It is also their nature to commit adultery if they can have their way without too much trouble. But Moses came and he said that if humanity wants to exist it has to follow certain rules no matter how difficult they are. I would say that even to this day we have not yet convinced ourselves that people can make such decisions and keep them. Even when they make them, they can only keep them if they make them as a collective. If people live together like the Jews in the ghettos they keep to their decisions. Why? Because one guards the other. In a collective, if a Jew wanted to commit adultery, there were many in the little ghetto who would have learned about it and they would have made a great outcry to stop it. There was a case where Tolstoy in his old age got a strong desire for some peasant woman and he went to a friend and said, "Please do me a favor and guard me." This means he knew that by himself he didn't have enough free will to take care of himself. These are the problems which interest me deeply.

Burgin: You mentioned that you often feel you are wasting time. What do you consider *not* wasting time?

Singer: When I speak about wasting time, I don't speak from a philosophical point of view but from a practical one. I assume that if I get up in the morning and do my work, three or four hours, and I accomplish something, write a story which I can later sell or which I will enjoy having published, I haven't wasted my time. But if I get up in the morning and I read yesterday's newspaper or look out the window for hours, or have a long telephone conversation of no value, this is wasting time. Of course, it is relative, but I'm not speaking here from a philosophical point of view. Like every writer, I would like to do my work well, to write and rewrite, but when I neglect my job, I feel that I have broken my decision. That is why when we betray our decisions, we all have these regrets. The word "regret" itself shows that we assume that we have some free will, because if we didn't believe in free will, we wouldn't regret anything.

Burgin: I'm wondering if you ever feel that everything is a waste of time. And if so, why is the practice of literature, which, in your view, only serves to entertain people, more important than entertaining yourself or entertaining writers with conversation in a writers' club?

Singer: Well, it has a pragmatic value.

Burgin: We've talked quite a bit about philosophy, but there is one last question I'd like to ask you about it. What can a fiction writer gain, if anything, from a study of philosophy?

Singer: If the novelist is not curious about philosophy, there is no reason why he should read philosophy. But he is never curious about philosophy, even when he's young. This shows there's something small about him. A larger person is interested in the so-called eternal questions: Who am I? Is what we see reality? Is there any way of reaching *true* reality? If he sits down to read philosophy because he thinks that a writer should know philosophy, I'd tell him, "Don't read it." If he's a real writer and a thinking man, he will be curious about it and maybe, after a while, disappointed in it. He will say, "I've had enough of it," and return from abstraction to the world of the senses.

Burgin: How can a novelist effectively use ideas? For example, Dostoyevsky dramatized philosophical ideas. How have you yourself used them?

Singer: I would say if he needs them in his stories, if he is the kind of writer who likes to write about ideas, he can find a million ways of using them.

Burgin: How have you used them?

Singer: Since I often describe people like myself and I am interested in human ideas, I let my people ponder the eternal questions. I could never make the protagonist of a novel a person who would not be interested in those questions. In other words, I don't make use of philosophy with a pertinent scheme or plan. Those writers who imagined that they found the final answer were sooner or later a disappointment to others and often to themselves. In my time, Tolstoy could serve as the example par excellence. There is no question that he died a disappointed man. His disenchantment would have been greater if he had lived to see the Bolshevist Revolution. Just the same, I have great admiration for him and for his struggle with God and with human nature.

I myself try to think that I have made peace with human blindness and God's permanent silence, but they give me no rest. I feel a deep resentment against the Almighty. My religion goes hand in hand with a profound feeling of protest. Once in a while, the old Jewish hope for the coming of the Messiah awakens in me. There must come the time for revelation! How long should we wait? My feeling of religion is a feeling of rebellion. I even play with the idea of creating (for myself) a religion of protest. I often say to myself that God *wants* us to protest. He has had enough of those who praise Him all the time and bless Him for all His cruelties to man and animals.

I have written a little book which I call *Rebellion and Prayer* or *The True Protester*. It is still in Yiddish, untranslated. It was written at the time of the Holocaust. It is a bitter little book and I doubt that I will ever publish it. Yes, I am a troubled person, but I am also joyful when I forget (for a while) the mess in which we are stuck. I may be false and contradictory in many ways, but I am a true protester. If I could, I would picket the Almighty with a sign: "Unfair to Life."

Isaac Bashevis Singer . . . Shrugs Off Fame
William Robertson/1988

From *The Miami Herald* (17 November 1988), sec. Living Today, 1B. Reprinted by permission.

Shortly before Isaac Bashevis Singer went to Stockholm to collect the Nobel Prize in literature, an interviewer asked him whether he had met many writers after he came to America from his native Poland.

"I will tell you, no," Singer replied. "When I was young I used to read books, and I never really looked at who was an author. I didn't care. What's the difference? When I was a boy of 12, I read Tolstoy. But I didn't know it was Tolstoy. I was interested in the story, not the author. A real reader, especially a young reader, never cares too much about the author. He wants to read the book and he enjoys it. When people begin to be less interested in art, they become more interested in the artist. . . . When literature becomes overly erudite, it means that interest in the art has gone and curiosity about the artist is what's most important. It becomes a kind of idolatry."

Like so much of what Singer says and writes, his thoughts on the celebration of the author as personality rather than artist have the authority of implicit good sense.

But that won't stop Singer, 84, from being idolized tonight at 8 when he is honored at the Miami Book Fair in the auditorium of Miami-Dade Community College's downtown campus.

In the age of publicity, rare and precious is the writer who shrugs at the perquisites of fame. But that is precisely what Singer has done. Over the years, he has made public appearances sparingly. In South Florida, where he lives during the winter, he has spoken with writing students and appeared on behalf of Jewish groups, but mostly he has preferred to stay away from the bright lights to work on the stories and novels that have won him worldwide acclaim. Although fortune has smiled on him, it hasn't changed the essential nature of a courtly man. Style as style per se is not in Singer's personal or artistic repertoire. Wisdom is his style.

Part of wisdom is that when you are the subject under discussion, it's best to let others do the talking. And tonight they will. Singer's publisher, Roger Straus, of Farrar, Straus, Giroux, will speak about the author, and Isaiah Sheffer, a New York actor with the company, Symphony Space, will read from his work. What Singer will have to say in response provides the evening's suspense.

Since he won the Nobel Prize in 1978, the contours of Singer's life and art have become fairly well known.

He grew up in Poland. He rejected his parents' wish that he, like his father and grandfather before him, become a rabbi, choosing instead the slightly disreputable life of the writer.

He emigrated to the United States in 1935, and, after years of writing in Yiddish, mostly for the Jewish daily *Forward,* he began to find a growing body of readers for his work in English translation. The best known of them include *The Magician of Lublin, The Manor* and *Gimpel the Fool and Other Stories.* As readers discovered him, so too did an increasing number of friendly critics who saw the underlying complexity and insight in his seemingly simple stories.

Singer believes strongly in a direct narrative line and, unlike many contemporary writers, has never abandoned the old-fashioned idea that action is character.

His work often combines myth and fantasy with Jewish folklore. But he also has acute powers of observation and with astonishing realism can take a reader into the streets of New York or Miami Beach or anywhere else he has traveled. That's another old-fashioned technique to legions of modern writers caught up in the psychoanalytical approaches to life and art.

At its best, Singer's writing has the force of parable. But it is easy to be misled by reading it too quickly. His are not necessarily nice little stories from a kindly old gent. Although Singer has criticized the reliance of contemporary art on psychology, what often comes through in his fiction is a deep understanding of psychological man, especially in the area of sexuality.

"I would say that the best contact with humanity is through love and sex," Singer has said. "Here, really, you learn all about life, because in sex and in love, human character is revealed more than anywhere else. Let's say a man can play a very strong man: a big man, a dictator. But in sex, he may become reduced to a child or to an imp. The sexual organs are the most sensitive organs of the human being. The eye or the ear seldom sabotage you. An eye will not stop seeing if it doesn't like what it sees, but the penis will stop functioning if he doesn't like what he sees. I would say that the sexual organs express the human soul more than any other limb of the body. They are not diplomats. They tell the truth ruthlessly."

Singer's stories convey this thought without stating it directly. Freud once noted that he developed his psychoanalytical theory in large part from what he learned about the human psyche as expressed in literature. He was talking about Singer's kind of writing.

In a magazine article not so long ago, a despairing Singer complained that "with all his refined ways, modern man remains the wildest animal" and that "the best novel will not change things."

It was one of the few times that he has been wrong, and the evidence is in his own work. He re-creates an ancient culture in conflict with the contemporary. He shows rational beings in conflict with the mystical. And in the process he demonstrates through his characters the necessity of believing in something beyond ourselves.

And revealing these things, he gives his readers the power to make a choice as to whether they want to remain the wildest animal.

That is the highest calling a writer can aspire to.

Isaac B. Singer on Writing, Life, Love and Death

Valerie Wells/1991

From the *Sun-Sentinel,* Miami (4 August 1991), 1F. Reprinted by permission of Valerie Wells.

Isaac Bashevis Singer, who died July 24 at age 87, wrote passionately about life in his books and short stories. In *In My Father's Court,* he wrote, "All was mixed up together: life, death, lust, boundless loyalty and love."

In his final years, Singer granted the following excerpted interview on the subject of life and death to Miami Beach author Valerie Wells. The Poland-born Singer, who won the Nobel Prize for Literature in 1978, wrote in Yiddish and his works were translated. Here he comes across as simultaneously vulnerable and invincible, innocent and wise.

Q: What has brought you joy?

A: The same things as anybody else: nature, sex, love and sometimes creativity. All the things which are important to us, which bring us some joy, also bring trouble, but you have to take it as it is.

Q: How do you feel about your writing? Are you happy with it?

A: One is never happy. If a writer is too happy with his writing, something is wrong with him. A real writer always feels as if he hasn't done enough. This is the reason he has the ambition to rewrite, to publish things, and so on. The bad writers are very happy with what they do. They always seem surprised about how good they are. I would say that a real writer sees that he missed a lot of opportunities.

God has given us strength and spiritual powers, but we don't make complete use of them. I would say that every human being uses only a small part of . . . his potentialities. Of course, before you begin to use them, you have to know what you want to do. If by nature you are not a writer and you try to be a writer, you can use all your

powers and the results will be nothing. It is very important for a
person to find out from experience, and from pondering, what he
would really like to do. Once you make up your mind, try to do your
best.

Q: You knew what you wanted to do at a very early age?

A: Yes, in my case, I knew. I think I was about 16 or 17 when I decided I would like to be a writer. I made up my mind early because
my older brother was a writer, and my father bought religious books.
I began to write in Hebrew and later turned to Yiddish because it was
more of a living language in those times. Everybody I knew told me
that to be a Yiddish writer means to go into failure from the very
beginning because the number of Yiddish writers was diminishing,
and most of them were very poor. But I said to myself, "I don't care; I
want to be good in a language which I know best. Even if I write for a
small number of readers—and some of them may even be primitive
readers—I will still try to do my best."

I went on like this until today. Of course, good things began to
happen to me. I was translated into many languages and I got prizes.
I received the Nobel Prize. I did not foresee this, and it was not the
most important condition. I would have continued to do my writing
even if I would have had no honors and no awards—not that I want
to show that I am an idealist. Even from a practical point of view, a
writer should be true to his roots and try to do his best. Many of the
great writers like Dostoevski and Strindberg never got any awards or
prizes, and they still did their best work to the last.

Q: Did it give you comfort to know what you wanted to do, and to
do it?

A: It gave me comfort and it also gave me a feeling of great responsibility, because between knowing what you want to do and
doing it well, there is a far cry; there are many inhibitions. In every
human life, you want to do things and they don't come out right.
It's a struggle, but to me it's a pleasant kind of struggle. I keep on
struggling today as I did 50 years ago because there is no guarantee
that even if you have written 10 good books, that the 11th is going to
be good. You have to work on it, rewrite, and improve, and ponder
about it, until it comes out right.

Q: What was your first experience with death?

A: Every human being has a lot of experience with death. In the

olden times, many children died in the neighborhood where I lived
in Poland. The death of grown-ups did not impress me so much
because I did not know them, but when a child died, it was often a
child I knew. Death was a quite frequent guest in the old country,
especially in the houses of the poor people.

Q: Did you ever become accustomed to it?

A: No one gets accustomed to death. For instance, the owner
of a funeral parlor—you might think that such a man is hardened
enough to get accustomed to death. No. They get accustomed to
other people's deaths, but they certainly don't get accustomed to the
idea that they will die. This is true about every human being. The fear
of death exists in every human being from childhood to the grave.
The only time when people stop being afraid of death is when they
die.

Q: Do you fear death?

A: Everybody does. If you cross the street and a car is running
toward you, you run for your life because you know what that car
can do to you. A person who says, "I'm not afraid of death at all," is
either lying to others or to himself—sometimes both.

There is a fear of death and it is useful to everything which is alive,
because if people weren't afraid of death, they would destroy their
bodies mercilessly. They would overeat, and overdrink, and over-
work, and oversex. They would do many things which now they
sometimes refrain from doing because of this fear. This fear of death
is a kind of protection God has given to everything alive so that it
should take care of its system. Without it, they would all destroy
themselves completely.

It is not true that only old people are afraid of death; the young are
just as much afraid. I know this from my own experiences and from
talking to other people. The fear of death is always with people and
this makes them more or less live. Those animals, those primitive
creatures which have no fear of death, will do anything. The fly will
run into fire.

The fear of death has made it so that people now live longer than
they have ever lived. Because people are afraid of death, they have
created medicine and hygiene. . . .

It is my personal conviction that the whole universe is alive. To say
that only human beings are alive, or the creatures that are on the

surface of the earth are alive, and the whole of the universe is dead, is only the idea of the materialists.

If a man dies, he stops doing his business and his body falls to pieces. But I believe that there is some spirit—call it whatever—which is alive. We may die privately, but as far as we are part of the universe, we are very much alive. The universe doesn't look to me like a dead body; it looks full of wisdom and purpose. Life is not a kind of chemical accident—certain chemicals met and combined.

Spinoza, who was considered a materialist, maintained that there is some part of everything which exists, which remains. I think that the chain of life is very much alive. The links of this chain may change, stronger links may take the place of weaker links, but the whole chain is alive. I think if people know they have to turn back to the universe, they feel somewhere that death is not a final thing.

In other words, life is alive. Since there is nothing but life, I assume that the fear of death is a good protection for us not to destroy ourselves.

Q: How do you feel about your life?

A: I feel like everybody else. We make a lot of mistakes. Sometimes we do something good. We all think that if we could relive the same life again and have the memory of our mistakes, we would avoid them. But I am not even sure of this.

Q: What would you change?

A: Well, I would still like to be a writer. I wouldn't want to be a dogcatcher or something like this.

Q: How do you want people to remember you?

A: I would like them to remember me as a good writer, not as a bad writer. I would like to be remembered as a good man, not as a bad man. But whether this will come out is a big question.

Index

256